Dreaming
and the
Self

SUNY series in Dream Studies
Robert L. Van de Castle, editor

Dreaming
and the
Self

New Perspectives on Subjectivity,
Identity, and Emotion

Edited by

Jeannette Marie Mageo

STATE UNIVERSITY OF NEW YORK PRESS

Published by
State University of New York Press, Albany

For information, address State University of New York Press,
90 State Street, Suite 700, Albany, NY 12207

Production by Marilyn P. Semerad
Marketing by Anne M. Valentine

Library of Congress Cataloging in Publication Data

Dreaming and the self : new perspectives on subjectivity, identity, and emotion / edited
by Jeannette Marie Mageo.
    p. cm — (SUNY series in dream studies)
    Includes bibliographical references and index.
    ISBN 0–7914–5787–7 (alk. paper) — ISBN 0–7914–5788–5 (pbk. : alk. paper)
    1. Dreams. 2. Dream interpretation. 3. Self. 4. Identity (Psychology) I. Mageo,
Jeannette Marie. II. Series.

BF1091 .D735 2003
154.6′3—dc21

                                                                    2002030973

                    10 9 8 7 6 5 4 3 2 1

CONTENTS

PART 1

Overview

CHAPTER 1

Theorizing Dreaming and the Self

JEANNETTE MARIE MAGEO

> I am accustomed to sleep and in my dreams to imagine the
> same things that lunatics imagine when awake, or sometimes
> things which are even less plausible. . . . I realize so clearly that
> there are no conclusive indications by which waking life can be
> distinguished from sleep that I am quite astonished, and my
> bewilderment is such that it is almost able to convince me that
> I am sleeping.
> —Descartes, *First Meditation*

In Western intellectual history, René Descartes is the prototypical pro-
ponent of the model of the person as the "I" who is identical with his
reasoning capacity—a capacity carefully disarticulated from affect and
embodiment. Descartes begins his first meditation with a reflection on the
dream. The evidence that experience is real in dreams, Descartes insists,
comes from the senses ([1637] 1952, 76–77). There the senses give false tes-
timony about the physical situation of the dreamer and misreport on the
world. This serves for Descartes as reason enough to retreat into a logic
denuded of rather than enriched by other elements of the self. In retreating
from these elements, Descartes must retreat from the dream. Indeed, he

poses it as his counterexample, recognizing the dream inevitably implies a more complex geography of the self and of the experienced world than can be inferred from conscious life. In this volume we seek a model of the self that includes embodiment and affect, as well as reflecting culturally and historically variable dimensions of being a person. We seek this inclusive model at the site of the original repudiation of embodiment and affect in Western thought—the dream.

I begin with a brief overview of the history of dream studies in anthropology. I then ask how one might reconceptualize the self from the perspective of the dream and contextualize the volume's chapters in relation to this question. This chapter also provides commentary on those to follow, relating them to the theme of the volume and offering critical reflections.

The Dream in Anthropology

Some early anthropologists tended to view dreams as a venue for the creation of culture. Tylor (1873), for example, believed that religions arose as a kind of dream interpretation—that is, as attempts to account for the events of dream life, which were looked upon as real experience. Lincoln (1935, 189) distinguished between ordinary dreams and "cultural pattern dreams." From the latter, he believed, people took inspiration for religious cults, but also for rituals and the arts. Influenced by psychoanalysis, other early anthropologists tended to see dreams as involving "only a minor reworking of already existing [cultural] material" (D'Andrade 1961, 298–99) and as a stage for the symbolic dramatization of universal psychological problems and cultural defense mechanisms. Rather than being mutually incompatible, a number of the authors in this volume propose that dreams are a venue in which people recreate culture precisely because the "psychological problematics" that people share in a culture are central to dreams. By this phrase, I mean that cultural psychologies are always to a degree problematic. People strive to organize and resolve recurrent but variable human problems (like incestuous feelings, sibling rivalries, identity, death, and so forth), but succeed only in partial ways. These ways are distinctly cultural and leave people with painful affective and embodied experiences with which they must struggle and out of which they continue to change their cultures.

More narrowly, many early-twentieth-century anthropological dream studies were influenced by two psychoanalytic tenets.[1] First, there were certain symbols that had a universal meaning, usually of a sexual nature. Second, dreams had a two-tiered structure. The surface stratum was the *manifest content*, which might be culturally variant; the deep stratum was the *latent con-*

tent, which was universally the same (Kluckhohn and Morgan 1951, 120). In psychoanalytic theory, the manifest content was the dream as dreamt and was borrowed from the shifting images and occurrences of daily life. It was the remains of the day—"day residues," Freud called them (1963, 83–135, 213–177). These remains were enlisted to represent anxiety, guilt, and desires that were linked to the complexes of early childhood. These feelings were likely to be disguised in the manifest dream, for example through displacement (sign substitutions), condensation (sign combinations), or symbolization (multifarious use of a single sign). The disguise was necessary, according to Freud, because dreams operated to maintain sleep; desires could disturb it because they incited action toward satisfaction and anxiety. Desires might also incite anxiety and guilt because they were often in conflict with social mores or with the individual's self-esteem. Just as the senses conveyed only illusions in Descartes's view of the dream, the manifest content was a ruse in Freud's view: its deformations and bizarre combinations were distractions from the dream's real meaning.

The mid-twentieth century saw the formation of the Culture and Personality school in anthropology. Revolving around figures such as Margaret Mead and Ruth Benedict, this school was interested in a range of personality theories and in how ethnography might contribute to and critique psychological theory. Mead's *Sex and Temperament in Three Primitive Societies* (1963), for example, spun off of Jung's idea of psychological types (1963; 1972b, 217). Mead's *Coming of Age in Samoa,* ([1928] 1961) on the other hand, was both informed by and aimed as a critique of Freudian theory.[2] I have argued elsewhere (2001a) that through her ethnographic work Mead was forging a "critical cultural relativism"—an anthropology that combined comparative psychological theory with critical theory.

The Culture and Personality thinker who made the most significant contribution to dream studies was Dorothy Eggan.[3] She, like Mead, saw her work on dreams as "a challenge to the social sciences" (1949, 469). I review several of what I regard as her major ideas about dreams here both because of their importance in shaping anthropological studies of the dream that followed and because these ideas are directly linked to many of the themes of this volume.

Like Mead, Eggan began by using ethnography, specifically her studies of the Hopi, to critique Freudian theory and its usage in anthropology. Eggan criticized the "oversimplified procedure" of dream analysis that had been employed by psychoanalytic anthropologists who often made "equation-like interpretations of dreams" (1952, 473). In this endeavor, she quoted Freud to the effect that dreams "possess many and varied meanings; so that, as in Chinese script, only the context can furnish the correct meaning" (1952, 474). For Eggan, of course, the context was a culture, or more precisely an interrelational setting within a culture (1952, 474)—an insight echoed in Vincent Crapanzano's afterward (chapter 10).

Freud used free association to analyze the dream ([1900]1953). For Eggan, "dreams in themselves are a from of projective phenomenon and represent a process of free association, both in sleep and after awakening" (1949, 197). The dream report, then, by continuing the projective processes of the dream itself, embeds dreams ever further in cultural modes of narration and cultural meaning systems. The manifest dream was composed of "culturally derived symbols" (Eggan 1949, 179). Variant cultural experiences would lead dreamers to symbolize events quite differently and this might lead to differences in cultural symbol systems (Eggan 1952, 479–480). Eggan's interest in dreams anticipates the turn in anthropology toward a concern with cultures as meaning systems that became salient through the work of Lévi-Strauss.

Eggan tells us that the dream is a "released image energy" that creates "a new inner world" (1952, 469). Similarly, several authors herein argue that dreams speak a different language than the conscious mind—the language of the imagination—and investigate the nature of that language as it bears upon dreaming and the self. Eggan believed that what transpires in dream narratives themselves "affords a deeper understanding of culturally conditioned affects, particularly as regards the disharmony between the cultural ideal" and what people actually experience in a culture (1952, 478). She saw the dream narrative as particularly useful in understanding culture change because of a "distinct lag" between people's consciously held models of culture and their actual historical circumstances (1952, 478–79). Chapters 2, 3, 4, and 5 also argue that dreams are continually forging symbolic bridges between these two.

According to Eggan, during the first half of the twentieth century "the concept of culture" had been "intentionally restricted to exclude material pertaining to the individual as such" (1952, 469). In more contemporary terminology, Eggan believed that dreams were a way toward person-centered ethnography and potentially offered insight as to the relation between culture and subjectivity. Dreams allowed informants to talk about themselves in what they assumed to be a "safely cryptic manner," which was nonetheless revealing of intense concerns and feelings they might not otherwise be willing to share with an itinerant anthropologist (1952, 477–78). Hopi "tend to work out a personal delineation of their problems at the manifest level in dreams in surprisingly complete and honest detail" and these problems "are of more than passing concern to the individual" (Eggan 1949, 179–80). Anticipating Hall and Van de Castle's method of content analysis (1966), Eggan held that people had a "pattern of dreaming" that was uniquely their own and that dream series evinced themes that were seldom finished in one dream (1949, 180).

By the mid-1970s, inspired by Geertz's brilliant explorations of personhood and culture, anthropologists turned toward "local knowledge"—studying folk theories in culture as alternative knowledge systems.[4] Local ways of dreaming, of narrating dreams, and of interpreting them became examples, both as forms of ethnopsychiatry and, more broadly, as alternative knowledge systems. This tack on dreaming and culture was wonderfully developed and illustrated in Tedlock's collection on dreaming (1987). As anthropologists studied dreams as local knowledge, they became increasingly aware of the part dreams played in communicative processes in culture and as a social performance, of either a ritual or an informal nature.[5] The essays in this volume share a commitment to perspectives on the dream grounded in long-term ethnography and a belief in the necessity of seeing culture form the local point of view.

The renewed emphasis on cultural relativism manifest in studying local ways of knowing was significant in cracking open Western universalistic paradigms in preference for studying cultures as unique cases—unique instances of being human. Along with this emphasis, however, came a hesitancy among some researchers to read dreams as indicative of cultural psychology, particularly as indicative of psychological problems in cultures, which tended to be seen as disrespectful. But all cultures, I argue above, have psychological problematics; to suggest that these problematics exist is not to presume inferiority, but rather a dynamic and vital element in culture, which must be considered in person-centered ethnography. The present volume considers psychological problematics and how studying cultures can provide anthropologists and others with new perspectives on dreaming and the self.

Theories of the Self and Dreams

As in prior work (1995, 1998, 2002a), here I take *self* to be a domain term that refers to all aspects of being a person. Identity, on the other hand, is the cumulative result of affirming "That is me" and "That is not me"; it develops through acts of identification and disidentification with elements of internal experience and with persons, groups, and representations in the cultural world (Mageo 2001b; Mageo and Knauft 2002). Inasmuch as identity is that sense of self that derives from successive acts of identification, it is fluid and ever in transformation, and the transformations are effected in part, many of the authors in this volume argue, in dreams. Recent anthropological insights about spirit possession (Boddy 1989; Lambek 1981, 1996; Mageo 1996a)—that it is a venue in which to think through waking experience of a cultural and historical nature—can also be applied to the dream. Dreams progressively work through our experience as cultural beings and as

such contribute, however subtly, to how people construct identity in daily
cultural life.

How does dreaming, cross-culturally considered, reflect on prior theories of the self? Take, for example, George Herbert Mead's (1934) idea that
the self is composed of an "I" and a "me." Mead's "I" is the individual who
feels, desires, wills, and acts. The "me" is the presence of social others within
the self. The "me" endlessly offers its opinion about the "I" and dialogues
with it. Who, then, is the self that acts in dreams? Is it the "I"? Are all other
dream figures the "me"? This seems likely from L. S. Vygotsky's viewpoint.
For Vygotsky, the child's internal life is an introjection of its social life:
"Every function in the child's development appears twice . . . first, between
people . . . and then inside the child" (1978, 57). The people we meet in
dreams would then be doubles or combinations of those we have related to
first in social life (some remembered, some forgotten in surface consciousness). It is unlikely, however, that dream figures are all actual people
(although they have relations to actual people); they are also the characters
who populate the world of stories in which we develop (Mageo 2002c). This
world of stories is interiorized in childhood, just as are social relations, and
establishes the fundaments of our imaginations and our dreams (Mageo
1998, 76–79; Miller, Fury, and Mintz 1996).

If Mead's concept of the "me" recognizes the presence of society in the
constitution of the self, it nonetheless locates that self within—in internal
events like feeling and thinking and in internal dialogues, rather than in
social transactions. Similarly, in Western cultures we place the dream within
a person's head. Many of the peoples who anthropologists study, however,
see dreams as an alternative social world, as much outside the person as a
convivial party, even if what goes on there is often far from convivial. For
them, dreams are the gate to a sphere inhabited, like our own, by powers and
people with which and with whom they live and cope—as is the dream world
for Erika Bourguignon's Haitians (chapter 7). These peoples also locate the
self in social role-playing rather than inside the person.

In Samoa, for example, agāga refers to the constitutive self believed to
survive death and to travel in dreams.[6] Agāga, however, is a doubling of the
word aga, which means "persona" (Mageo 1998, 10). A persona is a face we
show to others. Deriving from the masks of Roman theater, this word also
refers to the role that goes with a particular mask. Like Samoans, the Quiché
Maya have a concept of the constitutive self as a non-corporal being that
inhabits the body at birth and leaves in dreams or visions and at death. This
self is said to be one of twenty possible "faces" (Tedlock 1987, 110, 115; cf.
Mauss 1990, 39).

The divergence reflected by variant folk models of the self was much
discussed in late-twentieth-century anthropology and cross-cultural psychol-

ogy. Folk models of the person as a context-transcendent individual have been called egocentric; folk models of the person as an ensemble of social roles or personae have been called sociocentric.[7] These terms represent hypothetical extremes—north and south poles of a map where the ground is always to one degree or another intermediate and more complex than any map can show.

Carl Jung mapped the self in a manner that at first glance resembles more sociocentric folk models—that is, as multiple (1963). For Jung, at birth people were a vast sea of potentiality. The work of the first half of life was to make portions of that potentiality into an actual self (Jung 1971). This was accomplished by cultivating stronger aspects of self at the expense of others—splitting off aspects less well favored by temperament, society, or family relations and coming to regard them as "not me."[8] Jung (1963, 8–22; 1967, 29–38) believed that we often construct our vision of others by projecting onto them unacceptable aspects of the self. Men split off an anima and women an animus, for example, when forming their gender identity. Despite disidentification, these "archetypes" remained important aspects of the self, although they operated independently of consciousness. Similarly, current constructionist theories suggest that the self is a complex system, composed of conscious subsystems that are integrated to a degree, but also of less conscious subsystems that "may or may not remain separate from other parts of self-organization and function relatively . . . autonomously" (Hollan 2000, 539). Jung (1968, 3–41) and Perls after him (1971), thought that we encountered these parts in dreams.[9]

At critical life junctures one might meet what Jung called "the Self" in dreams, by which he meant the reintegration of all these potentials, in the form of an elevated or semidivine personage, such as a king or Christ (1963, 25–71, 184–221; 1970a, 110–28, 343–55, 497–505). Thus, in classic Euro-American theories, even multiple views of the self tend to privilege a unitary self—or at least a self that is striving to be unitary. Many ethnographers and cross-cultural psychologists have critiqued this model of the self and demonstrated that it is by no means universally prominent.[10] Katherine Ewing (1990) argues that the belief that the self is whole is a fiction people invent and reinvent to represent themselves in the ever changing circumstances of their lives. Ewing shows that often these "wholes" include admired parts of others whom the person has encountered in social life.

We meet these evanescent holistic selves in dreams, I suggest, as figures that are condensations of several people we have known in life or in fiction. As in Bakhtin's idea of heteroglossia (1981), in dreams the self has multiple voices. These voices are those of people appropriated from waking life, who represent our own subself fragments. The dream is the self as other(s), with whom we seldom have unproblematic relationships. Here the presence of alterity in subjectivity is exposed. Dreams continually splice self with other, complicating "me"/"not me" recognitions. Dream characters are composites of people we know or have known in life and in tales, but also our feelings/thoughts in other guises and those of others about us that we have interiorized. In this regard, dream symbols are at once about the subject and the social world; everything in them has both allegiances.

The self, then, is much larger than its conscious identifications; dreaming provides insight into the congeries of identities that it encompasses. Combining Vygotsky's and Jung's ideas, one might view the self as involving a continuing process of incorporating others to make an identity. In dreams this identity is then splintered into part selves who derive from these others and who carry our emotional reactions to them. Upon waking, the part selves we meet in dreams are projected back onto others, who later enter our dreams re-presenting our own feelings for us—and so on ad infinium.

Part 2: Revisioning the Self and Dreams

Cultural psychologists and psychological anthropologists have long been interested in how the dream's manifest content reflects cultural and subcultural differences. Cross-cultural psychologists investigated dreams quantitatively through Calvin Hall's and Robert Van de Castle's system of content analysis (Domhoff 1996, 99–129). By and large, anthropologists investigated the manifest dream through qualitative and in-depth ethnographic studies that considered variability in belief systems and narrative practices surrounding dreaming in a culture.[11] In "Diasporic Dreaming, Identity, and Self-Constitution" (chapter 3), Katherine Ewing, like Eggan before her, begins to deconstruct the idea that dreams' important symbolic work occurs only on a latent or hidden level. Ewing argues that the dream narrative itself updates culture. As an example, she discusses the dream of the Seneca prophet Handsome Lake. Handsome Lake was instructed in dreams to change the matrilineal transmission of political office and status in his society into a patrilineal system so that it would better articulate with the Euro-American world in which the Seneca had come to live.

Dream narratives, Ewing believes, can be understood as offering analyses of a present social situation in the language of metaphor. Many peoples that anthropologists study believe in the predictive values of dreams. Just like any other good hypothesis, Ewing tells us, a good dream may have predictive value. There are forward looking and problem-solving dreams, as Jung argued. Not all dreams are merely iterative of unresolved childhood conflicts, but are efforts to reposition the self in the social world and to constitute identities by fitting new experiences into existing narratives of self. Ewing illustrates this point through a dream of a Sufi teacher in Pakistan who lived for some time in England. In the dream, a Sufi saint feeds the dreamer spiritual food in an English basement. Ewing points out that basement apartments are typically where the economically disadvantaged live in England. The dream relates the man's current elevated religious identity with his dystonic identity experiences as a migrant. Transnational cultures are characterized by hybridity. Transnational dreams offer insight into how people are psychologically affected by and synthesize cultural incongruities.

For Douglas Hollan, the reconfiguration of the self in dreams stems from an articulation of existing self schemas with daily experience (chapter 4). These articulations take place in "selfscape dreams." These dreams are the "nightly news" of the self—registering within us the current state of our personhood, our body, and our relations with others. Selfscape dreams are universal, Hollan believes, but their content varies from person to person and culture to culture. Illustrating this cross-cultural recurrence and variability, Hollan discusses his ethnographic work with dreams among the Toraja of Sulawesi and his psychoanalytic work in Los Angeles.

In Sulawesi we meet Grandfather Limbong, a Toraja elder politically influential in his time, but suffering declining health and fortunes. Limbong dreams of his stomach emerging from his mouth, which he likens to dividing meat at community feasts and to being divided like meat at a feast and distributed. Hollan sees these dreams as articulating revolutions in Limbong's body and social standing with his identity.

In Los Angeles we meet Steve, a forty-year-old high tech specialist who is emotionally dependent upon and psychologically crippled by his parents. In dreams, often a parent is driving or back-seat-driving Steve's car and the car is impeded or damaged. The car, Hollan suggests, is an image of freedom/mobility in American society and represents Steve's identity in dreams. I suspect the car represents not only physical mobility, but social mobility: cars display socioeconomic identity, particularly for men, as one advertisement after another attests. The car is also the phallus in a Lacanian sense: it is a detachable symbol of masculine identity and privilege that can be lost by men or appropriated by women. Steve's relations with his parents may not only have impeded his freedom/mobility, but also compromised his gender identity. I wonder, are selfscape dreams aimed at charting a course out of an oppressive sense of self, of embodiment, of others, and of the world?

Limbong's dreams, Hollan concludes, show that the demands and expectations of others can be experienced as annihilating the self even in a culture that valorizes sociality, like the Toraja. Steve's dreams show that, even in a society that valorizes independence, internal representations of significant others can be destructively interfused with self. Hollan's selfscape dreams intimate modes of being outside these two cultural worlds and reflect

upon them critically. Limbong's dream caricatures sociocentrism as cannibal-
ism. Steve's dream places the putatively exhilarating freedom/mobility attributed to cars in late-capitalist American society (or more precisely to owning
them), as well as to white males who usually drive them in advertisements, in
quotation marks. Here cars are like the oozingly fluid clocks in Dali, betray-
ing the seemingly reliable cultural order they represent. For Limbong and
Steve alike, dreams are a key venue for the life of the self, and the dreaming
self appears as an essential counterpart to the waking self.

In "Race, Postcoloniality, and Identity in Samoan Dreams" (chapter 5),
I explore imaginal processing in dreams through consideration of a powerful
public symbol—skin color. Imaginal processing is aptly characterized, I
argue, by Derrida's concept of *différance* (1982). Derrida's idea is that symbol
systems operate via a continual slippage of meaning. Hegemonic colonial
worlds attempt to halt this slippage because they are built upon fixed meanings ascribed differentially to advantaged and disadvantaged groups. Yet
Samoan dreams indicate that even meanings critical to purposes of domination are dissolved by and reconstituted in dreams.

Hegemonies are only persuasively naturalized through internalization,
by becoming the structural categories through which we perceive, think,
feel, desire, and so forth. In this regard, a state of mind that continually
undermines internalized cultural categories is particularly important.
Dreams, the Samoan case will demonstrate, reflect critically on racial categories while showing them and (indeed cultural schemas generally) to be
inherently unstable.

From a political perspective, the idea that dreams corrode hegemonic
categories like race sounds salutary. But the nightly dissolution of our cultural universes is potentially disquieting as well. Discomfort with and sometimes terror in dreams can be read as a reaction to this dissolution of all fixed
meanings. Through the analysis of a teenage Samoan girl I call Penina, this
chapter shows that in postcolonial and transnational circumstances this
dynamic instability tends to bleed through into the waking world, undermin-
ing stable conventionalized meanings. This permeation can make people feel
victimized—as if the world is unreliable and there is no fixed point from
which to exercise leverage. Yet this historical situation also affords a richness
of possibility. It is after all people themselves, the primary processes of their
imaginations, that precipitate this continual transformation of meanings and
within it a quest for new opportunities to realize themselves and their desires.

This chapter also addresses the role dreams can play in discovering cultural psychology. As Eggan points out (1952, 477–78), ethnographers
seldom know their subjects as do psychoanalysts, yet dream analysis relies
upon the subjects' willingness and ability to open themselves (cf. Spiro, chapter 9). I illustrate how traditional analytic techniques can be converted into

projective exercises. These exercises permit subjects a greater degree of openness that can provide them insight and can allow ethnographers to use dreams to give thickness to studies of culture.

The relation of memory to dreaming is an important question in contemporary psychology.[12] In sleep, as sensory stimulation recedes, we recoup what we are in danger of forgetting by integrating daily memories into existing cognitive structures (Hunt 1989; Foulkes 1985). I connect personally to this idea: often as I start to slip off to sleep, I remember with alarm tasks I had meant to accomplish, but had forgotten in the whirl of daily existence. It makes sense that dreams should continue what the hypnagogic period begins.

In "Memory, Emotion, and the Imaginal Mind" (chapter 6), Michele Stephen proposes that dreams are a special form of remembering. Daily remembering articulates experience with a semantic code. Dreaming articulates emotionally significant events with the imaginal mind's configurational memory system. Similarly, Lacan believes we live conscious life predominately in a world of words where sequential thought is the basis of our identities—the Symbolic (1977b). But there is another form of mind that is backgrounded in early life—the Imaginary (Lacan 1968). This is where we live in dreams. In the gap between the semantic and the imaginal mind lies the unbridgeable distance between the dream-as-dreamt and the dream-as-told.[13] This distance, Stephen believes, explains why it is difficult to remember dreams and trances in our normal waking state. To me, Stephen's model further suggests that in order to translate dreams back into words (first in remembrance, later in relating them to others), we mediate between these forms of mind.

Spinning off Stephen's memory map, I suggest the remembered dream and the reported dream are similar to the recall of someone recovering from amnesia. As in amnesia, memory plays a hide-and-seek game in dream reporting, which could be attributed to the problems of translating an image-based form of memory into verbal memory. Remembered and reported dreams, then, would appear as a middle way between forms of mind.

Stephen's chapter raises further questions for me. Are the memories of artists and mystics (or left-handers) different from most people's? Are their semantic and imagistic memories less separated? Contrary to Lacan (1977b), Obeyesekere argues in *The Work of Culture*, (1990, 65–68) that in some places, for example Sri Lanka, the imaginal mind is not backgrounded. There the division between waking life and dream life is not emphasized and dream experience is looked upon as valid. Would the semantic memories and the configurational memories of Sri Lankans be as radically demarcated from one another as those of Westerners? In some cultures, American culture, for example (Lutz 1990), women are regarded as emotional. Is emotive-configurational memory less backgrounded for them? Probably everyone's memory needs to be charted as running between the semantic and the emotive-configurational poles of a larger spectrum. Activity along this spectrum may be as characterized by differential dual processing or, as in the images of modern physics, by moment-to-moment oscillations (sparked by context or biology) from one position to another.

Although Stephen's chapter constitutes a theoretical reflection rather than an ethnographic study, she illustrates her points through several dreams—for example, that of her housekeeper in Bali, Wayan. Wayan dreams that Stephen's big beautiful white dog, Timpal, has nothing to eat. This dream represents what Wayan needs to remember. At the time of the dream, Wayan was neglecting Stephen's house because she was terribly busy with preparations for the ceremonial adoption of herself and three siblings by her previously neglectful extended family (along with a tooth-filing ceremony for the youngest one). The dream articulates these events with several emotion-charged memories: (a) Wayan's parents were not able to care adequately for her as a child; she was often hungry and commented to Stephen that Timpal ate better than many Balinese people. (b) Stephen had become a mother figure for Wayan since her mother's death. (c) Wayan mothered the younger sibling who was to get the tooth-filing.

Balinese file the canines because these teeth (and presumably actual canines as well) represent to them humans' aggressive animal-like nature. It is likely that Wayan felt aggression throughout her life toward the significant others on whom she had depended, but who had so often left her unsatisfied. Probably she also felt guilt in her relations with them because of this aggression, as well as in her relations with those others to whom she now owed mothering (such as Timpal) and whom she herself at times neglected. By neglecting Timpal, Wayan implicitly identifies herself as a bad mother and *with* her parents and extended family. But inasmuch as Wayan was a neglected little girl who went hungry, she is also like Timpal. In my terms, Timpal can also be seen as a counteridentity—an animal with his canines intact who would still like to bite back. Ironically, the neglected Timpal seems also to represent all those Balinese who go hungry while white visitors lavishly feed their beautiful white dogs. This dream, then, may also be what I call in chapter 5 a "black and white" dream, in which postcolonial emotions are represented through color symbolism.

Part 3: Self-Revelation and Dream Interpretation

All chapters herein consider the nature of dreaming as well as the activities of dream telling and interpreting. In parts 1 and 2 the accent falls

on the former and in part 3 on the latter. In parts 1 and 2 we also emphasized the self and intrapsychic relations; in part 3 we explore, invoking Jessica
Benjamin's words, "what happens in the field of self and other" (1988, 20)
vis-à-vis the dream. Benjamin develops an intersubjective view of the self as
developing out of mutual recognition. The dream is, perhaps in every society,
a complex context in which recognition is negotiated because in dream
telling people both reveal and disguise themselves. Recognition is negotiated
in dream recounting through this dynamic of hiding and showing—for the
dream circulates around silenced and inarticulate aspects of self and of
self/other relations with the power to breach social relations. Let us turn to
psychoanalysis as a Western prototype of the work of interpretation and for
engagement with others in the context of the dream.

In psychoanalysis, interpretation occurs in the context of the therapy
session; the dream is taken as a guide to the dreamer's psychological problems. The interchange between public culture and the private self is represented, acted out in microcosm if you will, between analyst and analysand.
Transference and countertransference are an indirect dialogue between these
two, which takes place partially through dreams. This dialogue is indirect in
that it occurs between the lines—hidden in nonverbal messages and dream
images—rather than in transparent verbal messages. It is indirect because it
is communication with inextricably mixed motives.

Lacan, for example, characterizes Freud's analytic relationship with a
lesbian who tells Freud dreams of heterosexual love. Her homosexual desires
are represented in her dreams by reversal. Her dreams, then, seem to be a
deceit aimed at expression (of her forbidden desires), but not at communication. Yet, according to Lacan, through these dreams the woman says to
Freud, "*You want me to love men, you will have as many dreams about love of
men as you wish.* It is defiance in the form of derision" (1977a, 39, emphasis
in the original). Lacan believes that Freud symbolizes her father to this
woman, who she would defy; he also represents Lacan's "law of the father"—
the normative cultural world that insists she should be heterosexual. The
dreamer is mocking Freud (and the public world with him) by leading him
astray, and making a mockery of the analytic encounter as well. If the
dreamer might like to get away with this deceit, what good is derision and
mockery if its object does not get the message? Interpretation is an inevitable
part of such rich and circuitous communication. It is like the dream itself—
multi-layered, multivocal, and ambiguous.

For Lacan "the experience of the dream" is "that which floats everywhere, that which marks, stains, spots the text of any dream communication"
with one overriding sentiment: "I am not sure, I doubt" (1977a, 35). This
essential ambiguity is a "colophon" in the margins of the dream that points
to its significance (Lacan 1977a, 44). The irremediable ambiguity of dreams,

their inability to become a conventional and hence transparent form of communication, instigates hermeneutical activity that transports dream symbols out of private reality and back into social life. Crapanzano (chapter 10) argues that dreams' ambiguity provokes "interpretive anxiety"—a compulsion to ascribe a graspable meaning to them that circumvents their refusal to accommodate mundane norms of thought and action. Alternatively, one may react to dreams' irreducible ambiguity by denying legitimacy to the process of interpretation—dismissing interpretive activity in principle. The insistence that if dreams do not have one true meaning, a meaning that fully preexists the interpretive act, they have no meaning worth thinking about, is simply another form of interpretive anxiety. Evidence of both types of anxiety can be found in cultural approaches to the dream, as we will see below.

In "Dreams That Speak: Experience and Interpretation" (chapter 7), Erika Bourguignon discusses dreams that, from the local perspective, do not require interpretation. Interpretations are so much a part of the fabric of these dreams that they seem to come preinterpreted. What is actually seen in the dream is regarded as secondary, if not irrelevant. Preinterpretation, Bourguignon tells us, bypasses the manifest level of the dream in favor of a dream message. What indigenes see as the message is likely to dramatically diverge from what a psychoanalyst would consider the dream's latent meaning. Yet this message inspires a course of action that might well be undertaken if, from a psychoanalytic viewpoint, the dreamer had understood this latent meaning. Thus the Haitian Annette, visiting the country with Bourguignon, dreams of her boyfriend in the city. Annette sees the dream as a message from the female spirit Ezili: namely, a complaint from Ezili that Annette is neglecting her shrine back in the city. From the psychoanalytic perspective, the latent content is still encoded; it is Annette's desire to return to her home and boyfriend, despite having led a Western authority figure (Bourguignon) to the country purportedly to work with her on trance. In response to the dream, however, Annette tells Bourguignon that she must return to the city—acting as she would if she had understood the latent meaning.

Ezili and the several other spirits Annette meets in her dreams could be seen as representing the essential multiplicity of personhood in those societies where spirits and possession are salient. People in cultures that treat the self as unitary tend to preach faith in one God; people in cultures that see the self as role based and multiple tend to experience a plethora of spirits (Levy, Mageo, and Howard 1996). In these spirit cultures, communication in dreams and elsewhere flows freely between divine and human worlds (Shulman and Stroumsa 1999, 5). This communication relies on being able to translate the language of spirits into human language, that is on a system of preinterpretation.

Traditional western psychotherapeutic styles are confessional (Foucault 1990). Confession is a largely unidirectional form of communication in which the confessor speaks and the listener—a priest or psychoanalyst—occasionally makes pronouncements that grant absolution. Absolution retrospectively amends the division between internalized precepts and lived action. In Haiti, by way of contrast, it is the spirits who make pronouncements through dreams and through the mouths of those who relate them. These dream pronouncements at once displace and support the agency of the dreamer, prospectively sanctioning what would otherwise be a socially censured course of action.

From a western psychological perspective, Ezili is a subself fragment—a dissociated aspect of Annette that is not conscious and with which she does not identify. Annette's case suggests that the dream, like a trance state, is a venue in which people can (unbeknownst to their conscious self and wearing different personae) express and even find recognition for repressed/repudiated elements of self without the onus of personal responsibility. Ezili could also be seen as what I call a counteridentity: the agentive self in a society that valorizes deference. Rather than struggling against this counteridentity, Annette simply follows its injunctions.

In trance-possession cultures many people, like Annette, seem more comfortable with agency in the third person—agency attributed to a spirit whom they serve as "horse" or devotee. Displacing agency onto a spirit allows for independent action, while the individual, at least publicly, defers to social relationships and responsibilities. In Annette's dream, it is the spirit Ezili who exercises agency by commanding her to return to the city. This displaced agency permits Annette to honor the Haitian value of deference in hierarchical relationships while doing precisely what she wants. Haitian dream interpretation intimates that ways of thinking and acting provoked by dreams counterpoint internalized cultural schemas even while they appear to validate them. And yet rather than offering a radical critique of the Haitian world, Ezili allows Annette to accommodate complex feelings about Westerners as colonial authorities (owed a high degree of deference) within the Haitian cultural order. Haitian dream interpretation seems to position the dream as an antistructural moment that supports social structure by keeping it supple (cf. Turner 1977).

Waud H. Kracke, in "Dream: Ghost of a Tiger, A System of Human Words" (chapter 8), draws parallels between verbal communication and dreams. Dreams, he tells us, often borrow not only vocabularies, but also syntax and thesauruses from culture. An example of a vocabulary borrowed from culture would be someone whose latent dream thoughts concerned a condom, but who dreamed about a condom as a raincoat. When a culture contributes syntax, a dream paradigm is inscribed within the dream itself.

Thus it is often said that people in Jungian analysis have archetypal dreams, while those in psychoanalysis have dreams replete with the kind of symbolism central to Freud's view of the dream. Haitians, we have seen, think they dream of that world the Haitian system of dream interpretation suggests they will find—even when the surface story of the dream does not obviously reflect it. Dream thesauruses are standardized equivalencies between a dream image and a preestablished meaning, which Bourguignon calls preinterpretation. Then dreaming of A is consistently read to mean that the dream is about B as, for example, in Freud's view of concave and convex objects as signifying sexual body parts, or in the Haitian equation of identifiable types of dream figures with certain spirits. Dream thesauruses bring the evocative and indeterminate character of dream images closer to a language-like code.

Symbols and symbol systems appropriated from culture (like raincoats and paradigms of dream analysis) may be inscribed in the dream. But what about equivalencies between dream images and standardized meanings: aren't they in the interpretation? Parintintin shamans use their culture's dream thesauruses within the dream itself. By intentionally dreaming of a symbol, the shaman seeks to create an event in the world that this symbol would ordinarily predict.

I suggest in chapter 2 that dreams have critical implications for the cultural order: they reveal our embeddedness in and also our resistance to this order. But systems of dream interpretation may subvert these resistances. In this vein, Kracke shows that dream thesauruses can distance dreamers from anxiety-ridden conflicts, particularly when they appear on the surface of the dream, and hence may be a way of avoiding underlying dream thoughts. Kracke recounts the case of his Parintintin friend Manezinho, who dreams of his comrade's big penis and of getting a haircut (in psychoanalytic terms, signifying castration anxiety). Using a dream thesaurus learned from his father, Manezinho interprets both the penis and the haircut dreams as prophesying hunting success. Kracke believes these dreams are really about guilt and fear constellated around Manezinho's desire for his cousin (a union that the Parintintin see as incestuous) and his concomitant desire to get rid of his father (who represents the societal law forbidding incest). Unlike Haitian dreams, Manezinho's dreams do not abet a subterranean form of agency and an antistructural moment of acting out. Rather, the conventionalized system of equivalencies through which his dreams are understood merely distracts him from troubling feelings about others that could potentially undermine his relationships to them.

There is, I suggest, a range of possible attitudes towards the dream reflected in styles of interpretation. At one extreme one finds attitudes that reject interpretation and dismiss dreams as an errant form of mind. Along with the dream, these attitudes dismiss those reactions against the cultural order that are often symbolized in them. In the middle range are attitudes that honor dreams in name, but use interpretation to camouflage the dreamer's discontents and the implicit cultural critique they offer. At the other extreme are attitudes that honor dreams and use interpretation to listen to all the messages that they convey. Haitian and Parintintin cultures support middle-range attitudes. Yet the Haitian system of dream interpretation—which camouflages the dream's anti-structural message while encouraging the dreamer to act upon it—seems to support listening to the dream better than the Parintintin system.

Melford E. Spiro's "The Anthropological Import of Blocked Access to Dream Associations" (chapter 9) examines the case of Ms. B., one of his psychoanalytic clients. Ms. B.'s dreams suggest that public value systems, no matter how benign, generate intrapsychic conflicts that pose difficulties in discovering and abiding with oneself. Ms. B. has feminist values, yet has dreams of sexual enslavement that are a source of shame. She puts off telling Spiro about her dreams of forced fellatio and intercourse with sailors until the seventh month of analysis. Ms. B. also dreams of being poked, eaten and groped by witches. One could see in Ms. B.'s dreams internalized images critically representing both the schemas of feminism (the witches) and of male dominance (the sailors). These two schemas become mediums for pleasure and humiliation—a brew that Ms. B.'s dreaming mind continues to stir. The psychoanalytic endeavor aims at the development of critical self-awareness. In this tradition, Spiro challenges Ms. B., and us with her, to face all our contradictions, whatever their relation to culturally idealized models of the self.

What is consistent in Ms. B.'s dreams is a radical lack of agency: it is always her alters, either female witches or male sailors, who undertake or compel action. One is reminded of Jessica Benjamin's analysis of the problem of domination in the pornographic novel *The Story of O* (1988, 55–62). In O's story, as in B.'s dream, the female is always an object acted upon by others. O again and again acquiesces in the transgression of her body's boundaries and to her lover's demands that she be "always available and open" (Benjamin 1988, 57). Benjamin believes these sentiments derive from an early relational situation in which only the father is seen as a powerful agent. The girl, then, has no model for agency in her own sex and can only acquire it through identification with a powerful male other. Bondage and slavery are symbolic for O of relinquishing all sense of difference and separateness in order to remain connected to the Other (Benjamin 1988, 59). Where O's story and B.'s dreams differ is that both males and females represent powerful others for B.

Might the drunken sailors and the witches be Ms. B.'s counteridentities—her own capacity for agency in alienated form? Like Annette's dreams in Bourguignon's chapter, Ms. B.'s dreams suggest that she has in some measure dissociated her capacity for agentive action. Just as Ezili can be seen as a dissociated aspect of Annette's personality, the sailors and witches may be repudiated/repressed aspects of Ms. B., which she can express in dream life without the onus of personal responsibility. She is compelled rather than free to act in both these dreams; dreams themselves may serve, as does spirit possession in many cultures, as a denial that she is responsible for what these subself fragments do. One wonders if a dissociation of agency will work as well for Ms. B. in American society as it does for Annette in Haitian society.

Spiro's chapter also raises the question I confront in chapter 2: Where is agency? Is it in the conscious intention of the actor? Or is agency in the denied/hidden movements of the self against the demands and contradictions of a cultural world? Or, possibly, does agency lie in negotiating the dynamic interactions of these two?

Vincent Crapanzano's "Concluding Reflections" (chapter 10), can be viewed as a phenomenology of dream relating. Phenomenology begins with deconstruction—the dismantling of cultural categories that normally structure, but also limit perception. Crapanzano begins by deconstructing the category of the dream, underlining that all we have is dream accounts, not dreams themselves. The dream "seizes us . . . like any trickster," Crapanzano tells us, "by slipping away."

Dream accounts are performative. Interpretations, like accounts, reperform the dream. Reperformances are always within a particular social context, which leads us to recast dreams in the conventions of that context, however unwittingly.[14] Reperformance that does not recognize itself as such may lose track of the original context, which Crapanzano believes has much to tell us about culture and the self, as well as about the place of the dream in relation to them. To be within a social context is to be engaged with others, embedding the dream in what Crapanzano calls "a series of interlocutory nestings." If dream performances are multiply situated in and engaged with the cultural world, Crapanzano tells us, potentially they retain the dream's ability to enact breach, permeability, and fluidity within it.

Out of all these chapters comes a view of dreaming and of the self. The self appears as multiple and the dream as doing the work of mediation. This mediation is not directed at making a unitary self, but at crafting open systems of communication. The various chapters show communication that takes place in dreams to be between people's preobjective perceptions and their cultural schemas, existing narratives of self and experiences that do not fit these narratives (such as migrants' transnational experience), self schemas and daily life, hegemonic social categories and the free play of imaginal thinking within the person, emotional experience and the configurational memory system. Dream interpretation appears as a context in which the person's capacity for agency, creativity, and reflection are to varying degrees exercised or abrogated. But in every instance the agency, creativity, and reflection that we find through dreams and their interpretations are not those of Descartes's "I"—identified solely with the ratiocinative individual. Rather they are authored interrelationally in the context of complex emotions and of subtle, often hidden and subliminal, social communications in which we exercise influence on one another.

Notes

I thank Robert Van de Castle for his comments and generous support for this volume. I also thank Mary Bloodsworth for reading and commenting on this chapter. I thank Troy Wilson for his excellent work on the index.

1. See for example C. G. Seligmen 1924, 1932; Lincoln 1935, 107–131; Róheim 1946, 1949, 1950; Devereux 1951.

2. On Mead's Samoan work and Freudian theory see further Mead 1959 and Mageo 1988, 28–37.

3. Other Culture and Personality anthropologists who investigated dreams were A. Irving Hallowell, George Devereux, and Weston Le Barre. Samples of their work can be found in Von Grunebaum and Caillois's *The Dream and Human Societies* (1966).

4. See for example White and Kirkpatrick 1985; Lutz 1988.

5. See for example Homiak 1987; Graham 1995.

6. The belief that people's spirit doubles travel in sleep is common in many of the cultures anthropologists study. See for example Basso 1987, 88–89; Herdt 1987, 58; Levy 1973, 374.

7. On egocentrism and sociocentrism, see for example Murray 1993; Hollan 1992, Markus and Kitayama 1991; White and Kirkpatrick 1985; Shweder and Bourne 1984; Levy 1983, and Mauss [1938] 1985. For critiques of the egocentric/sociocentric dichotomy see Spiro 1993; Mageo 1998, 1995, 2002a; Mageo and Knauft 2002.

8. Sullivan (1953) called those aspects of experience lost to awareness as a result of encountering strong negative evaluations in the course of socialization the "not-me."

9. See also Hofstadter and Dennett 1981; Tedlock 1987, 26; Price-Williams 1987.

10. See for example Lutz 1988; Strathern 1990; Markus and Kitayama 1991; Wagner 1991; Battaglia 1995; and Benjamin 1988. Cultural theorists also argued that the idea that people are unitary and autonomous is illusory. See for example Althusser 1971 and Derrida 1978.

11. For an overview of this work see D'Andrade 1961. D'Andrade himself believes that there is "no simple relation between the culture and the manifest content of dreams" (1961, 313). Rather the manifest dream reflects the needs and conflicts of individuals in particular societies.

12. For a synopsis of contemporary psychological research on the relation of dreaming to memory see Van de Castle 1994, 274–76.

13. On the difference between the dream experience and the dream report see further Crapanzano chapter 10 and 1980; and Van de Castle 1994, 280–81.

14. On the effect of social context on dreaming and dream reporting see also Van de Castle 1994, 281–87 and Hunt 1989, 12.

CHAPTER 2

Subjectivity and Identity
in Dreams

JEANNETTE MARIE MAGEO

> The ancients recognized all kinds of things in dreams, including, on occasion, messages from the gods—and why not? . . . [W]ho knows, the gods may still speak through dreams. Personally, I don't mind either way. What concerns us is the tissue that envelops these messages, the network in which, on occasion, something is caught. Perhaps the voice of the gods makes itself heard, but it is a long time since men lent their ears to them.
>
> —Jacques Lacan, *The Four Fundamental*
> *Concepts of Psycho-Analysis*

*B*eing on the edge, as it were, of normative reality, re-presenting it, dreams highlight its anatural character and our "encounter" with this reality. For this reason, the way cultural processes play upon and shape the self is more palpable in dreams than in many other venues. My intent in this chapter is to reflect theoretically on how dreams engage us nightly in what might be called a phenomenological descent into the self.

There are hints of a relationship between phenomenology and the dream in that classic Western perspective on dreaming, psychoanalysis. We saw in chapter 1 that for Sigmund Freud, dreams are littered with "day residues." These are symbols of events from the past day, events that were ambivalently significant to us when they took place. At the time, this significance was swept from conscious mental and emotional life by our need to avoid anxiety-provoking stimuli. From a psychoanalytic viewpoint, then, we are always reacting to experience more strongly and with interest than we know, but in daily life our deeper psychological reactions are clouded.[1] The clouds begin to dissipate when we fall asleep. Then the defenses that are usually so vital to psychological well-being (and ill-being) relax, allowing what is normally elided from consciousness to arise. This psychoanalytic portrait of the relation between the waking and sleeping mind implies that in dreams a more immediate level of existence, closer to moment-to-moment experience, is arising too; it also presupposes levels of the self—all colored by enculturation, but some less effectively, more tenuously, than others.

In anthropological terms, the clouding elements of daily life are those shared, patterned understandings that compose the normative world and can be inferred from discourse, which anthropologists call cultural schemas (Strauss and Quinn 1997). As Ricoeur (1981, 41–42) says of language, cultural schemas give us access to experience—a certain purchase upon it. But this access occludes and fails to provision other possibilities for experiences in the self and in the world. The anything-but-normal reality of dream life suggests that in sleep cultural schemas sustain a degree of slippage. I am not saying they go away. The chapters to follow will show that, in a sense, cultural schemas become more dramatic. Dreaming, in Shulman and Stroumsa's words, is "a cultural act" (1999); its landscapes, scenes, figures, objects, problematics, and solutions, as well as ways of recounting the dream, are all appropriated from culture.

In Bali, for example, krises are family heirlooms that symbolize secular and spiritual authority (Stephen, chapter 6). Komang dreams of carrying his family's kris to a temple and pointing it at each family member. In chapter 5 I present a young Samoan who dreams of going to heaven and meeting his great-grandfather, a paramount chief, in the act of signing away American Samoa to the U.S. Navy. In Kracke's chapter on the Amazonian Parintintins (chapter 8), Manezinho dreams of killing a jaguar. All of these—sacred krises and visiting temples, paramount chiefs and treaties with the United States and hunting jaguars too—are schemas that come from cultures. Ethnographic reports of dreams verify that cultural schemas dictate what people expect to, and do find, in their dream worlds.[2] Yet if culture shapes our dreams and our reports about them, it is also true that in dreams the apparently seamless interdigitation of cultural schemas and our experience frays, and our discomfort with these schemas, for most of us submerged in the onrush of daily living, surfaces. Let me give an example from Samoan dreams.

I taught at a small college in American Samoa for many years. My Samoan students used to tell me that they knew their parents loved them, but parents never expressed love except when childen were hurt or sick; then parents betrayed real distress and deep concern.[3] Grandparents more openly expressed affection, students said, and often took the most active role in childcare.[4] I realized when I looked at these students' dreams that this discourse was what Bourdieu calls "doxa" (1992, 164–171)—tenets of the taken-for-granted social world that legitimate given relations between people. My students' dreams told a different story. Take for example the following, in which a teenage boy dreams of his childhood:

> [M]y friends and I were playing marbles in front of our house. . . . Suddenly, out of nowhere, I saw this big, hairy monster. . . . My friends got scared and ran away. Somehow this monster . . . wanted to eat me. . . . [W]hen I ran around the house I saw a trash can. . . . I jumped into it. . . . [T]he house door it was open, so I ran for the doorway. As I got closer, the door slammed shut. . . . I screamed and yelled and pounded on the door. . . . Right when the monster was about to reach the back of my shoulder, my grandmother opened the door. I found myself face first in front of my grandmother's feet. . . . I told her about the monster. . . . She said, "What monster? I don't see any monster. . . . [G]o back and play marbles."

I call this dreamer Fefe. Fefe role-played a dialogue between himself and the monster. The monster said, "I might as well eat you. It seems like no one cares." Just as my other students had stressed that their elders did care despite appearances, at first Fefe rejoined, "No, Monster, you're wrong. They do care!" But after this dialogue he remarked, "I feel like the monster is right about my family. . . . [T]he monster is forever chasing me. To compare that to my family—they're always chasing me and telling me to do this and do that. Oh, a thought just passed through my head. . . . I remember my grandmother always telling me if I don't pick up the trash . . . she's going to send me to my mother. And she knows I don't like my mother's family."

The doubts Fefe suffers, we will soon see, have as much to do with cultural history as with the Samoan family. My point here is that Fefe's dream "talks back" to Samoan cultural schemas about parenting, asking: Do parental figures, his grandmother in this instance, really care?

The differences between dream images and their waking originals betray secret feelings we hesitate to share with others and even with ourselves. Dreams offer images of how we feel and think about the cultural world beneath ordinary awareness, as Fefe's monster offers an image of how he secretly thinks and deeply feels about his family chasing him and telling him "to do this and that." Dreams expose the way we experience cultural life, as well as the possibility of comprehending this experience.[5] Our suppressed and denied tribulations, our infantilisms, but also our humanity are there in emotions that are ordinarily cast into the "trash can" of dreams (to combine Freud's and Fefe's imagery). This is why one suspects people who habitually forget dreams, and cultures that encourage or validate this forgetfulness, of avoiding reflexivity.

On the individual level, Carl Jung anticipates the idea that a critical perspective is potentially offered us by dreams. For Jung, dreams take positions directly opposed to those dreamers take in waking life and thereby highlight precisely what they have neglected or overlooked, to their cost (1970b, 136–56). Dreams offer an incipient critique of cultural reality, and people within it, by mirroring that reality. The mirror world, which so many peoples imagine as the hereafter, is also the dream world.[6] This is obvious in Bourguignon's essay (chapter 5), where the worlds of spirits and dreams are one and the same. Bourguignon's dreamer, Annette, sometimes enters the Haitian spirit world in sleep and sometimes in trance: it is merely a question of different foyers. The idea that spirit worlds are entered in dream states is a common apprehension among peoples who believe in these worlds, as anthropological studies of shamanism have long shown.[7] One finds this idea in Western societies as well. Ewing (chapter 6) writes of a young Turkish German woman whose brother dies. Her family believes in an afterlife and that those who have died visit them in dreams. "Now," she says of her brother, "we see him only in our dreams."

The Bizarre and the Uncanny

In the dream, waking reality appears alien, even bizarre (States 1993, 13–45). The kinship between the bizarre and the dream was a major focus of the most famous surrealist, Dali. In his series "Dream Approaches," the cultural webs of significance in which humans live are rendered, but are far from seamless.[8] These paintings capture the nature of dream images by offering us abnormalized copies of our waking worlds. The schemas of ordinary life are juxtaposed with contradictory contents: most famously, oozing (which we associate with formless objects or experiences) and clocks (which we associate with structured objects or experiences). Art and the dream are forms of mimesis: they copy or repeat the ordinary worlds in which people live, but the copies differ tellingly from their originals.

Stephen (chapter 6) and I (chapter 5) argue that dreams are a form of imaginal thinking, like art.[9] Imaginal thinking operates via contradictions (Mageo 2002a): images are reproduced with contradictory additional or subtractive marks that differentiate them from their originals; the contradictions offer a commentary on the originals. Dreams have marks, additional and subtractive, that distinguish their images from those of everyday life. In Fefe's case, for example, there is an image from the ordinary world, playing marbles; additionally, there is a hairy monster. Fefe's grandmother is an image from the ordinary world but, subtractively, she can't see what's right in front of her face (the monster). These differences—from ordinary marbles games and grandmothers who see just fine—offer commentaries. In the first case, the dream image suggests that Fefe is trapped in an outside world that does not feel safe to him. Indeed, in Samoan childrearing schemas girls are expected to stay inside or in the immediate environs of the house; boys are expected to roam farther afield and to need less protection. In the second case, Fefe's grandmother's vision is adequate, but the dream implies her emotional perception is not. Obviously, she is not attending to the monster or to Fefe and here again there is a gender difference in Samoan childcare schemas. Girls are closely watched to safeguard their virtue; parent figures pay less attention to Samoan boys.

Surrealists used the bizarre to create a sense of the uncanny (Breton 1972). Following this lead, we must also consider the uncanny to unravel the bizarre nature of dream life. Levy's Tahitians describe uncanny feelings, which they called *mehameha* (1973, 151). When one is *mehameha*, one's head feels swollen, one's hair stands on end, one's limbs get gooseflesh. Tahitians take these sensations to mean a spirit is present. My Samoan informants gave me similar accounts in which they knew they had been in the presence of a spirit because after feeling spooked they went home and looked in the mirror: their hair was standing on end.

Mehameha, Levy remarks, occurs "in the context of the 'unknown'" (1973, 151). Building on Jerome Bruner's work (Bruner, Goodnow, and Austin 1956, 12), Levy maintains that categories are the means by which we identify the events and objects of the world about us. "When an event cannot be categorized," Levy says, we "lose our anchor in commonsense reality" and "experience terror in the face of the uncanny" (1973, 152). In contemporary psychological anthropology, we speak not so much of categories, which imply lexicons for experience, but schemas, which imply larger conceptual structures of which lexicons are a part.[10] But it is also true that when we cannot fit an experience into a cultural schema we lose our moorings in the commonsense world.

The uncanny occurs in sensory deprivation contexts (Levy 1973, 152). In Tahiti and Samoa, people live in extended families and small villages; everyone is around lots of people all the time. Tahitians and Samoans often experience the uncanny when they are out alone at night. Remember, they believe they sense the uncanny because they are in the presence of a spirit.

One might infer they go on producing the schema "people" even when no one is there (Whitehead).* The uncanny can be thought of as cultural schemas reproduced without sensory content, as when the schema "people" is reproduced as a mere ghost of its former self—as a spirit, that is. The uncanny gives us a momentary unverbalized sense and sensation that those schemas with which we construct daily experience are merely conventional. What we normally take for reality is thus breached and we stand there without the usual protection staring in terror, glimpsing something that makes our hair stand on end, for, as T. S. Eliot says in the *The Four Quartets*, "human kind cannot bear too very much reality" (1971, 14).

The dream, too, is a sensory deprivation context. There, our cultural schemas are reproduced as the uncanny: that is, without real sensory contents.[11] Rather than being used to construct sensory content as in waking life, in dreams sensory content is recruited to support schemas. It follows that in dreams we inhabit a world of pure meaning, for which the spirit world, all alternative realities perhaps, are metaphors.[12] While dreams borrow the residual images of the day to supply schemas with a sensory content, it is a patchwork job that never looks quite right—letting us, potentially, see through our schemas like transparent ghosts. The anxiety and quickening of the dream derives in part from this momentary possibility for transparency, a moment in which we perceive what Merleau-Ponty (1962) calls the "preobjective."

Dreams and Preobjective Perception

For Merleau-Ponty, the world, as we normally perceive it, is a conventionally agreed upon one. The agreements are registered in the way that world is objectified in conventional forms of expression, "which reveal my thoughts to others *only* because already . . . meanings are provided for each sign" (Merleau-Ponty 1962, 166, emphasis mine). Language and discourse are the most obvious forms of expression that operate *only* through conventionally agreed upon meanings. Objectifications obscure dimensions of phenomenal life that are unacknowledged in conventional expression; however, they do not exhaust the possibilities of perception, which are rich and indeterminate (Csordas 1990, 8). Merleau-Ponty tells us there is a preobjective form of perception that is "anterior to conventional means of expression" (1962, 166). Preobjective perception, like normal perception, takes place in the cultural world with which "we are in contact by the mere fact of existing" and "carry about inseparably with us before any objectification" (Merleau-Ponty 1962,

---

*Harriet Whitehead shared this insight with me on a hike in the spring of 1992.

362). While preobjective perception is not precultural, Csordas says, it is "pre-abstract" (1990, 10). But if culture is, in Max Weber's terms, "webs of signifi-cance," then to inhabit culture at all is to inhabit a world of signs, which are inherently abstract. Some distinction needs to be made here between kinds of symbols in relation to conventional expression and to perception.

Merleau-Ponty equates preobjective perception with "a primary process of signification" (1962, 166). Freud, of course, equates dreaming with his own model of primary process thought ([1900]1953, vol. 5, 599–611). For Merleau-Ponty, what characterizes these primary processes is that "the thing expressed does not exist apart from the expression and . . . the signs themselves induce their significance." Like art? Like dreams? I do not mean to suggest that dreams are coincident with preobjective percep-tion. Dreams are objectifications. The images of dreams, like the signs of language and discourse, abstract elements of daily life, framing certain expe-riences in specific ways. Yet dreams can fracture the conventionally agreed upon world by reshuffling conventional meanings. In the Samoan dream mentioned earlier, in which the young man goes to heaven and meets his great-grandfather, he gets to heaven via a spaceship. "Going to heaven" is a cultural schema and has a conventionally agreed upon meaning in contem-porary Samoa, which is universally Christian. "Spaceships" have a shared meaning too, given all the movies and TV programs contemporary Samoans watch. But their combination is original, contradictory even, combining sci-ence with a mythological destination.

Freud sees the ego as the mediating element of self—reconciling con-science and desire, and bridging between the self and the world (1961a). But symptoms and dreams may also play this mediating role (1963, 394, 358–60). When the ego is undermined in mental illness, a symptom mediates between conscience and desire. In this psychoanalytic view, however, symptoms are merely pastiches that never achieve reconciliation between these elements of self. When the ego is absent in sleep, the dream takes on the ego's mediating role. Like symptoms, Freud sees the dream as a potpourri of elements, rather than doing the work of reconciliation. In this sense, for Freud dreams are the universal symptom. But it is also possible that the combinations of desire and conscience we find in the dream and related states, such as trance, are genuine compromises made in images rather than in verbal terms that point the way to working out conflicts (Mageo 1998, 79–80, 164–190; 1991a, 366–367).

And so in my chapter on Samoa (chapter 5), Penina dreams of stealing jewels that she shares with her aunt. The jewels symbolize their close per-sonal relationship. Samoans tend to downplay such relationships in favor of responsibilities to, and social relations with, their extended family groups. In the dream, a policeman comes to get Penina, but her aunt hides her in the closet. Penina was afraid of her father (who she compared to the policeman in the dream) and in consequence hides feelings of wanting to live with her aunt. When working on the dream, Penina decided (without any comment from me) it meant she had to persuade her father to let her return to her aunt. By representing conflicts between conscience and desire, dreams themselves begin the work of mediation. Indeed Calvin Hall (1966) saw dreams as a record in images of the dreamer's conflicts and as attempts to resolve them.

Dreams' mediating effect is accelerated when people recount them after waking, but there is no reason to believe that dream images and scenarios do not exert influence on us even when we do not recount them. Dreams do more than mediate between elements of the self. Dreams, I will show, mediate between the forms of awareness inherent in cultural schemas and preobjective perceptions of possibilities for being a person and for being in the world that we register, but are often unable to communicate or even to think about in words.

While dreaming is a mode of abstraction in images, it does not, in Merleau-Ponty's words, "reveal my thought . . . only because already . . . meanings are provided for each sign" (1962, 166). Dreams are capable of producing their own nonverbal significance—as the images of art also do. Because dreams and art share this productive capacity, Bert States calls dreaming the "ur-form of all fiction" (1993, 3) and Jean Paul Richter calls it "involuntary poetry" (1973, 151n). Dreams haunt us because they are so often pregnant with immediate yet evanescent meanings. The post-Freudian Lacan says in the dream something "demands to be realized. . . . [W]hat is *produced*, in this gap, is presented as *the discovery*. . . . This discovery is, at the same time, a solution—not necessarily a complete one, but, however incomplete it may be, it has that indefinable something that touches us . . . namely *surprise*, that by which the subject feels himself overcome, by which he finds both more and less than he expected—but, in any case, it is, in relation to what he expected, of exceptional value. Now, as soon as it is presented, this discovery becomes a rediscovery. . . . [I]t is always ready to steal away again, thus establishing the dimension of loss" (1977a, 25).

This sense of discovery derives in part from the fact that, more so than linguistic signs, the imagistic signs of dreams are original. Dream images combine symbols that are generated by the social world or by psychological processes into unique configurations. Dream images, like those of art, can afford originality because they re-evoke experience in the world and are themselves a kind of experience.[13] Experience produces its own meanings. But the images of art and dreams are to varying degrees conventional as well: they re-evoke experience more readily for those who share a common cultural and historical situation.

D. H. Lawrence (1936) characterizes the conventional world as a sky-dome that people take for the sky. He portrays the role of the artist as making gashes in that dome so that everyone sees the stars. Dreamers, too, make gashes in the assumed world, so that in sleep we evanescently glimpse the sky—although it is more often stormy than starry. Fefe's dream, for example, makes a gash in Samoan childcare conventions by asking, Do his elders really care? In Lawrence's sky-dome image, society is personified by workmen who repair the dome by painting the image of a starry vision over the gash. Dream visions are ever-so-instantly painted by our minds into the cultural vision. Fefe's gash has already been painted into the Samoan sky: there are cultural schemas in contemporary Samoa that give a conventional form to just the sort of doubt that Fefe feels.

Samoans have many terms for "care," but a word they often use these days is a pidgin term, *kea*. *Leai se kea*, meaning "I don't care," or just *lē kea*, meaning the same, are common expressions. When my Samoan students role-played their dreams, characters were often described as exhibiting *lē kea* attitudes (Mageo 2001c). Lack of care is for young Samoans conveyed in an idiom that bespeaks the culturally hybridized context that has exacerbated care concerns in recent decades. Those resistances to cultural life Fefe realizes through his dream are already part of his cultural patterning. J. S. Lincoln distinguishes between "cultural pattern dreams," in which the dreamer receives a message for the community, and personal dreams (1935; see also Fabian 1967). Fefe's dream could not be more personal, yet it is recursively drenched in culture.

Shared, patterned understandings—our cultural schemas—deeply tinge and structure our dreams, painting over the possible vistas of perception. In this sense, the dream is, as Lacan tells us, "an act of homage to the missed reality—the reality that can no longer produce itself except by repeating itself endlessly, in some never attained awakening" (1977a, 58). Yet consciousness is inherently expansive. If we can never get out of conventional reality, we are always trying to see over its edges. Dreams are one of its edges.

Dreams and Hypocognition

What then is the nature of this "missed reality"? In what sense is it "repeated" in dreams? Levy maintains that Tahitians are unable to conceptualize and verbalize the experience that in English we call "sadness" (1984, 219). Shared inabilities of this sort point to areas of experience that are missed by the culture's linguistic/discursive system (Levy 1973,324). Levy calls these areas "hypocognized." Hypocognized experiences are outside of epistemes, but Levy tells us (1984, 225) they are represented in dreams—an insight Fefe's dream confirms. Fefe's dream points to a hypocognized area of Samoan cultural life: close personal relationships, which are undermined in early childhood. Traditionally in Samoa, newborns were constantly carried and nursed on demand; however, as early as six months of age a transit to sibling care began and elders gradually suspended physical and verbal demonstrations of affection.[14] Called "parental distancing," this practice is common throughout Polynesia and fosters limited emotional investments in later relationships.[15]

The "missed reality" represented in dreams is not only cultural, but historical. People share problematic historical experiences that are new to their cultures and that their linguistic/discursive systems are ill prepared to handle. These experiences cannot be easily talked about, but can be represented in dreams. Fefe's problem derives from Samoan traditions of childcare, in which children attend to adults rather than vice versa (Ochs 1982). But his problem is also the historical convergence of these traditions with Western models of relationship, which feature interpersonal engagement. Thus, the interchange between Fefe and his grandmother occurs around a door. Traditional Samoan houses lacked both walls and doors, which symbolize a host of new possibilities for inclusion and exclusion. The grandmother does not answer the door because she is watching television. (If she is like other Samoan grandmothers, she is likely to be watching soap operas, which celebrate, ironically, the very Western models of interpersonal engagement to which she does not seem to subscribe). *Fefe's problem is his historical moment*, it is one that he shares with all his generation. During my eight-year residence in Samoa, I collected over five hundred dreams. I had many young people role-play their dreams, just as Fefe did (Mageo 2001c). In the dialogues that ensued, care, or the lack thereof, was these dreamers' most recurrent and pressing concern.

I am not saying dreams operate to assist us. Dreams are a kind of thinking done in sleep—imaginal thinking—and "as necessary to the mind as beating is to the heart" (States).* While awake we often think about practical problems; in dreams only the psychological residues of these problems remain—those residues created at least in part by a lack of fit with our cultural-historical worlds. The dream "repeats" this lack of fit. Hollan's Los Angelian client, Steve (chapter 4), inhabits a cultural world that expects him to be autonomous and dreams of his overbearing parents, with whom he is entangled in a symbiotic relationship. Stephen's Balinese housekeeper (chapter 6) inhabits a cultural world that freights her with extensive care responsibilities and dreams of neglecting to feed a pampered dog. My Samoan student, Penina (chapter 5), inhabits a cultural world that expects her to render obedience in accord with her position in her social group, but dreams

---

*This quote is from an e-mail from Bert States to me dating from the fall of 2001.

of being free in America with her indulgent aunt. Buddhists say life is suffering. Cultural life is full of problems. Our minds, whether waking or dreaming, are preoccupied by these problems and work on them like the oyster works on the pearl.

Dreams, Cultural Work, and Creativity

What is the nature of this work and what is its relevance for the self? Dreams perform what we might call the primacy stage of "the work of culture." Obeyesekere calls the work of culture crafting "personal symbols" (1981, 1990). Personal symbols mediate between private and public symbols. Following Leach (1958), anthropologists distinguish between kinds of symbols. *Private symbols* are those that relate to individual psychology and to bodily life. Hair, for example, can be a private symbol; it is one of those extending and easily cut-off body parts that to psychoanalysts represents the penis, as well as sexuality and desire more generally.[16] *Public symbols*, alternatively, are private symbols that have been denuded of psychological meanings by people in society and used to convey social messages. Hippies conveyed social messages through their long hair: they were part of a group that had a friendly attitude toward desire. *Personal symbols* are public symbols that individuals articulate with their personal psychological suffering, thereby renewing or recreating them. These symbols can then be taken up by others and may lead a culture in new directions.

Ecstatic female priestesses in Sri Lanka, according to Obeyesekere take a public symbol that is important in Sri Lankan religious traditions—matted locks—and reinvest it with intense idiosyncratic meanings (1981). Psychologically, their matted locks signify the resolution of their own private childhood conflicts through the sublimation of desire. But these matted locks are more than private in their significance: publicly they are regarded by many as proof of these women's vocation—that they have been chosen by a god. Personal symbols, then, inhabit a liminal position between private and public symbols; they are psychologically charged and yet are also shared, and thus to a degree communicative and removed from purely personal psychological problems.

These distinctions map a territory that is private (albeit also universal) and another that is public. On this map are mediators (like religious specialists) who transit these domains. I find this map clarifying, as so many scholars have, but I also question it. For Obeyesekere, the work of culture, and presumably personal symbols, are symbolically removed from "deep motivation"—those enduring compulsions that derive from the family dramas of early childhood. Dreamwork and dream symbols are not (1990, 54). The further removed symbols are from deep motivation, Obeyesekere tells us, the more they approximate "the Saussurean idea of the arbitrary relation between signifier and signified" (1990, 58)—in other words, the more they participate in the conventional nature of language and discourse. It follows that the closer symbols are to deep motivation, the more experiential and evocative they are.

While closer to the preobjective than the personal symbols of art or religion, like them, dream symbols occupy a liminal space between language and emotive/embodied reactions. "Private" and "personal" can be understood as different registers of dream images: a dream image is a private symbol inasmuch as it relates to deep motivation; it is also a personal symbol inasmuch as it relates to public cultural reality and brings preobjective responses to this reality. Fefe's case illustrates that family dramas are situated in and shaped by sociocultural worlds, particularly when hypocognized aspects of these worlds are brought into greater play by historical circumstances. Just as personal symbols, the image of the door that slams in Fefe's face articulates a public symbol that contemporary Samoans understand (indeed, that everyone who lives in cultures with closed doors understands) with monstrously powerful feelings that Fefe ordinarily hides even from himself. If the personal symbols mystics and artists promulgate move us, it is because these symbols represent solutions to shared cultural and historical problems. Their personal symbols are contributions to a common work we all undertake initially in dreams and secondarily in our attempts to comprehend them. Dreams, Globus rightly holds, are a form of "creative consciousness" (1987, 62). For this reason, they can provide an entrance to a "space of authoring" (Holland et. al. 1998) in which people begin to reenvision their world.

Thinking about his dream, Fefe later concluded, "This dream is telling me the answer. . . . I have to talk straight up with my family and grandmother about my feelings." In Samoa the high chief is a model of ideal conduct; he plays his role nobly and his speech is sa'o, "straight." Aiming at this ideal, one woman said, "I always have to face straight and say straight," meaning without prevarication. Several young Samoans with whom I worked on dreams arrived at the same solution: it was original, but also logical in Samoan cultural terms. Another woman, for example, thought she needed "to be straightforward with people . . . and tell them what I feel without being afraid of . . . hurting the other's feelings and disregarding mine." To enlist Richard Shweder's phrase (1991), what these dreamers were doing was "thinking through culture," that is, thinking not only with cultural schemas, but also through them to new possibilities.

Dreams are imagination in action. They can be seen as a virtual reality—a mock-up for a trial run of semiotic possibilities inherent in cultural meaning systems vis-à-vis personal articulations. Experimenting with these semiotic possibilities, dreams can help us make discoveries that fill in meaning voids in culture. Jung believed that in dreams our imaginations propel us into the future through symbols that capture the past and reveal within it possible directions (1972b, 237–280). Ellen Basso (1987) has suggested this is why many traditional cultures see at least some dreams as portentous. In dreaming, we are discovering the future—perhaps not the literal future, but ways we can move into it, ways it invites us forward—articulated in symbolic form. Western dream research indicates that dreams help people master new individual experience (Palombo 1978; Cartwright 1977). By transforming shared meanings, dreams also help us master new cultural experience.[17]

What I am suggesting is that dreams do not simply carry meanings in an epiphenomenal way—accidentally, as it were, by virtue of their nature—as knowing a Samoan inevitably conveys some information about Samoan culture. Dreams are continually creating meanings, and they do so by lending our life experiences fresh interpretations. All thought, dream conceptualization as well, by virtue of its symbolic nature, is unavoidably interpretive. The act of representing a hypocognized area of culture, as Fefe's dream does, is a kind of symbolic work that makes an interpretation. We interpret dreams, but first they interpret us. This is, of course, in a manner of speaking, for we are our dreaming selves just as truly as we are our waking selves.

Dreams, Agency, and Counteridentities

If dreams are a quintessentially creative aspect of self (Globus 1987, 3–62), then it is strange that one often feels in dreams as if one is merely reacting to shifting scenes and circumstances beyond one's control.[18] In the dream, our agency is decentered and we count the cost of acting only in a moment-to-moment retrospect. This is one explanation as to why dreams are so anxiety provoking. Lacan calls this quality of the dream "it shows," and tells us that it consists in "the absence of horizon . . . and, also, the character of emergence, of contrast, of stain, of its images, the intensification of their colours. . . . [I]n the final resort, our position in the dream is profoundly that of someone who does not see. The subject does not see where it is leading, he follows" (1977, 75).

Positionally, gazing encodes a difference between subjects (who gaze and who act) and objects (who are gazed at and acted upon). In Western art and cinema, women have been portrayed as the embodied object of male gaze and thus as lacking subjectivity and agency—nudes being the prime example (Berger 1972, 47–57; Mulvey 1975). But in Lacan's characterization of the dream, there is a reversal of positions we normally associate with gazing: gazing is synonymous with passivity and responsiveness (not seeing, following); its antinomy, display, becomes agentive (the "it shows," leading). If we are our dreaming minds, then we exercise agency in dreaming, however limited in efficacy we feel. How might one resolve this contradiction between our actual agency and our sense of being "profoundly one who does not see"? The answer to this question, I believe, lies in another: Who is this self who inhabits the dream?

For Freud, the dream is the muffled voice of the id. The id refers to the embodied and emotive aspects of self motivated by "the pleasure principle," a principle that seeks to satisfy desire (1961a). Dreams express desires, in the psychoanalytic view, but these desires are muffled: dream logic (primary process thinking) represents desire in disguise. This is because desires can disturb sleep because they incite action (towards satisfaction) and anxiety. The reason desires incite anxiety is because they are often in conflict with the individual's values, self-image, or self-esteem. If the id is a part of the self that is often at odds with fundamental features of conscious identity and is represented in dreams, then Jung's idea that dreams compensate for the conscious attitude of the dreamer (noted earlier) makes perfect sense.

Freud's portrait of the self as being divided between an emotive and embodied id expressed in dreams and a waking rational ego iterates and perhaps hinges on the mind/body dualism ushered into Western thought by Descartes. At the opening of chapter 1 we saw that Descartes took the dream as a prime example of how the mind could be deceived by the senses and as evidence, therefore, that the senses could not be trusted. With Descartes's "I think, therefore I am," the self for Western peoples came to be located in the mind as opposed to the senses or sensibilities. In her book *Volatile Bodies*, Grosz writes of the tendency in Western societies to conceive of "the human subject as a mind housed or encapsulated in a quasi-mechanical body, the 'captain of the ship'" (1994, 86). It is just this map of the self that Merleau-Ponty seeks to change. Grosz goes on to quote him: "The perceiving mind *is* an incarnated body" (Merleau-Ponty 1964, 3–4, emphasis mine).

Is an oppositional arrangement between conscious identity and the dreaming self peculiarly Western? In chapter 1 we saw that in many other cultures the dream self is taken to be the constitutive self that survives death. In these cultures the dream self, like the waking self, tends to be conceived of as a social persona rather than as an internal "I." The idea of a dream double that survives the life of the body *also* suggests that people believe the self is divided between one part that is constitutive and another that is affiliated with the body

Along these lines, Lakoff (1996, 98–103) shows that one can discover a "divided person" metaphor for the self in phrases like: "I'm beside myself," "I'm debating with myself about that," "Be kind to yourself," and so forth. One part of the person, according to Lakoff, is seen as the "true self" and as a way "we really are" and the other as not real, that is, as merely contingent rather than constitutive (1996, 106–110). Taking the English phrase "I'm not myself today" as his definitive example, Lakoff (like Descartes and Freud) identifies this real self as inner and equates it with consciousness and rationality. The contingent elements of self he sees as body, emotion, needs, desires and passions. And so in the phrase "being at war with oneself," Lakoff says we mean we are at war with the passional, embodied self. He also identifies this contingent self with social roles (1996, 94).

Contra Lakoff, the ethnographic data suggests that the part of the self people consider constitutive and the part they consider contingent varies between cultures. In the introduction, I argued that in Western societies the inner self was to one degree or another highlighted and the social self to a degree shaded. As such, connectedness between people is likely to be more remote from conscious life, as Lakoff says. But in many cultures, sociality is highlighted and subjectivity is then inaccessible to the linguistic/discursive system. Thus the Zapotec say, "We see the face, but do not know what is in the heart" (Selby 1974, 62–63). The Ilongots, say "One can never know the hidden reaches of another's heart" (Rosaldo 1984, 146). In Samoa, *loto* refers to deeply personal thoughts and feelings, but literally this word means "depth" (Mageo 1989, 191–192). Samoans say, "One cannot know what is in another's depths" (Gerber 1985:133).

Whichever part of the self is alienated from the linguistic/discursive system is conflated with passion and the body. The Samoan word *lotoa*, for example, is a word that derives from *loto* and means "passion" or "passion-ate." To feel a yearning in one's *loto* (*momo'o i loto*) may serve as an explanation for passionate behavior that verges on the involuntary. Samoans also believe the *loto* is a physical organ located in the chest. Although it is sometimes glossed in English as "heart" (because there is no word to refer to that organ Samoans call *loto* in English), *fatu* is the actual word for the organ English speakers call the heart.

What all this means is that Westerners are not alone in alienating an affective and embodied self. Cultures tend to highlight either subjectivity or sociality, and to associate the other (whichever it is) with body and emotion. This is not to suggest that cultures are equally alienated from affect and the senses—the id in psychoanalytic terminology. People's relation to dreams (which represent these parts of the self) is an index of the degree of alienation they suffer. But everywhere, I suggest, emotive/embodied responses testify to experience missed in cultural schemas and are a preobjective form of perception. The dream is an attempt to translate those perceptions into images. In this sense, there are "on occasion, messages from the gods" in dreams—messages from a broader reality than our own, as Lacan says the "ancients recognized."

For Freud, the embodied and emotive aspect of self was the id and was often experienced as a radical other within the self, compelling actions about which the person, as subject, might be highly ambivalent. The id was also an aspect of the self that resisted "civilization" and was discontent with it almost in principle (Freud 1961b). From a more current perspective, the id could be reconceived as a potential form of affective and embodied agency that visits us in dreams whether we identify with it or not.[19] Nightmares eloquently illustrate that our affective/embodied selves can become as mad or as destructive as any other part of the us; this potentiality has been documented by Freud, by the psychoanalysts who succeeded him, and by many others.[20] Nevertheless, this dimension of the self and the form of agency it exercises have the potential to make us genuine interlocutors with our cultures.

The form of agency manifest in dreams is what Lacan calls the "it shows"; it may also appear as what I call "counteridentities"—identities that go against the grain of established hegemonies, like the hairy monster in Fefe's dream. Is this why we see these figures as monstrous? Monsters may represent potentially empowered yet alienated parts of our selves that challenge our positions in and ascription to cultural worlds.

The monster is the one character who actually seems to be enjoying Fefe's dream and who has a sense of humor in subsequent role-playing. This monster represents Fefe's family constantly chasing him, making him feel like trash. But the monster also embodies a hidden self that testifies against the sociocentric demands of Fefe's society—a possibility that lies in wait in his dream and that he discovers by working on it. Fefe later commented, "Whoever was inside [the house] should have heard me. . . . My grandmother has to take the time to sit down and hear me out." Normally silence is enjoined upon Samoan children; this is how they show respect for elders and for those hierarchical relations that are the bones of their cultural world (Mageo 1998, 49–50; 1991b, 410–12). But by confronting the monster and hearing its message about family relations ("no one cares"), Fefe develops a counteridentity, an identity that counterposes his own culture's orientation and that summons up life possibilities that are relegated to the fringes of his world. The idea of counteridentity is reminiscent of Michel Foucault's countermemory (1977), which draws upon memory streams that are incongruent with epistemes.

Because of Pierre Bourdieu's seminal work (1992) and of praxis theory more generally, agency was a salient aspect of self in late-twentieth-century cultural theory. Praxis theory shows how people use structures of meaning as self-interested strategists, yet leaves obscure the person as an experiencing subject.[21] The form of agency one finds in dreams and counteridentities in particular can help us remedy this obscurity by offering an idea of agency that includes within it preobjective responses to cultural reality, which are registered in our senses and feelings.

In sum, dreams render cultural schemas in visible form, but also "talk back" to these schemas by altering them in meaningful ways. These alterations grant us critical perspectives on everyday life and whisper to us that our schemas are not reality, but a particular perception of it. In this regard, dreams straddle important territories along a continuum between conventional and preobjective perception, bringing us sometimes uncomfortably close to unmediated experience. Out of these territories dreams craft personal symbols that can point us and our cultures in new directions and counteridentities that point out unrealized possibilities for being and living more fully. Dreams also help to prepare the ground for an interlocutory theory of culture and the self by tuning us into the background noise generated by people's lack of attunement to their cultural system and showing us how people are forever recreating their cultures out of this lack.

Notes

I thank Bert O. States, Mary Bloodsworth, Thomas J. Csordas, and Kathryn Geurts for reading and commenting on this chapter.

1. In Heideggerian terms (1996), one could say that these reactions are the impression, the trace, of our openness to existence (*Dasein*).

2. The chapters in this volume demonstrate this point. See particularly Bourguignon (chapter 7) and Kracke (chapter 8). Bourguignon writes of a voodoo priestess, Annette, in Haiti. Annette dreams of a man she knows, but tells Bourguignon this man is actually a female spirit; she is a devotee of this spirit and is sometimes possessed by her. This female spirit, Annette says, can take any form she likes, including that of the opposite sex or friends. One of Kracke's informants dreams repeatedly of his friend's "big penis," but takes his dream to be an omen that he will catch a tapir. Parintinin typically look for hunting omens in dreams. For further examples, see Shulman and Stroumsa 1999; Stephen 1995; Ewing 1994; Tedlock 1991; Degarrod 1989; Crapanzano 1975; D'Andrade 1961; Eggan 1955; and K. Stewart 1951.

3. On not expressing love to children in Samoa, see Mageo 1998, 48–49, 1991b, 407–408, Gardener 1965, 145–146, 153.

4. On grandparents' role in childcare, see Mageo 1998, 40–51; Gerber 1975, 51, 53; Gardner 1965, 145–46, 153.

5. An important contributor to the subject of dreams and phenomenology was Medard Boss. Boss saw dreams as portraying the dreamer's existential experience (1958). Basso (1987) argues similarly that dreams reveal a hidden personal reality that is only dimly perceived in normal life.

6. See, for example, Schieffelin 1976 and Herdt 1987, 58.

7. On shamanism and the dream see, for example, Tedlock 1987 and Kracke 1987.

8. On these paintings and the cultural history of their time, see Stich 1990, 90–93.

9. On dreams as imaginal thought, see also Stephen 1989a, 1995; Kracke 1987; and Price-Williams 1999.

10. See, for example, D'Andrade 1995; Shore 1996; and Strauss and Quinn 1997.

11. See also Eggan 1949, 471. Globus argues that because the "senses are mostly closed down during sleep" dreams are generated by "intentional meaning," that is, by unconscious wishes and defenses (1987, 61, 90).

12. D'Andrade (1961, 308) points out that in dreams there is for most people little conscious control and an absence of external restraints, so that only those cultural patterns and norms that are most deeply internalized are likely to be present.

13. A number of researchers on phenomenology and the dream look at the dream itself as real experience, as opposed to illusion, as Descartes sees it (cf. chapter 1). This is the perspective taken by Gordon Globus in *Dream Life, Wake Life* (1987). Following in this tradition Watson (1981) and Watson and Watson-Franke (1977), working among the Guajiro in Venezuela, and Hallowell (1976), working among the Ojibwa of Manitoba, tell us these peoples regard dream experience as an actual experience. The Parintintin (Kracke, chapter 8) speak of dreams as real experience rather than as quasi-objects, as Westerners do when they say, "I had a dream."

14. See Mageo 1998, 40–51; Sutter 1980, 31–41; Schoeffel 1979, 102, 126; Gerber 1975, 45, 51; Gardner 1965, 145–146, 153; Mead [1928] 1961, 22, 128.

15. See Beaglehole and Beaglehole 1938, 1946; Ritchie 1956; Ritchie and Ritchie 1979; Mead [1928] 1961, 128, 199; cf. Gerber 1975, 12.

16. In chapter 8, Kracke's informant, Manezinho, has a dream in which he is skinning a jaguar and a friend says, "Cut me here on the forehead." He then calls another friend who has just cut his hair. When you skin an animal you effectively remove its hair; getting cut on the head is like a haircut (although more threatening); these two indirect references turn explicit when the second friend shows up with a haircut. For psychoanalysts, all of these images represent castration anxieties. On the psychoanalytic significance of hair, see Leach 1958, Spiro 1970, and Mageo 1994.

17. There are, of course, cultures that actively draw upon dreams to think about existential and social problems. See Graham 1995 for a fascinating example. Alder (1931, 99) believed that dreams sought a solution to the dreamer's problems. Bulkeley (1996) argues that dreams provide practical solutions to social problems.

18. The lucid dream cultivated in some cultures is exceptional here. Lucid dreamers feel they are at least to a degree creating the dream. For an overview of studies of the lucid dream see Van de Castle 1994, 439–458.

19. For Calvin Hall, dream images are "the embodiment of thoughts" (quoted in Van de Castle 1994, 188). I am arguing that dreams are embodied reactions/perceptions translated into images as a means to think them.

20. On embodiment and agency, see Csordas 1990; Haraway 1991, 198; and Mageo and Knauft 2002.

21. For related critiques, see Mageo and Knauft 2002, Quinn and Strauss 1997, 47; de Certeau 1984; and Ortner 1984, 144–48.

PART 2

Revisioning the Self and Dreams

CHAPTER 3

Diasporic Dreaming, Identity, and Self-Constitution

KATHERINE PRATT EWING

*T*he effort to understand globalization and the diaspora experience has challenged anthropology's theoretical apparatus. We can no longer understand culture as a system of meanings that constitutes social reality and shapes the experience of individuals. Anthropologists are now preoccupied with flows of goods, ideas, and people, and with borderlands, where culture is a fluid, often inconsistent and disjunctive process. From this perspective, the idea of the individual as possessing a cohesive self—whether understood to be culturally constituted, innate, or a psychological, developmental achievement—has also been challenged. In its place we now see multiple identities, shifting selves (Ewing 1990a), and even an ever fluid process of identification in which an individual never fully inhabits a stable identity, but is continually escaping into new positions (Hall 1997; Ewing 2000).

While virtually no one today is isolated from the interpenetration of the local and the global and the constant juxtaposition of cultural difference, for migrants this experience of dislocation and the juxtaposition of differences is a core element of life. If we understand migrants to be negotiating inconsistent identities and shifting selves in the midst of cultural and social disjunctions, this question arises: how can we observe migrants negotiating these inconsistencies and shifts? Just as Freud saw dreams as the "royal road

to the unconscious," I suggest that we can look at migrant dreams as a manifestation of the process of adaptation—and as a key site where culture and
identity are negotiated. We can look at the process of dreaming as a primary
way in which individuals negotiate the experience of being caught between
worlds and resynthesize self-conceptions in their new situations.

In this paper I argue that dreaming is an important process in managing the disjunctions generated by the experience of migration and reconsti-
tuting self-organization in the diaspora environment. But to recognize and
understand this cultural dimension of dreaming, we must attend to aspects of
dreaming that Freud's psychoanalytic approach ignored or downplayed.
Specifically, we must look at the surfaces of dreams and not just to their deep
structure, where Freud located primal conflicts. It is on these surfaces, I
argue, that new cultural meanings are generated and acquire emotional
salience. Furthermore, we must look at the significance of dreams to those
who dream them in order to understand how dreams may contribute to the
ongoing process of the cultural construction of meaning and even to the
ongoing reconstruction of culture.

Freud's Quest for a Scientific Approach to Dreams: Looking Backward

Though there are significant differences in how dreams are attended
to, understood, and interpreted from one cultural tradition to another and
even within traditions, the corpus of ethnographic research suggests that in
indigenous dream theories, dreams are often used to predict the future.
Dreams are part of folk healing. Dreams are a social phenomenon. As the
anthropologist Ellen Basso has put it, folk dream theories tend to be progressive or forward looking, in contrast to the regressive nature of Freudian-
influenced Western dream theory; this theory uses dreams as a window
through which can be seen the repressed desires and conflicts stemming from
the individual's idiosyncratic personal history and from universals of the
human condition (Basso 1987).

Freud's work on dreams was revolutionary because he brought the
dream into the scientific realm without dismissing it as a mere epiphenome-
non, a by-product of brain activity. He broke with his more biologically
minded colleagues by recognizing that dreams have a *meaning* that must be
interpreted, an idea that he borrowed from traditional dream theories. But
for Freud, finding meaning in dreams was a way of understanding the past in
order to identify the determinants of the dreamer's ongoing conflicts. He
thus engaged in the paradoxical project of seeking past causes for dreams in

the meanings they had for patients.[1] He found these causes in the history of unresolved conflicts, neuroses, fixations, and traumas that could be exposed through the technique of free association. The patient could be cured of the neurosis that manifested itself through dreams and symptoms (which he also recognized as meaningful) by means of psychoanalysis as a medical practice.

Freud thus clearly distinguished his scientific search for causes from traditional forms of dream interpretation, which often claimed to be oracular or predictive. Suggesting that dreams could predict the future was, in his opinion, necessarily unscientific.

Freud's own approach was firmly grounded in a discourse of modernity that included cultural assumptions that prioritize the individual, articulating for the individual a private interior or inner self, and pathologizing and med-icalizing the experience of distress and conflict. But focusing only on latent meanings for the individual not only breaks up the socially communicable text of the dream; it also projects the dreamer backward, away from the social present and future trajectory of his or her life. Though Freud dismissed tra-ditional dream theories because of their emphasis on the future, the dichotomy between traditional dream interpretation and psychoanalytic interpretation actually embeds and confounds two contrasts that can be dis-entangled: a forward-looking versus backward-looking approach to interpre-tation on the one hand, and a social versus an individual understanding of dreams on the other. When we disentangle and foreground each of these two axes, it is even possible to understand how dreams can be in some sense pre-dictive, in the way that good hypotheses in the social sciences are predictive: because they involve astute analysis of a social situation and hence provide a kind of map of how people may act in the future. Even further, in certain cases, dreaming is a social act that has the power to create a future. Dreams can be transformative, even mythical, not only for the individual dreamer, but also for others in the dreamer's social world.

In foregrounding the transformative and social possibilities of dream-ing that are so visible in the ethnographic literature, I am not talking about an obscure social phenomenon to be found only in unmodernized, traditional areas, but one that is particularly likely to occur among those who are in complex social situations negotiating inconsistent identities and expectations, such as immigrants and many other inhabitants of the modern world for whom the interpenetration of the local and the global has affected most aspects of daily life. I suggest this because many of the transformative dreams that I have been told in my own fieldwork or have read in the anthropologi-cal literature have occurred in individuals caught between cultures, as in the well-known dream of the Seneca prophet Handsome Lake analyzed by Anthony Wallace (1952), which I will discuss further below. Such dreamers have, in effect, found their own solution to a conflict, a solution that in some cases works for others as well, thereby making it a cultural solution. Such dreams dramatically demonstrate the fact that the dream is not necessarily just a symptom; it can also be a creative act that affects the dreamer's identities, social positioning, and self-constitution. In such situations it is often the dream's overt content and its narrative structure that are significant. But even more mundane dreams, when told in significant contexts, can have transformative social significance that does not merely reflect tradition, but creates new forms of cultural meaning. These dreams can be an important way that migrants socially create "home" in their new environment.

The Loss of Manifest Content

In *The Limits to the Possibility of Interpretation*, Freud distinguished mental activities into two types: those that pursue a "useful aim" (that is, have a social purpose) and those that pursue "an immediate yield of pleasure." The former includes intellectual judgments, preparations for action, and conveyance of information to other people; the latter are play or fantasy and essentially private. It is the business of preconscious thought to be concerned with the tasks of life. Dreaming, in contrast, is an activity of the second kind, according to Freud. Its only useful function is guarding sleep. While even few psychoanalysts today would accept this very narrow theory of human motivation, the causal aspect of Freud's theory of dreams rests on it.

The conflicts that Freud identified, however, were not immediately visible in the manifest content of the dream narrative. Freud saw the manifest content of the dream—the actual images and events that constitute the dream as narrative—as merely a taking-off point for revealing the dream's latent content. Much of the dream's manifest content fell into the category of "day residue," incidental stimuli that become the vehicle by which the mind expresses otherwise repressed wishes, which are the cause of ongoing intrapsychic conflict.

In Freud's distinctive approach to deciphering the meaning of dreams, the latent meaning was to be uncovered through the process of free association. This hermeneutic method of interpretation proved to be a brilliant technique for uncovering the multiple layers of meaning that he found dreams to have. In trying to understand what he called "dreamwork," the processes by which underlying wishes and conflicts were transformed into dream images, he identified several strategies of interpretation: condensation (the combination of multiple ideas into a single image), displacement (the substitution of one image by a related, less disturbing one), considerations of representability (how dream thoughts such as negation can be expressed by images), symbolization (use of a neutral image that bears some kind of iconic relationship to a sexual thought), and the principle of overdetermination (the fact that a single image is linked to and evoked by several different dream thoughts). This approach to dream interpretation and the parallel process of understanding neurotic conflict have had a profound influence on Western culture, including academic disciplines such as literature, history, film theory, and other humanities and social sciences. These strategies continue to be a powerful interpretive tool.

But is something lost in this kind of dream interpretation? Despite Freud's powerful influence on twentieth-century thought, later scholars and even some of Freud's immediate followers sensed something missing in this approach. Perhaps the most famous and controversial dissident was Carl Jung, who broke with Freud over Freud's insistence that the latent content of a dream expresses, above all else, a sexual conflict. But he also challenged Freud's tendency to move too quickly from the manifest dream images and symbols to the dreamer's free associations and their infantile roots. Jung placed greater emphasis on the dream imagery itself, encouraging the dreamer to "amplify" the dream by entering into the atmosphere of the dream, reexperiencing and examining its images more fully instead of moving away from the images through free association. Jung also felt that dreams seek to express something that the ego does not understand (1967–1978, Vol. 7, 177). They are, in other words, forward looking, even problem solving.[2] Because of Jung's greater involvement with religion and mythology as fundamental components of his dream theory,[3] his approach, though influential in religious studies and among New Agers, has never been taken as seriously in psychiatric and clinical circles or even in academic and literary circles as Freud's was.

Other more recent scholars have also turned to a reconsideration of the manifest content of dreams. For instance, Bert States, a literary theorist who has written a study of dreams as narratives, takes a position that, while not contradictory to Freud's, has a very different emphasis: "Narrative is a persistent characteristic of dreams, and a persistent characteristic of dream narratives is that its consistency—its aesthetic coherence, so to speak—is the evolution of an emotional tension as opposed to the evolution of a causal sequence" (1993, 101).[4]

The business of the dream, then, is not to point cryptically to, or away from, the primal source of a particular emotion, but to enact the emotion in its entirety as a psychic state that can only be represented cubistically—that is, as a fusion of past and present experience (States 1993, 102).

Freud used the term "secondary revision" to characterize and account for the narrative flow of the dream, and Freud's method quickly set aside the product of this secondary revision, the dream's (more or less successful) coherence, in his quest for meaning. But for most of us, it is precisely the narrative flow that makes a dream so interesting to recall and even to recount. Dream telling can be a social event, even in Western societies that do not recognize dreams as significant.[5] Psychoanalytic theory has removed the social dimension of dreaming except in the highly circumscribed setting of the private psychotherapy session—because it is an approach that is itself intellectually shaped by our cultural understandings, social pressures, and scientific perspective, all of which presume and constitute individuals with private interiors.

The Anthropology of Dreaming and the Cultural Myth

A look at how dreams are understood and managed in other societies may help restore this missing dimension to our understanding of dreams and give us more powerful tools for looking at the significance of dreams for migrants in diasporic settings. The focus in psychoanalytic interpretations of dreams is on intrapsychic conflict between what Freud saw as basically antisocial wishes (egoistic and libidinal impulses) and the constraints of civilized society. Early psychoanalytic anthropologists and psychoanalysts who did field work took this approach and applied it to the analysis of myths and rituals. They interpreted myths as if they were the dreams of an individual, as if they were a compromise formation, simultaneously expressing an unacceptable sexual or aggressive wish and its prohibition. The primary meaning of these cultural products was thereby reduced to a collective defense against infantile, antisocial wishes. Myths were seen as symptoms of a culture's basic conflicts, and were even labeled by some as manifestations of a culture's specific pathology. This was an approach to which many nonpsychologically oriented anthropologists took strong exception. It has always been evident to other kinds of anthropologists that myths meant other things and did important social work. While many anthropologists rejected psychoanalytic approaches altogether, others have tried more productive syntheses of anthropology and psychoanalysis. Victor Turner (1967), for instance, drew heavily on Freud's work (while at the same time distancing himself from any self-identification as psychoanalytic in orientation) to show how ritual symbols carry multiple layers of social meaning. Ritual symbols, in Turner's view, simultaneously expressed and resolved conflicts between inconsistent social principles, while at the same time drawing their emotional charge by expressing basic infantile wishes. He called such symbols "multivocal."

With respect to dreams themselves, anthropologists have found many instances in which dreams, too, are an important dimension of social interaction and serve functions that go well beyond the modest one of preserving sleep identified by Freud. Certain dreams may actually produce social transformation. These socially and personally significant dreams are not important because of a hidden latent content (though this latent content is presumably also present), but because of their powerful overt content and narrative structure. In this vein, Anthony Wallace, writing in the 1950s, discussed the case of the Seneca prophet Handsome Lake, a down-and-out, alcoholic, early-nineteenth-century Native American who, it is reported, had a visionary dream that not only transformed his own life, but also that of his reservation-dwelling community (Wallace 1952).[6] The case of Handsome Lake is particularly well documented because Handsome Lake narrated his experience that same day to three Quaker missionaries, who recorded it. This act of narration and documentation thus occurs across a cultural divide. In the dream, Handsome Lake was instructed to alter basic aspects of the community's social organization: to switch from matrilineal transmission of political office and status to a patrilineal system that would be more compatible with the American system that was impinging on the community. Wallace explained the impact of the dream in terms of wish fulfillment, understood in psychoanalytic terms, and in terms of cognitive restructuring. It satisfied some of Handsome Lake's personal emotional cravings, including the experience of stable and benign authority figures in the form of three men who appeared like angels, offered him branches of curative berries to eat, and reassured him that he was not on his deathbed. They also gave him a strict moral code to preach to others. But Wallace also emphasized a cognitive restructuring in the face of cultural contradictions and crisis. This type of explanation is consistent with a dominant theme among researchers from several different disciplines today. Dreaming is one way in which the mind organizes itself, sorting and categorizing recent experience, analogous to what Piaget called "assimilation" of experience to existing cognitive structures. A significant dream like this may be an expression of a more basic reorganization, a kind of "accommodation" in Piaget's terms (1985), in which perceptual and interpretive structures themselves alter and adjust to handle new experiences that do not fit into the old categories. It is as States put it, "a fusion of past and present experience" (1993, 102).

For Freud, the manifest content of a dream serves no function but to prevent such conflicts from arousing too much anxiety and thus to preserve sleep. The dream is not meant to be a communicative act at all. But dreams such as Handsome Lake's are clearly meant to be such a communicative act with important social ramifications. Wallace, influenced by Freud's approach, pointed out that dreams such as Handsome Lake's differ from ordinary "symptomatic" dreams in the following ways: they often (but not necessarily, it is important to note) occur in a waking state as a hallucinatory experience or in a trance state; they impress the dreamer as being meaningful and important; the manifest content is often "rational" or coherent; and recollection is unusually rich in detail (Wallace 1956, 271). Such dreams are a major social phenomenon when they result in the formation of a religious movement such as the religion preached by Handsome Lake, and even more influential religions such as Mormonism and Islam, which could be said to have been initiated in a similar communicative process. But it is important to realize that such dreams are not as extraordinary and rare as one might believe from these examples. Furthermore, it is misleading to create a sharp distinction between symptomatic dreams and such formative experiences.

Many anthropologists have concerns that psychoanalytic interpretations reduce the meaning of social phenomena to the expression of individual psychological conflict, so that myths are treated as if they were individual dreams. Those who do attempt to look at the relationship of dreams and myths have been careful, therefore, to assert that they are distinct phenomena. Barbara Tedlock, for example, has written of some excellent examples of synthetic dreams analogous to the dream of Handsome Lake (1992). Because of a dream in 1991, a young man became the inspiration for a major religious and political movement among a Mayan people in a region of Guatemala. This people was caught in intense civil war and was being threatened with cultural extermination under pressure from Catholic evangelists. The dreamer, a young man, had a visionary experience.[7] According to his narrative of the experience, he had learned that Jesus Christ did die for us, as the Catholic Church preached, but that we should also worship the earth deities because they care for our bodies and are guardians of our crops, even though not equivalent to Christ. After the dream, he made a tape recording of his narrative and set out to spread the word.

Tedlock also presents a myth that clearly shares elements with this dream. Though the dream and myth shared elements, they differed in certain key features. These differences paralleled changes in social organization of the community in recent years. For example, the status of women had changed in the community. In the myth, a product of an earlier era, the female deity has a fairly low status and is portrayed in somewhat negative terms, while in the recent dream, the female deity is depicted as being on a par with a male deity, a depiction that parallels the rising status of women in the society.[8]

Before she presented the myth, Tedlock was careful to give the disclaimer, now standard among psychological anthropologists, that dreams and myths are different cultural phenomena, thereby differentiating her work from that of psychoanalysts who interpret myths as if they were collective dreams. The distinction avoids reductiveness, but we also need to reexamine some of the assumptions about the nature of myth that are embedded within the disclaimer itself. I suggest that if we reconsider the nature of myths and the nature of dreams, we will find that a clear line distinguishing them cannot be drawn.

Following States's emphasis on the narrative structure of dreams (1993), we can say that dreams are like myths. This approach reverses the old psychoanalytic tendency to see myths as dreams. Unlike the old equation, this blurring of the boundary is not reductive, since such a recognition does not rule out the multilayered significance of the dream, by means of which it also expresses the individual's desires and intrapsychic conflicts. Myths, too, have multiple dimensions: in addition to a myth's social meanings, it can also be a vehicle for expressing personal conflicts for the individual who tells a myth (Obeyesekere 1981). Nevertheless, we cannot simply look at a myth as a text and read out a society's typical intrapsychic conflicts. The individuals within a society have a wide range of psychic organizations, an array of strengths, deficits, and conflicts, and a single myth may affect these individuals and serve as an expressive vehicle in very different ways (Crapanzano 1975; Ewing 1990b). The key difference between a decontextualized narration of a myth and each of the dream/visionary experiences presented in this chapter is that the dreamer is explicitly positioned with respect to the actions of the dream, and the act of having and narrating the dream repositions the dreamer in the social world. Because the dreamers I discuss below are migrants or children of diaspora, their dreams also show how they manage their experiences of cultural difference and social repositioning.

Dream of a Returned Pakistani Sufi

One characteristic of dreams that is often noted is their tendency to create bizarre juxtapositions, juxtapositions that often strain or disrupt the dream's narrative structure. In Freud's approach—taking each dream image and tracing out its associations—these juxtapositions play little role in the search for meaning, since narrative structure is deemphasized in favor of the significance of each dream element. But if we see these dreams instead as efforts to reposition the self and constitute identities by fitting new experiences into old narratives of identity, often transforming both in the process, the narrative structure, specific dream images, and disjunctions take on central importance. From this focus, bizarre juxtapositions are significant. In diasporic dreaming, these juxtapositions may be an expression of cultural differences and an effort to synthesize disjunct experiences. This diasporic experience of disjunction and the way that dreams may express it is represented in Gurinder Chadha's 1994 film *Bhaji on the Beach*, which depicts a multiaged group of South Asian immigrant women in Britain on a beach outing. One middle-aged woman is presented as being acutely torn between cultures. The film maker conveys this sense of conflict through a series of visions or dream-like sequences of jarring juxtapositions of Hindu religious imagery and her current experiences. Often one image is superimposed on another, suggesting her unsuccessful efforts to synthesize two very different self-representations.

But many migrants are more successful at coming up with a viable new synthesis of their different identities and self-representations. The following dream was narrated to me (in English) by a man who was, at the time I met him, a *khalifa* (designated spiritual successor) of a Sufi teacher/saint (*pir*) in Pakistan. It is a striking dream for several reasons. 1) It has a clear narrative structure. This structure bears a strong resemblance to examples of dreams that can be found in Sufi literature over the centuries, in much the same way that the Mayan dream/vision that Tedlock recorded bore a marked resemblance to a local myth. 2) The dream had a lasting significance in the life of the dreamer, as evidenced by the fact that he narrated it to me thirty years after experiencing it. 3) As a young man, the dreamer had undergone significant intercultural dislocation, having spent an unplanned eight years in England, trapped there during World War II, and he experienced the dream immediately after returning to South Asia from England.

> I first met my Master in 1958, but I saw him in 1946. I searched for him from 1946 on. . . . From my childhood I had been looking for a teacher, but I couldn't define my thoughts clearly. Then the war years interfered. I went to the United Kingdom for studies and stayed through the war, eight years in all. But always I had a yearning beyond the material aspects of life. In 1946 I came back to Calcutta and saw a dream. It was very vivid, as if it had actually happened.
>
> I dreamed of a basement room, with a street passing outside at the level of the ventilators. It was a long narrow room with a low table and a carpet. There was food on the table. I was at the door waiting for a guest to arrive, sitting cross-legged in a spirit of great expectation. Then I saw two people coming, and they stood on the stairs. One was my *pir*. I didn't know him. The other was very saintly, tall, fair, with curved eyebrows and a white turban. Both were dressed in white, with black shawls, as the Prophet wore. I suddenly realized that these were the people I had been waiting for. I was awe struck. I couldn't move. They came and sat at the low table. My *pir* beckoned to me and told me to sit with them. I crawled up to them on hands and knees, with great respect. The saint was on one side, my *pir* was in the center, and I sat on the other side. My *pir* said to the saint, "This is my son. Take a good look at him." The food on the table was *dal* [lentils], curried spinach, and *chapattis* [flat bread]. The saint took a morsel of *chapatti*, dipped it into the spinach and *dal*, and then put it into my mouth. I can still taste it, a heavenly taste. It filled me with longing and love. I ate it, and as the morsel went down my throat, both of

them disappeared. I ran up the road, like a madman on the public street, shouting and crying for them. I knew that they were my life. Then I saw a telephone booth and a thick telephone directory. I flipped through it as if I were searching for his number. I was saying Khwaja Moin-ud-Din Chishti [founder of the Chishti order of Sufis] over and over again. When I awoke I was actually saying this. Ever after that I searched for the *pir* who told Khwaja Moin ud-Din, "This is my son."[9]

This dream, like the Mayan visionary experience, clearly recreates what can be called an existing template or myth. The dreamer is visited by two Sufis. These represent the continuity of this Sufi spiritual genealogy. The dreamer is initiated by partaking in a meal, the elements of which are typical of the food distributed at the annual death commemoration (*urs*) of a saint.

Among the Sufis I worked with in Pakistan, I met a number of people who had had dream experiences that were in many respects quite similar to this dream, which is striking in its clarity and culturally patterned structure. Though explicitly dream narrations, they bear a remarkable structural similarity to a number of dreams and visionary experiences that have been recorded by Sufis in the Muslim tradition, which provide a cultural template analogous to a myth.

One example of such a dream in the Sufi tradition, a mythlike template, can be found in the spiritual diary of the Persian Sufi Ruzbehan Baqli of Shiraz (d. 1209 C.E.). This visionary experience affirmed to him his high spiritual rank among Sufis.[10]

> All created beings. . . are enclosed in a house; numerous lamps provide a brilliant light, but a wall keeps him [Baqli] from entering. So he climbs onto the roof of his own lodging where he finds two very beautiful people in whom he recognizes *his own* image. They appear to be Sufis and smile at him affectionately. He notices a hanging pot under which a delicate and pure fire is burning without smoke and fed by sweet-smelling herbs. At this moment one of the visitors unfolds a cloth and brings forth a bowl of very beautiful form and several loaves of pure wheat. He breaks one of the loaves into the bowl and pours over it the contents of the pot, an oil so fine as to appear a spiritual substance. Then the three together eat a kind of communion meal. (Corbin 1966).[11]

The marker of Baqli's high status is the fact that he climbs to the roof of his house, thereby standing above all of creation enclosed within. His equal status to his illustrious visitors is marked by the recognition of his own image in their faces and by the fact that they eat a communal meal together. The Pakistani *khalifa* who told me his dream, in contrast, marked his own positioning as one of low status with respect to his Sufi dream visitors by, for example, finding himself in a basement room in contrast to an open roof or a more neutral positioning in which the level of the room is not marked.

He crawled toward his visitors on hands and knees, and was fed like a disciple or child.

But this *khalifa*'s dream is far from a simple mechanical reproduction of the template that has shaped both of these dreams, with only structural transformations in the Levi-Straussian sense marking differences in spiritual status. On the contrary, the dream imaginatively updates the template, the myth, with details that reflect the particulars of the dreamer's experience and social world. Freud might consider such details to be day residues or otherwise mere symbolic vehicles that the psyche found useful for communicating the dreamer's underlying conflict. I argue, in contrast, that the incorporation of such details serves as an important vehicle for synthesizing otherwise radically disjunct aspects of his life. This dream occurred shortly after his return from wartime Britain to South Asia. He alludes to the sense of disjunction and his effort to create personal continuity in his preamble to the dream: "The war years interfered. . . . But I always had a yearning beyond the material aspects of life." His subsequent actions—the search for "his" *pir* and taking on a Sufi identity—suggest that this dream marked a significant and synthetic reorganization of identity. When I first heard the dream, the narrative was so coherent (undoubtedly polished during the course of thirty years of telling and retelling) that I noticed only one salient incongruity: the idea that he would flip through a phonebook to find the identity of his future Sufi teacher. This was an obvious juxtaposition of an element of modernity and the Sufi tradition. But it is a juxtaposition that he and other Sufi teachers now experience every day: when he receives his followers for instruction or spiritual healing, he is seated cross-legged on a carpet, surrounded by pillows, a telephone by his side.

Only on later reflection did I realize that the images in the dream were not images from a modernized South Asia at all, but rather represented an inclusion in the dream of details of his newly distant everyday life in Britain. These include a thick phone book (not to be found in Calcutta in 1946!), a telephone booth, and a basement room with street ventilators. The basement room does considerable symbolic work: it marks his spiritual status within a Sufi structure of signs, in which basement and roof are contrasted, as I have previously mentioned. But it also undoubtedly marks his comparatively low student status in Britain, since basement rooms are not exactly prime real estate in the British rental market. It thus condenses two structures of meaning into a single image, repositioning the dreamer with respect to the dichotomy of materiality and spirituality in the process. The phone book operates in a similar way: the physical, mechanical search for names by turning the pages is to be replaced by a spiritual search that will take many years.

The dreamer's shift of self-orientation and identity is suggested by the statement, "I ran up the road like a madman on the public street, shouting and crying for them." The phrase "like a madman" indicates that he was looking at himself from the outside, as others would see him and judge him, expressing a fear that he might be taking up an identity as a madman by following this spiritual quest, especially on the streets of a British city. Within the Sufi tradition, however, madness is often a sign of closeness to God. The most salient, disjunct experiences that are manifest at the surface of his dream are thus his concern with reestablishing a relationship with his Muslim religious heritage, specifically with a Sufi teacher, and a concern with how this would be possible given his identity, formed in the diaspora, as a Western-educated, modern, and materially oriented postcolonial. His dream predicted that he would one day find his Sufi teacher. It offered him a new identity as a Sufi disciple and a new basis for integrating his diasporic experience into a self-concept rooted in his South Asian past and future.

The Dreams of a Diasporic Turkish Family

Predictive dreams are a cornerstone of Islamic dream theory. The basic elements of this theory are shared across the Muslim world. Though reformist Muslims have sought to purify Islam of many local practices that they label superstitious and un-Islamic, the art of dream interpretation and a belief in the ability of dreams to reveal the future is felt to be an important aspect of one's relationship with God. My recent work has been with diasporic Turkish families in Germany who are active in an organization that is dedicated to teaching a form of Islam that they consider purer than the practices and beliefs that the majority of Turks now living in Germany brought with them from villages in rural Turkey. I had come to know one family quite well when they were struck by tragedy: the eldest son died suddenly in an accident. In this time of extreme distress, dreams and dream sharing became a central element of the family's mourning process. These dreams, at least in the form that I heard them later, were not elaborate narratives, but they did play an important role in locating the dreamers in a social and existential space, transcending the cultural/spatial disjunctions of diaspora.

One of the sisters of the young man who had died told me the following summer (that is, nearly a year after the accident) about a dream that she had had the night before her brother was killed. In the dream, she and other students were gathered around a prominent professor who spoke of something of extreme importance. In telling me the dream, she commented that he was a German professor, but he was also like a religious teacher. Though this dream was not a long and elaborate narrative obviously based on a cultural template, it did combine elements from her two worlds, situating her in relationship to both. She is a devout Muslim who wears a headscarf and devotes considerable time to the study of Islam. Born in Germany, she is also a student at one of Berlin's major universities. One way that the dream synthesized her worlds was through condensation. Condensation is a key element in what Freud called "dreamwork," the process by which multiple trains of thought are synthesized into a single image. The image of the professor and that of the religious leader or teacher are superimposed, creating an equivalence and suggesting that far from seeing the world of her secular education and the Islamic world of the mosque as antithetical and incompatible, she experiences an analogous relationship to each of these types of authority figure.

But the key element of the dream's meaning for her was the fact that this teacher in the dream was saying something important. Remembering and telling this dream occurred in response to the trauma of her brother's death, and it was in this context that the dream acquired its significance. She saw the dream as predictive, as anticipating what was about to happen to her brother if only she had realized it. In contrast to a synthetic dream such as the Sufi initiation, which has a powerful predictive quality because it shapes the dreamer's subsequent identity and goals, this predictive dream and its interpretation occurred in response to an otherwise unforeseeable and arbitrary event. What can we make of her emphasis on a predictive dream? A first answer, based on Islamic dream theory, is that the dream was to her a message from God that she came to understand after her brother's death. Such messages from God resituate the self in the world.

Just how they do so is suggested in a long e-mail message she sent me after she had returned to Germany with her family from Turkey, where they had taken the body for burial. In the message she described the family's reactions to the death. Predictive dreams played a key role in her narrative.[12]

> It is now more than two months ago that my brother died, but we miss him every day more and more. It is very hard. OK, everyone will die, but if the person was young and had her/his life before, it is much harder. My brother had so many plans, he liked traveling, meeting different people, he planned to found a firm after his schooling, he wanted to help people, he wanted to learn more about Islam and also tell people about Islam. He did it, but he wanted to do more, and up till that time he had not had much time to do it because of school. How could he know that he would die so early? If we think such things we get crazy. But on the other side, we think that he left the world before gathering many sins. Could you guess what he said two or three days before he died? He said: "To die young is good on the one side, you die before having many sins." I or my other brother replied: "You can also think the other way; if you die early you can also not do many good things (savab)." Could you imagine, we had this conversation two or three days before he died, between both my brothers and my mother. I forgot this conversation—my mother reminded us. Some events and conversations we understand better now. Also some

dreams. For example, my mother dreamed one month before my brother died, that she gave something (she thinks bread) to her dead grandparents. My mother had heard before that giving something to dead persons is not good, but she didn't have misgivings, because her grandparents were smiling in the dream. And some days before the accident my father saw in a dream his sister, who died as she was fourteen years old. In his dream she was giggling in her grave. Now we can understand these dreams better. The dead persons were happy that my brother will come to them. We buried my brother next to my father's sister, because she is our nearest relative who has died. I had never seen her—she died one and half years before I was born. Not anyone from my nearest relatives or friends died that I remember, only one aunt of my parents died last year. (My parents are cousins.) All my grandpas and grandmas are living, even the parents of one grandpa are living. Then suddenly my brother died. I had also never seen a dead person before. My brother's best friend died four years ago of a tumor (cancer). My brother was very sad about that, but if my mother cried (we all knew his friend) he would say: "Why you are crying? He is my friend, and on the other side, do you think that people who have died are really dead? No, they are living but we cannot see them." And my brother was not afraid of death. But he could also not know that he would die young. Now we see him only in our dreams.

This message conveys the agonies of a family trying to make sense of and come to terms with a seemingly senseless death that challenges human notions of purpose and tears apart the fabric of everyday life. A basic strategy the family used was to look for signs of the impending rupture, the sudden death, in the events leading up to it. These events, signs, could be fully understood only after the death, thereby recasting the death as a completion rather than as a rupture. The message identifies two basic sources of these signs—earlier conversations with her dead brother and dreams experienced by family members. Though she repeats that her brother could not have known that he would die so suddenly and so young, she describes conversations in which he spoke of the advantages of dying young, thus suggesting that he had been prepared for death, as a good Muslim should be.

The second source of signs was dreams. In the message she describes two dreams that are quite similar. One was a dream of her father's, dreamt a few days before the accident. The other was her mother's, from a month earlier. In each dream, there is an image of a dead relative smiling or laughing. This image is one that appears in Islamic dream interpretation books (I had heard the same interpretations of dreaming of the dead during my research in Pakistan). The e-mail message indicates that her mother was familiar with such interpretations but had not understood the dream's significance because she had focused on the dangers of giving food to the dead and didn't realize the ominous significance of the dead smiling. The interpretation of her father's dream—that his dead sister was laughing because his son would be joining her—explains the logic of this inverted image. As it turned out, the boy was buried beside her in Turkey.

In the *Interpretation of Dreams* (1900) Freud explicitly dismissed this interpretive strategy of taking a specific dream image and assigning it a meaning based on a code that is set out in a dream book.[13] Freud's criticism was based on the fact that this way of interpreting dreams is decontextualized and does not take into account the specific situation or associations of the individual dreamer, which would reveal its latent meanings. But in this dramatic situation, Freud's criticism is hardly to the point. It is evident to the dreamer and the audience for the dream sharing what the significance of the dream is at the time of narration—it anticipates the death and thus is a moment of connection between the past and future. The dream acquires its significance through the death: "Now we can understand the dreams better."

When I visited the family in the summer following the death, I heard more about the boy and about how the family had been managing their trauma. I heard details about the accident and their dealings with the German police, the hospital, and especially the courts, as the criminal case against the driver who had hit him dragged on for more than a year. I also heard that there had been many more dreams. The mother, for instance, had also had a significant dream the night before her son died. The details located the accident in the everyday world of German urban space, in which the grown children in the family were more competent to deal with the family's affairs because of their fluency in German. But as the family struggled to regain equilibrium, this space was overlaid by another. Or perhaps it would be more accurate to say that the contours of diasporic space became more visible to me as the family absorbed the trauma into its webs of significance. According to Muslim dream thought, there is an unseen world. The living catch only glimpses of that world. God and the dead are unconstrained by conventional space and time. Through dreams God communicates with the living. Just as the whole family flew back to Turkey to bury their loved one in a family grave site, in these dreams long dead relatives not only speak with the living across the barrier of death, but they appear to dreamers in Germany.

The children in this devout Muslim family thus reconstitute themselves as members of a family that transcends geographical and cultural distance and occupies a single imaginal space that can be experienced in dreams and shared through their narration. In the anguished days of mourning following the young man's death, his family and relatives told and retold these dreams.

The accident and its aftermath were experienced in a fully German context, with its police, courts, hospitals, and so forth, but the meaning of the young man's death was understood with reference to God and Islamic systems of meaning, in which dreams and their sharing involve modes of communicating and relationship that transcend these German settings and institutions. The dream creates a continuity between German and Turkish worlds.

Dreams, the Self, and Diasporic Identity

Dreams are synthetic. In some dreams the dreamer weaves together discrepant impressions and experiences into some kind of narrative that may reposition the self in the world. In the case of the Turkish family confronting an unexpected death, the dreams that I heard were not extended narratives, but they clearly came to have great importance to the family during this traumatic time. At times of crisis, when people's sense of control and order is challenged, strategies of self-organization may be more visible. I would even suggest that the family's mourning process, with its dream sharing and reinterpretations of past events, is similar to what goes on in the synthetic dream. In both cases, the self (and the family) undergo reorganization.

This chapter opened with a discussion of the challenges to models of culture and the self as stable, cohesive entities that have arisen in a world in which we can no longer blindly assume that tradition is the stable background of people's lives. And I have argued that we actually manifest shifting self-representations but that most of us experience an illusion of wholeness because these shifts of self are highly contextualized and automatic. At times of crisis or major changes such as those associated with the loss of a loved one or migration, existing self-representations are challenged. Dreams are one way in which one's existing self-organization responds to these challenges. New identities are taken up, old ones may be discarded, and others are resynthesized and integrated in new ways. But even further, dreams, like myths, are creative productions that not only resituate us in the world but also recast the world around us.

Notes

A portion of this chapter is based on a previously published paper, "Dream as Symptom, Dream as Myth: A Cross-Cultural Perspective on Dream Narratives." A preliminary version was originally presented at the International Symposium on Cross-Cultural Psychiatry, September 6–7, 1999, in Trabzon, Turkey. I would like to thank the staff at Wildacres Retreat in Little Switzerland, North Carolina, who, through their generous Scholars Residency Program, gave me uninterrupted time in a mountain cabin, where I developed the ideas for this piece.

1. As Ricoeur (1970) has argued, Freud's juxtaposition of a causal model and a hermeneutic, interpretive one involves a fundamental incompatibility since causes are antecedents while meanings are intentional, forward looking, or teleological.

2. Stevens, comparing Freud's and Jung's own dreams, has pointed out that "Freud's dreams were relatively fragmented and disorganized in comparison with Jung's, which tended to have more coherent symbolism and a stronger narrative structure" (1995, 54), suggesting that such differences in personal experience may account for some of their disagreement.

3. Freud also dabbled in mythology, most notably in his use of the Oedipus myth, but his use of the myth is quite different from Jung's. Freud found in the Oedipus myth an explicit enactment of a fundamental psychological conflict, but he could have articulated his theory of psychosexual development and conflict even if the myth had not existed. Jung's approach, in contrast, identifies mythical archetypes as a basic source of the meaning of dreams.

4. States's pattern of citation demonstrates Jung's lack of academic respectability. Though States claims not to be addressing interpretive or motivational issues and is not interested in free association techniques that move away from the dream's surface structure, Freud is a frequent interlocutor in his text, while Jung merits only glancing mention in one footnote, despite the fact that States extensively explores and theorizes the phenomenon of archetypes, one of Jung's favorite concepts, and, like Jung, attends to manifest content.

5. It could be argued, though, that Freudian theory has created a fear in many of us that if we tell a dream, we may be revealing some psychological disturbance or neurotic conflict.

6. Wallace (1956, 264) has identified several other revitalization movements that similarly had their origins in the dream or visionary experiences of the movement's founder.

7. Though Tedlock presents it as visionary experience, it is unclear whether it was an experience he had while asleep, since the experience involved walking into a mountain, traveling around all the local villages while inside the mountain, emerging from the mountain, walking home without being able to feel the rain, and falling asleep in his hammock before awakening to report the experience.

8. See Bursik (1998) for an experimental study of how changing patterns of gender role socialization and the convergence of male and female roles in American society have affected the manifest dream content of men's and women's dreams.

9. For a different analysis of this dream, see Ewing (1990a).

10. For another example of a similar dream recorded in Sufi literature see Kugle (2000). Kugle translated the dream from the Arabic text *Kitab al-Mu'za fi Manaqib al-Shaykh Abi Yi'zza* by Ahmad al-Suma'i (Ali al-Jawi, ed. Rabat: Matba'at al-Ma'arif al-Jadida, 1996, 119). See also Ewing (2000) for a discussion of this dream.

11. Corbin (1966), a French scholar of Sufism, summarized this dream in English translation.

12. She wrote this message in English. Like most informal e-mail messages, it contained minor errors that I have edited to make it read more smoothly in the more formal medium of the published book.

13. Islamic dream books and those found in Western supermarkets have a common source that can be traced back to the Greeks.

CHAPTER 4

Selfscape Dreams

DOUGLAS HOLLAN

*D*reams appear to serve many biological, psychological, and communicative functions.[1] These include the imaginary fulfillment of unconscious wishes, the solving of problems, the integration of new experience into emerging schemas of self, the working through and mastery of traumatic experiences and other types of intrapsychic conflict, and the representation and expression of family and community relations. In this chapter, I explore the possibility that some types of dreams—those that are imagistically and emotionally vivid and easy to recall—serve yet another purpose. Some dreams reflect back to the dreamer how his or her current organization of self relates various parts of itself to its body, and to other people and the world. I call these "selfscape" dreams. They provide the mind with a continuously updated map of the self's current state of affairs: its relative vitality or decrepitude, its relative wholeness or division, its relative closeness or estrangement from others, its perturbation by conscious and unconscious streams of emotions, and so on. They are one of the ways in which the mind/body seems to assess itself.

Selfscape dreams, I suggest, will be found everywhere in the world because they serve a basic psychological function. Their content, on the other hand, varies considerably because the relationships of part-self to part-self and of self to world they map and represent will vary considerably from culture to culture and from person to person even within the same culture. My examples of dreams from Sulawesi and the United States will illustrate this variation in how the self is constituted and represented to itself in different cultures, but also suggest the similarity in psychological function I have outlined here.

I focus on dreams that are vivid, both emotionally and imagistically, and easy to recall—at least in the short term. Cultures vary in the extent to which they encourage the remembering of dreams. And we will find much variation in the ability of individuals to remember dreams even within given cultures. Nevertheless, my work in Sulawesi and the United States suggests that most people experience dreams that cry out for their attention, at least occasionally. These are the dreams that awaken people in the middle of the night or the emotional residues of which carry over into waking life of the following days, weeks, or years. In both Sulawesi and the United States, I have been struck by how often the manifest content and imagery of such dreams can be related to the dreamer's life circumstances and to his or her current conscious or unconscious state of mind, body, self, and emotion.[2] In this chapter, I illustrate how selfscape dreams in two very different parts of the world map out the relations of self to body and to other objects and people.

I begin by reviewing work that has influenced my thinking about selfscape dreams. I then discuss how and why I collected the dreams I present here, before turning to an analysis of the dreams of two particular men, one from Sulawesi (Nene'na Limbong) and one from the United States (Steve). I conclude with a summary of my argument and a discussion of its implications.

Background

My perspective on dreams has been influenced by a number of researchers. Following Pinchas Noy (1969, 1979) and a number of other scholars who share similar ideas,[3] I assume that the nondiscursive, emotional, and imaginal processes chacracteristic of dreaming are not necessarily more primitive than nor inferior to the cognitive, conceptual, and discursive mental activities charactistic of waking thought and consciousness. Further, I assume that while dreaming may come to represent, and be implicated in, processes of psychological regression, they also may play a central role in psychological growth and development. As Noy points out, processes such as displacement, condensation, and symbolization may be especially well suited to represent similarity and difference in the construction and modification of self-related schemas, and they capture well the timeless nature of the experience of self-continuity. Noy also points out that the nonverbal and imaginal processes characteristic of dreaming seem to develop, mature, and become more complex over time, like other cognitive and perceptual processes.

My thinking about dreams also has been influenced by recent work in the neurosciences. In *Descartes' Error* (1994) and in *The Feeling of What Happens* (1999), Anotonio Damasio reminds us just how deeply the mind is rooted in the body and its biological processes. Perceptions and cognitions of the world are always influenced by emotional states that mediate between neural representations of the body as it acts on the physical and sociocultural environment and as that environment, in turn, impinges upon the body. In effect, emotions are the glue that hold together representations of the body and the world.

Dasmasio emphasizes how dependent the mind is upon continuously updated representations of the body and how these representations qualify our perceptions of the world. In the later stages of the first book and throughout the second, he begins to speculate about the origins and maintenance of the self and consciousness. He suggests that neural representations of the self must be continuously updated and modified in a manner similar to that of bodily processes. Further, he speculates that the earliest representations of the self very likely emerge from, or coincide with, representations of the body as it interacts with the world. Thus according to Damasio, neural representations of the body, self, and world are inextricably tied together through complex emotional states and processes, all of which must be continuously updated and modifed as they stimulate and impinge upon one another.

Interestingly, Damasio barely mentions dreams in either of his books[4] even though dreaming clearly involves many of the emotional processes and representations of body, self, and world that are his central concern. My contention here is that dreams may provide a vantage point from which we can observe how the mind continuously updates and maps out the self's current state of affairs.

That this mapping out does indeed include the self's relation to its own body is supported by Oliver Sacks, who in a recent paper entitled "Neurological Dreams" (1996), reports how people may dream of damage or repair to their brains or bodies long before such injury or repair becomes manifest in physical or behavioral symptoms. He presents cases of migraine, sensory and motor seizures, lesions of the visual cortex, blindness, encephapitis lethargica, acute sensory neuronopathy, motor-neural reorganization, disturbances of body-image from limb and spinal injury, parkinsonism, Tourette's syndrome, and psychosis, all of which were foreshadowed in dreams before becoming manifest in symptoms. He comments, "One must assume in such cases that the disease was already affecting neural function, and that the unconscious mind, the dreaming mind, was more sensitive to this than the waking mind. Such premonitory or, rather, precursory dreams may be happy in content, and in outcome, as well. Patients with multiple sclerosis may dream of remissions a few hours before they occur, and patients recovering from strokes or neurological injuries may have striking dreams of improvement before such improvement is "objectively" manifest. Here again, the dreaming mind may be a more sensitive indicator of neural function than examiniation with a reflex hammer and a pin" (1996, 214).

Finally, my thinking about selfscape dreams has been influenced by the work of the psychoanalysts Heinz Kohut and W. R. D. Fairbairn. In *The Restoration of the Self* (1977), Kohut distinguished "self-state" dreams from those whose latent contents are rooted in repressed wishes, desires, fantasies, and drives. The latter dreams, those that Freud ([1900] 1953) described and analyzed, can be deciphered and talked about through the process of free association.

In contrast, self-state dreams are characterized by visual imagery that is not easily associated to or talked about. Rather, it can be manifestly and directly related to the dreamer's current life situation and to alterations in his or her conscious and unconscious sense of self-esteem and well being. Such dreams and imagery, according to Kohut, usually involve unconscious efforts to cover over dramatic shifts in self organization: "Dreams of this . . . type portray the dreamer's dread vis-à-vis some uncontrollable tension-increase or his dread of the dissolution of the self. The very act of portraying these vicis-situdes in the dream constitutes an attempt to deal with the psychological danger by covering frightening nameless processes with nameable visual imagery. . . . [F]ree associations do not lead to unconscious hidden layers of mind; at best they provide us with further imagery which remains at the same level as the manifest content of the dream" (Kohut 1977, 109).

The meanings of self-state dreams are on the surface, so to speak. Thus, people who unconsciously sense a disruption or dissolution of self-organization may dream of themselves in a rocketship shooting off into empty space (see Mageo, this volume, who relates similar dream imagery in Samoa to the disruption of colonization) or sitting precariously on a swing that is swinging ever higher and higher, and faster and faster (cf. Kohut 1971, 4–5).

Kohut thought self-state dreams are linked to dramatic and ominous shifts in the dreamer's self-esteem and overall psychological balance. However, later self psychologists, including Paul Tolpin (1983), believe they are related to less ominous shifts in the condition of the self as well. Many contemporary self psychologists now take self-state dreams to be more common than Kohut imagined, and may be used to express shifts in self-organization of all kinds—not just potentially traumatic or perilous ones. Tolpin and others also argue, in contrast to Kohut, that free associations may indeed be helpful in interpreting self-state dreams, though primary emphasis is still placed on how the manifest imagery can be related to the dreamer's current life situation.

Long before Kohut, Fairbairn (1952) was struck by the manifest content of dreams and their relation to the dreamer's self. After analyzing a woman who spontaneously described her dreams as "state of affairs" dreams, he came to view dreams as "dramatizations or 'shorts' (in the cinematographic sense) of situations existing in inner reality" (1952, 99). The manifest contents of dreams did not disguise the fulfillment of repressed wishes and drives. Rather, they accurately depicted the unconscious relationships among part-selves and of part-selves to the internalized representations of other people.

Both Kohut and Fairbairn came to believe that the manifest content of dreams could be related in a fairly direct way to the state of the dreamer's self. However, Kohut emphasized how dreams could illuminate the self's response to its relations with real people and objects in the world,[5] while Fairbairn emphaized how they could shed light on a dreamer's internal organization of self. In my view, both may be right: the manifest content of dreams often can be related either to the self's perturbation from the outside, or to its internalized state of affairs, or to both at the same time.

I use the concept of selfscape dreams to integrate some of these ideas about dreams and psychological processes, as well as to highlight both similarities and differences I have with particular researchers. The term obviously is a play on those used by Kohut and Fairbairn, which emphasize the manifest content of dreams and their relationship to self-organization. But along the lines of Damasio's work, I also wish to emphasize how dreams may provide a current map or update of the self's contours and affective resonances relative to its own body, as well as to other objects and people in the world. The self emerges and maintains itself in the biological and imaginal space between body and world. Selfscape dreams map this terrain. Thus the "scape" part of the term.

To summarize briefly, selfscape dreams involve complex, developmentally sensitive imaginal, emotional, and cognitive processes that reflect back to the dreamer how his or her current organization of self relates various parts of itself to itself, its body, and to other people and objects in the world.

How and Why the Dreams Were Collected

The dreams I discuss here were collected for different reasons and under different conditions. Nene'na Limbong's dreams were collected while I was conducting longterm fieldwork among the Toraja from 1981 to 1983. The Toraja are wet-rice farmers who live in scattered villages and hamlets throughout the central highlands of the province of South Sulawesi in

Indonesia.[6] They are famous throughout Indonesia, and now throughout much of the world, for their elaborate and complex funeral ceremonies.

Most Toraja currently consider themselves to be Christians. However, their religious and existential beliefs are still influenced by traditional ideas about the power and significance of ancestral figures, *nene'*, and spiritual beings referred to as *deata* (see Hollan 1996). Many Christian Toraja still encounter *nene'* and *deata* in their dreams, and many still believe that such entities intervene directly in human affairs. For most Toraja villagers, the question is not, which spiritual beings, including the Christian God, actually exist and which do not? But rather, which of these beings, at any given moment in one's life, has the power to influence the course of one's fate and fortune?

Toraja society is organized hierarchically, and social position and status are reckoned through both heredity and the competitive slaughter of buffalo, pigs, and chickens at community feasts (Volkman 1985). Many younger Toraja now leave the highlands to find work in the urban areas of Indonesia. But it is not uncommon for them to send much of their cash income back to the highlands, where it is used by their families in the competitive staging of ever larger and more elaborate feasts. These large and spectacular community feasts have, in turn, attracted ever larger numbers of international tourists in recent years, and tourism has now become a major industry in certain parts of the highlands.

My fieldwork in Toraja involved extensive participant oberservation of everyday lives and activities. However, it was focused around the collection of loosely structured, open-ended interviews in which Jane Wellenkamp and I asked people to describe and reflect upon their life experiences (see Hollan and Wellenkamp 1994, 1996).

As part of these interviews, we asked people to report current or past dreams to us. Our respondents were not surprised by our interest in dreams because the Toraja are one of those groups of people who believe that certain types of dreams can foretell the future. In fact, prophetic dreams—those that are vivid, emotionally charged, and easy to remember—are marked with a special term (*tindo*). They are clearly distinguished from other dream and sleep experiences in which the dreamer merely continues to have fragmentary thoughts about the previous day's activities or those in which he or she is attacked by spirits (*tauan*) (Hollan and Wellenkamp 1994, 101–107; Hollan 1989, 1995). The Toraja share dreams with one another, and they may consult people who are thought astute at interpreting dreams if they have a dream they find especially puzzling or upsetting. They are less likely to report or share dreams thought to portend good fortune, however, fearing that such good omens may be stolen by others.

Steve's dreams, on the other hand, were collected during a psychoanalytic encounter in Southern California begun in the 1990s. A white, a-religious man in his early forties, Steve is a high tech specialist who came to therapy complaining of depression and of feeling weak, incompetent, and broken inside. As part of a therapeutic process stretching over several years, Steve has reported scores of dreams to me.

In both samples of dreams, I examine the dream as narrated, not the dream as experienced—which, of course, we can never know directly (see Crapanzano 1980). And in both cases, the dreams as narrated are influenced by cultural and transferential factors (cf. Bourguignon, this volume; Mageo, this volume), which I discuss below.

The samples of dreams I present here are selective. In the case of Nene'na Limbong, they are selective because I have access only to a small number of dreams he narrated to me during our interviews together, most of which share a common theme. And of these, I have space to discuss only three. Steve's case presents the opposite problem. Steve has told me a great number of dreams over the time I have worked with him, the themes of which fall into several genres or subtypes. I select only one of these themes to discuss here.

Thus, the two samples of dreams are different in important ways. Nevertheless, they are both comprised of dreams that had great emotional significance for the dreamers involved, and were easily remembered and narrated.

The Dreams of a Toraja Elder

As part of an open-ended interview process I conducted with seven Toraja men, I asked Nene'na ("Grandfather of") Limbong, a high-status, wealthy elder, to discuss some of his dreams with me. In the last of our interviews together, Nene'na Limbong reported nine dreams from different stages of his life, eight of which he considered highly meaningful and prophetic, and one of which was a spirit attack nightmare.

In another paper (Hollan in prep), I discuss at length why I think Nene'na Limbong reported these nine dreams and not others, reasons that are related to transferential, intersubjective, and stage-of-life issues. To summarize that argument very briefly: Nene'na Limbong was preoccupied with old age and his approaching death at the time I interviewed him. Eight of the nine dreams he reported expressed a concern with status enactment or loss and the threat of death or bodily disintegration—the very issues he was most concerned with near the end of his life, as he was struggling to maintain his social position and influence. Further, the kind of person I was (white North American, male, relatively young and wealthy) and the kind of questions I was asked only intensified Nene'na Limbong's awareness of these issues, since my presence in the community was perceived by him as an implicit threat to his own status and position.

In any case, in the space I have here I must focus on the manifest content of only three of Nene'na Limbong's dream narratives and suggest how they are related to his life circumstances and organization of self. I begin by presenting the three dreams, and Nene'na Limbong's own interpretations of them. The dream narratives are taken from the interview transcripts. I have edited them for clarity, and have inserted explanatory comments in brackets.

Dream 1: When I was still young [around seventeen or eighteen, before he was married], I dreamed that there were many people, like at a feast. I sat on a mat while the people swarmed about me, petitioning me. Then my stomach started coming out of my mouth, pouring onto the mat in front of me. It didn't stop unil it was all out on the mat. I awoke, startled and afraid.

> Meaning of Dream 1: It meant that when I became an adult, I would become an *adat* expert [an expert on traditional custom] and divider of meat at feasts [a very important position, given that the quality and amount of meat a person receives is symbolic of his or her status]. When I divide meat at a feast, words come out of my mouth just like my stomach does in the dream: "Here is the piece for A, here is the piece for B, here is the piece for C."
>
> Dream 2: I was already an adult and had children when I had this dream. I dreamed that I was in an open field with many other people, and we saw a plane approaching that was carrying bombs. Then the plane dropped its bombs and I was hit and fell to the ground! Many of the people I had been standing with were also hit, but some were not. Those that survived began to say, "Nene'na Limbong is surely dead." But a hour after I had been hit and fallen, I stood up! I stood up and I said, "I am not wounded. I am not hurt. You can see for yourselves!" And then I was just like normal.
>
> Meaning of Dream 2: It foreshadowed the deaths of my parents and first wife, all three of whom died within a period of seven years. During that time I had to sacrifice many buffalo at their funerals. But I was able to survive financially without having to sell off my land. The dream predicted that I would survive that hard time without losing my wealth or position.
>
> Dream 3: One time I dreamed that my throat had been cut! There was a man who cut my throat. I fell down! And I was frightened. I woke up frightened thinking, "I'm dead!" A man cut me with a machete and I fell down dead and my eyes went dark. Then my body was cut up and distributed to A and B and C [He then whispers in a low, terrified tone of voice]. "Oh, this is my body being cut up!" But I could see it happen! I was cut up and distributed [his voice continues low, quiet, horrified]. I was very frightened.
>
> Meaning of Dream 3: The dream really meant that I would eventually slaughter many buffalo and become an important man.

Focusing for a moment on the actual imagery and content of these three dreams, and using Nene'na Limbong's interpretations as commentaries on them, we see a common theme emerge: in all of these dreams Nene'na Limbong suffers some kind of bodily assault, if not death, in the context of status enactment. In dream 1, he loses his entrails as he attempts to respond to his clients' petitions. In dream 2, expectations that he fulfill his ritual obligations become as destructive and damaging as an aerial bombardment. And in Dream 3, his achievement of status through the sacrifice of buffalo is linked to his own bodily disintegration and death. The dreams depict the social and ritual demands of others as a type of predation or attack. They liken the risk of the loss of status to dismemberment, disembowlment, and death.

Elsewhere (Hollan and Wellenkamp 1994, 1996) I have suggested that the Toraja pay a psychological price for their participation in family and social networks that emphasize status competition and the extensive use of reciprocity to maintain relatedness. Nene'na Limbong's dreams offer a window onto some of these widespread social anxieties, anxieties that for the most part are culturally hypocognized (Levy 1984) and suppressed, if not repressed, in daily life. But the intensity of the anxiety that we find in these dreams, and the graphic nature in which it is depicted, is also related more specifically to Nene'na Limbong's social position. Born to an aristocratic family and subject to innumerable social obligations and responsibilities, Nene'na Limbong has been struggling even more than most, and throughout his life, to assert and hold onto his status and sense of self-worth, even as the hereditary privileges to which he clings come under increasing attack in the political economy of modern-day Indonesia.

These dreams illustrate a part of Nene'na Limbong's self responding to a part of his environment with dread and fear. They depict a part of himself experiencing the boundaries among body, self, and other as fluid, permeable, and breachable—in fact, dangerously so. Even one's own guts are not really one's own, and are up for grabs. And one's image blends into that of a sacrificial animal. But they also show his underlying resilience and defensiveness. In Dream 2, he miraculously arises from the dead, showing that a part of himself refuses to succumb to the assaults upon himself. And his interpretations of Dreams 1 and 3, based on widely shared assumptions about the symbolic meanings of dreams, enable him to shore up his conscious sense of perseverence and transcendence (see Kracke, this volume, for another example of how cultural idioms of dream interpretation can be used to defend against the anxiety generated by distressing dreams).

The Dreams of a Southern California Professional

Steve lives in a large metropolitan area of southern California, works in a highly technical field, and commutes long distances to and from his work and social activities. Although he has lived in his own apartment since he was in his late twenties (he is now in his forties), he has never left the psychological grip of his parents, who conceived him late in their own lives and raised him as an only child in almost complete social and emotional isolation.

Steve is extremely ambivalent about his relationship with his parents: on the one hand he loves them and cannot imagine how he will live without them (both are quite old and in ill health). But on the other hand, he realizes that his inability to separate himself from them has been the root cause of much of his misery. He complains that it is as if he and his parents are stuck together in a huge pool of honey, unable or unwilling to free or separate themselves.

Unlike Nene'na Limbong, Steve does not remember and ponder his dreams because the larger, dominant culture of which he is a part holds them to be significant. Rather, he does so because he and I are engaged in a therapuetic endeavor in which dreams are thought to illuminate psychological problems and conflicts. He ponders his dreams because he believes that by doing so, he will understand himself better, and eventually change his behavior. But he reports his dreams also, at least in part, because he thinks I expect this of him, and because he wants to be perceived by me as a cooperative client. In other words, transference factors influence the way in which Steve reports his dreams, just as they influence Nene'na Limbong's dream narratives.

The content and frequency of the many dreams Steve has reported to me have varied. He has repeatedly dreamed of himself as an animal or as a mere speck of dust. And he has had dreams in which he is trying to avoid or escape the attention of others. But the most frequent and emotionally salient type of dream has been car dreams, dreams in which the car he is riding in or driving becomes blocked, stalled, broken down, involved in a crash, or in some other way impeded in its path.

The car is a ubiquitous, highly salient symbol of the self in North American culture. It is used by people to express their status aspirations, their sense of fashion, their sexuality, their wish for freedom, mobility, and autonomy, and so on. The identification between self and auto is promoted by huge advertising budgets, and is reinforced day in and day out by the amount of time most North Americans spend in their cars.

What kind of cultural understandings might the image "self as auto" entail? Perhaps the notion that life and people should run smoothly and without interruption; that when life and people do break down, they should be repairable; that life is a journey involving constant movement and progress, and that one is in trouble if one is stopped too long by the side of the road; that big, strong, fast, powerful cars are better than small, weak, slow, brokendown cars; that it's better to be the driver of a car than a passive passenger; that it's better to own a car than not; that one's car is one's castle and its boundaries are sacred; and so on.

Let me now present three of Steve's dreams that illustrate some of these cultural understandings (and others, no doubt). I choose the following three because they illustrate so well Steve's sense of being stalled and damaged, and the depth of his despair. The narratives are reconstructed from my notes, which I jotted down at the end of therapy sessions.

> Dream 1: He's driving towards work but as he approaches, he notices other employees driving away. They seem to be headed in the opposite direction. He begins to hurry, wanting to find out where everyone is going. But by the time he finally gets to work, almost everyone is gone. . . . As he drives off to find the others, two huge, dark locomotives cross the street in front of him, blocking his path. He must decide whether to race around them and then worry about running into other locomotives as he goes, or just give up and stay where he is. He decides to give up and just stay where he is.

> Dream 2: He's driving with his parents. He sits in the back while his mother drives and his father rides in the front passenger seat. He needs or wants to stop, but his mother is oblivious. He cautiously leans over the driver's seat to take the wheel from her and steer towards the curb. At first, his mother seems to be cooperating, but as they approach the curb, she fails to brake and they run into the rear of a parked car. He is greatly concerned about how much damage has been done to his car, which he thinks must be in the thousands of dollars. But his father downplays the whole incident, claiming that the damage couldn't be more than a few hundred dollars at most, which infuriates and disappoints him.

> Dream 3: He's driving down the road past a long line of parked cars. He suddenly realizes how easy it would be to turn into the cars and kill himself. And then he does crash his car. He wakes up in a hospital, barely conscious. His father or someone is there. He says to this person, "Kill me or put me out of my misery."

The manifest content of these dreams represents well the utter frustration and misery that a part of Steve's self experiences in relation to his parents, to me (on occasion), and to his current situation in life. In Dream 1, he is moving in the opposite direction from that of his peers, and when he finally seems to be getting back on track, he is blocked by impassible locomotives. Steve immediately related the two locomotives to his parents when he first reported this dream. In Dream 2, he is shown taking the back seat to his parents, even in his own car. Once again, his efforts to change directions and exert more control prove fruitless: his mother is oblivious to his need to stop, and her failure to brake results in a crash. And then to make matters worse, his father severely underestimates the extent of his car's damage and incapacity. In Dream 3, he seems to exert more control, but only that necessary to kill

himself. And even here, he fails in his attempt and must plead with his father
(or someone?) to put him out of his misery. Steve's character in the dreams is
hopelessly blocked at every turn, is incapable of action, suffers great misery
which is only exacerbated by the indifference of others, and longs for an end
to it all.

The dreams illustrate in a remarkably revealing and accurate way the
manner in which Steve struggles in his current relationships and situation in
life. However, from a Fairbairnian perspective, they also reveal how Steve's
internal representations of part-self and other have come to be organized and
experienced. Having internalized as part of himself parental-like images who
prevent his growth and development, are oblivious to his incapacitation, and
from whom he cannot escape, Steve engages the world from a position of
entrenched paralysis and passivity. He is a man who experiences himself to
be profoundly unfree, shackled, and dependent, despite his culture's valoriza-
tion of self-sufficiency and autonomy.

Discussion and Conclusion

I have argued that certain types of dreams—those that engage the
emotional and imaginal underpinnings of self-organization—reflect back to
the dreamer how his or her current organization of self relates various parts
of itself to itself, its body, and to other people and objects in the world. Both
sets of dreams I have presented here illustrate this function, though in different ways. In Nene'na Limbong's dreams, we see a self organizing itself
around the need to enact status and the risks that such enactment entails. By
fulfilling status obligations, one risks social effacement and death, which is
depicted in the dreams quite literally as the dissolution or destruction of the
body. Images of the permeability of the body's boundaries, accompanied by
the emotions of fear and dread, illustrate as well how the demands and
expectations of others can be experienced as an annihilation of self, even in a
society where the culture encourages a strong, conscious identification
between self and other in many contexts.

In Steve's dreams, we see a self-organization depicted with reference to
the possibilities for mobility, directionality, autonomy, and self-control.
Threats to these possibilities evoke images of brokendown, damaged, or
immobilized cars that are no longer capable of moving. Loss of control over
the course of one's journey, resulting from either extrapersonal or intrapersonal obstacles, can be experienced as so painful and unpleasant that a part of
oneself might prefer death.

Steve's dreams illustrate as well the extent to which internalized representations of self and other can become intermingled and fused, even in a

culture that valorizes independence and autonomy. Indeed, they demonstrate the special danger such fusings can pose for people who place a strong value on the integrity of the self, and fear its violation or influence from without. Steve seems unable to gain control over his own "car" (meaning "self") without the presence of a parental image there to thwart him, even though this internal control is what is demanded of him by his culture. Although Steve's struggle for self-control is particularly intense, could not many North Americans identify with the pain and difficulty of his effort to exorcise outside influence?

Following from this, selfscape dreams provide evidence that self organization may be much more fluid and less unitary than we had once imagined (cf. Bourguignon, this volume; Stephen, this volume), as emerging constructivist models of mind suggest (see Hollan 2000). According to these models, the self is not a seamless, unfractionated whole, but rather the end product of a complicated series of feedforward and feedback loops within a broad and open system of information exchange. This self system encompasses the synaptic structure of the brain, intrapersonal processes of memory and symbol formation, and interpersonal, self-other configurations as organized and shaped through familial, social, and historical processes.

Thus, the self system is organized hierarchically, dynamically, and temporally. Lower level subsystems may or may not come together to form a superordinate self (or selves) that is aware of its constituent parts. Lower level subsystems may or may not remain separate from other parts of self-organization and function relatively independently and autonomously. In any or all of these cases, the organization of the self system, and the border between what is conscious and unconscious, is highly responsive to both the intrapersonal and extrapersonal processes within which it is embedded. Selfscape dreams illustrate some of this complexity of self-organization.

Although selfscape dreams can probably be found everywhere, only some cultures seem to recognize them and take advantage of the feedback they provide (see Stephen, this volume). Cultures that focus attention on dreams, categorize them, and label them—especially those that identify some types of dreams as prophetic—recognize that some dreams can be related, either directly or indirectly, to the fate and well-being of the dreamer. In Toraja, what I am calling selfscape dreams (and what the Toraja refer to as *tindo*) may motivate a person to initiate or terminate some type of behavior that significantly alters how he or she experiences the world or parts of him or herself, such as the making of amends to family, neighbors, or ancestral spirits. For example, when Nene'na Limbong once dreamed of his deceased father attempting to drag him off to the afterworld (and so to certain death), he consulted a dream expert who told him to acknowledge his father's angry and hungry spirit by sacrificing a pig to him (Hollan 1989).

From a cultural point of view, Nene'na Limbong's sacrifice repaired and reestablished his relationship with the spirit of his dead father. From a psychological point of view, it allowed him to acknowledge and work through a sense of guilt.

The dreams I have presented here are dreams of affliction: they depict the self in fear and dread, and under assault. Although selfscape dreams may, in fact, represent the self in states of health, pleasure, and elation (see Sacks 1996), my anecdotal evidence from both the United States and Indonesia suggests that dreams of the self in states of pain are more common than those in which the self is experiencing pleasure. Damasio reminds us that the human brain "handles positive and negative varieties of emotion with different systems" and that there "seem to be far more varieties of negative than positive emotions" (1994, 267). Further, he suggests that as a species, we seem to utilize the avoidance of pain more than the attraction to pleasure as a determinate of behavior, or as a source of feedback affecting our behavior (1994, 267).

Perhaps selfscape dreams, entwined as they are with emotional processes, have come to be weighted in the same direction. Perhaps it has become more important for us to know when the self is in pain than when it is in pleasure. Perhaps the self in pleasure is not, from an evolutionary point of view, a problem in the same way that the self in pain is. In any case, selfscape dreams offer us a unique vantage point from which to observe how self-organization is affected by its interactions with other people and with the world.

Notes

1. See for example Barrett 1996; Breger 1977; D'Andrade 1961; Fishbein 1981; Fosshage 1983; Freud [1900]1953; Lohmann Nd.; Noy 1969, 1979; and Tedlock 1987, 1994)

2. For another much-cited work on the manifest content of dreams, see Hall and Van de Castle (1966).

3. See for example Tedlock 1987; Kracke 1987 and this volume; Price-Williams 1987; and Stephen 1995 and this volume.

4. There are no index entries for dreams in *Descartes' Error* and only six minor ones in *The Feeling of What Happens*.

5. More accurately, Kohut was interested in how the self experienced its relationships with other people, which he referred to as "selfobject" relationships. Self-state dreams, according to Kohut, illustrated how the self responded to changes in its selfobject relations.

6. There are only two large market and administrative towns in Toraja—Makale in the south and Rantepao in the north. As I have noted, the vast majority of Toraja still live in relatively isolated villages and hamlets.

CHAPTER 5

Race, Postcoloniality, and Identity in Samoan Dreams

JEANNETTE MARIE MAGEO

*I*n his seminal work on postcolonial psychology, Fanon (1967) argues that colonialism is a self-negating experience for the colonized that revolves around a symbolism of black and white. I resided in Samoa through most of the 1980s and collected over five hundred dreams. In many of these dreams there is a black/white motif. In this chapter, I use these dreams to explore Samoan postcolonial psychology and the symbolic traffic between culture and the self.

We saw in chapter 2 that, according to Leach (1958), private symbols originate in individuals' unconscious, but move into cultures, becoming public symbols. Hair, for example, is for psychoanalysts a private symbol expressive of the individual's sexuality. Long hair for hippies or shaved hair for monks, however, convey certain standardized meanings about these groups and about affiliation with them; they do not necessarily reflect individual psychology (Obeyesekere 1981, 42–44). But it is probable, following Vygotsky (1978), that many symbols originate in the social world and only secondarily move into the emotive depths of people. Samoan dreams testify that public symbols like black and white are indeed internalized.

According to Freud, secondary processes are privileged during the day; primary figurative processes prevail in dreams (1953, vol. 5, 599–611). Dream processes, I will show, evince the transformative play Derrida calls "*différance*." The signified concept, Derrida tells us, "is never present in and of itself. . . . [E]very concept is inscribed . . . in a system within which it refers to . . . other concepts, by means of a systematic play of differences" (1982, 11). Strauss and Quinn reject Derrida's model for meaning because they believe people need stable meanings to "get them through the day" (1997, 5). I concede that this is true of secondary-process thought; but what about getting people through the night? In dreams, I will demonstrate, there is a continual slippage of meaning such that meaning becomes a succession of transformations rather than a fixed point at which one could arrive.

Considering *différance* in the historical context of postcoloniality and in the semiotic context of black and white inevitably opens questions about power. If we internalize public symbols and, within the self, these symbols are subjected to transformative play, over time they are likely to move back into the public world, changing shared meanings. Power relations are at odds with this meaning revolution because they rely upon fixing the meanings assigned to persons and groups through racial, ethnic, or caste ideologies (Mageo 2002; Friedman 1992; Ricoeur 1981, 228–9; Williams 1973, 9). Charles Briggs believes that racism, and (post)colonialism in particular, "limit the ability of dominated communities to play with signifiers and to circulate their signs" (1996, 462). Despite a fixing of ideologically inflected meanings in the public/political sphere, Samoan dreams attest that these meanings keep dissolving back into a play of significance in dreams, power relations notwithstanding. Consider, for example, the following dream of a young man.

> I was at a party. . . . dancing and laughing and having fun. . . . Suddenly, the music stopped. . . . I started walking home. Then a car stopped on the side of the road. It was a black car. . . . I looked inside. There was nobody but it was white inside. Everything was all white. I got in the car, I started it and I drove home. When I got home, I got outside, and it was black inside and white outside. And then it changed again to black outside and white inside. It kept on changing back and forth. It drove me crazy. I started throwing rocks to the car, and then it stayed black for a long time. . . .

Admittedly, to truly understand this dream would require lengthy analysis. I take this dream only as a picture of several ideas I demonstrate in the course of this chapter and of several themes that recur in other dreams. A vanguard of the modern world, this dream car sits like an abandoned cargo, inviting the dreamer to take a joyride that turns out to be none too joyous. So colonialism must have seemed to many colonials, promising great wealth, but in the end offering little more than a confounding confusion that in many locales inspired a desire to aggressively reject colonial culture. The boy, sitting in the driver's seat, takes possession of this modernist cargo, which precipitates a color revolution. Through its chameleonic character, the car intimates that the conceptual process Derrida calls *différance* actually becomes more psychologically salient in postcolonial circumstances. This is because, I propose, in colonial and postcolonial times key public symbols tend to become emotionally cathected for many people. The result is that these symbols move into their imaginal worlds as reflected in dreams, are powerfully subjected to a play of meaning, and hence destabilized.

The relative fixity of public symbols lends stability to society, but also to the self. Inasmuch as we construct our identities in terms of shared cultural values (which are symbolic constructs), the stability of these identities depends upon the reliable character of public meanings. But if in postcolonial contexts internalized public meanings are not necessarily stable, what does this indicate about the self? The car's color revolutions can be read as a metaphor, not only for a slippage of meaning, but also for identity slippage. Taking possession is an act of identification. Indirectly, through the car's chromatic instability, the dreamer asks, "Am I black or am I white?" Black/white sandwiched in one identity is reminiscent of Fanon's title, *Black Skin/White Masks* (1967), which contrasts a genuine skin to a false face. The dream car conflates a confusion about black and white with one about inside (interiority) and outside (exteriority)—an association that will recur in later dreams. An inner/outer color contrast is evocative of the African-American name for blacks who act white, "Oreo," meaning black outside and white inside. Yet, unlike in Fanon's title or African-American slang, here which part is black and which is white is unreliable.

However tempted or encouraged postcolonial Samoans may be to align themselves with one side, one color, of a black/white opposition, the dreams presented in this chapter will illustrate that they experience themselves as relations between these opposites, which spin around them at dizzying speed. The experience of being a postcolonial subject, moreover, is one in which many fixed public meanings decompose, abandoning people to the semiotic fluctuations Derrida describes. This accelerated play leaves people in a perpetual identity crisis that, like the ceaseless transformation of the dream car, is possibly (borrowing a term from Gregory Bateson, 1972) "schizophrengenic." In the dreamer's words, "It drove me crazy." Let this dream also stand as a marker for one further premise: dreams are useful at revealing what people in culture actually experience.

I collected the dreams presented in this chapter within the context of a college class I taught over a number of years in American Samoa. Dream sharing and analysis was one of the major focuses of the class. Like all the classes at the college, it was conducted in English, supplemented by my increased understanding of Samoan as time passed. I taught students Freudian and Jungian analytic techniques, along with a technique of my own called "dream play," which involves role-playing (2001c). Three dreams will be explored in depth in this chapter. The first two dreams were merely recorded and were not subjected to formal analysis. I interpret them by relating white or black symbols that are salient in the manifest dream to these same symbols as they occur elsewhere in Samoan culture. These dreams show that the historical meanings of black and white in Samoa are embedded in these dreamers' emotive lives. The last and most significant of the dreams was interpreted by the dreamer. Her interpretation was structured by several projective techniques that I asked students to perform. Although I demonstrated these techniques in class with a few of my own dreams, I gave her no coaching. It is in her dream and projections that both the slippage of public symbols in private fantasy life and its consequences for the self are most stunningly visible.

My students were predominately from American Samoa, although some were from the westerly Samoas too. In some cases their family had moved to American Samoa; in others, they were staying with American Samoan relatives. While the westerly Samoan islands now form an independent country, American Samoa is a largely self-governing U.S. territory. There is virtually no U.S. administrative or military presence.[1] Many, if not most, of my students had transnational experience. The context of the last dream I consider is transnational. Traveling abroad is a very old Samoan practice. Samoans figure kinship collaterally and as far back as genealogical calculation makes possible. They are entitled to reside with any of their kin, and in the past would travel between islands to do so. Today most Samoans have relatives in Hawai'i, the mainland United States, New Zealand, or Australia, and often in a number of these places, which makes contemporary transnationalism easy and inviting. We will see that transnationalism, which is a part of postcoloniality in many locales, intensifies the slippage of meanings and identities I describe.

All the dreams discussed here have a strong storylike quality that may derive from the context of their recording. My presence, furthermore—an American Caucasian residing in American Samoa and married to a Samoan (Sanele)—probably enhanced my students' tendency to dream about colonial and racial themes. No doubt it also accented these elements in their dream reports. The dream-as-dreamt is not the dream-as-reported: dream reports are shaped by dreamers' conscious positions and attitudes. To an extent Jung believed, they also escape these positions and attitudes symbolically, by taking a position directly opposed to the dreamer's consciousness (1972a, 203–210, 1972b, 281–297).

Dream #1: The UFO Prince

First, let us examine the dream of a young woman I call Fia that carries those "white" significances one might predict from the politics of colonialism—mission and cargo symbolism. People tend to think of cargo cults as Melanesian, but in fact they were found in various Pacific locales, including nineteenth-century Samoa (Holmes 1980).

> I had an unforgettable dream last night. . . . A handsome prince from out of space came to my village and was on earth for the first time. His name was unknown and even the language he speaks was not understandable by most people. He dressed all white and . . . [no] one knew where he came from, except that he travels around in his UFO. . . . He was kind. . . . He never showed any hard face but he greets everyone with a big, friendly smile. He visits every family of my village and writes things down on his small writing pad. When he was done, he waved good-bye and was gone on this unidentified flying object. Two days later . . . the people of my village were no longer sad but just happy. They were no longer poor, but rich. Everyone has their free will to do anything they wish.

Samoans have been avid moviegoers at least since the 1960s and movie motifs often appear in their dreams. In this dream, the movie motif of contact with space aliens is imagined as an idealized colonial experience and merged with colonial themes. The foreign visitor lands in Samoa and has the language difficulties that characterized the initiatory experience of colonists and colonized.[2] The kind, smiling UFO prince is distinctly anthropological, writing down everything, visiting everyone. Indeed anthropologists are a component of this Samoan image of idealized colonialism. But the dream visitor is neither an ET nor an anthropologist; he is a prince, personifying the European version of status distinction. Precontact Samoa was a status-based society. Europeans and their accouterments were useful in the everyday status jockeying of Samoan life. For this reason, probably, images of Western royals became an enduring presence in Samoan fantasy life. Take, for example, two theatrical genres that were salient in the colonial period, *Faleaitu* (improvisational comedy skits) and *Koneseti* (biblical-mythic-historical dramas).

In one *Faleaitu* recorded by Shore, the Prince of Wales visits Samoa, speaking a nonsensical and ludicrous pidgin English (1977, 321–24). According to two of my Samoan friends, Nusi Mauala and Sanele Mageo (formerly my husband), in the 1950s and 1960s *Koneseti* plots often revolved around Western aristocratic figures.[3] There were princes and princesses, kings and queens, and soldiers with short dresses, Sanele told me, like pictures of Romans. Sanele described the soldiers escorting the king with drawn swords of tin foil, corned beef cans as handles, and tinfoil helmets. Nusi and Sanele remember their aristocratic costumes of chiffon and silky fabrics, bejeweled with rhinestones.

White Cosmology

When white people first came to Samoa they were called *papālagi*, "sky busters"; they were seen in quasi-outer-space terms. Obeyesekere maintains the colonized don't see white people as gods (1992), but there is a tendency in the UFO prince dream to project the power to make desires come true onto whiteness.[4] This projection is part of a cargo calculus. Various symbolic elements combine to define whiteness in the UFO prince dream: a foreign visitor, a first-contact language problematic, and white dress. They add up to "no longer being poor, but rich."

The cargo cult can be seen as a contagious cultural neurosis that was imported to many locales along with Victorian colonial culture.[5] McClintock (1995) analyzes wealthy Victorians' preoccupation with mirrors. Mirrors effortlessly multiply objects, reflecting a fantasy that one can amass wealth magically at no one's expense. Just as the servants who did the work that produced Victorians' fantastic domestic displays were hidden downstairs, so also the thought that one could augment one's own wealth only by exploiting people in remote places was repressed.

The white-robed prince also brings the psychological counterpart of this "no longer poor but rich" fantasy—free will for the villagers "to do anything they wish." The Enlightenment ideal of the free individual who entered into contracts or into religious beliefs of his own accord was a missionary import. From their arrival, missionaries to Samoa emphasized the importance of free will in relation to God, rejecting demonstrations of faith resulting from chiefs edicts and imploring chiefs not to convert their people by command (Turner [1861] 1986, 23).[6] "Freedom" translates in Samoan as *sa'oloto*, which also means to be "self-willed." *Loto* is the word for "will," but also for the personal inner self, which up until the middle decades of the twentieth century Samoans typically depicted as a dark unknowable territory (Gerber 1975, 133). In modern Western contexts—state nationalism or getting out of jail, for example—*sa'oloto* is good. Thus now that the westerly Samoas are an independent nation they are *sa'oloto* and this is good. In more traditional milieus, however, *sa'oloto* suggests that people run loose rather than acting in accord with the hierarchical structure of Samoan respect relationships. In the UFO prince dream, "freedom" is a pie-in-the-sky, getting-without-giving sweepstakes entity; it is what one might call the colonial mythopoetic of whiteness.[7]

White Religion

The dream prince is of unspecified race, color-marked only by garments. Missionization robed Samoans in white. White is the color Samoans commonly wear to church, encouraged by the missionaries, who were forever preaching against heathen benightedness, which "the light of the glorious gospel" would "chase away" (Williams [1830–32] 1984, 77). An occasion called "White Sunday" is an icon of Samoan Christianity. On that day everyone wears white to church. Samoans compare White Sunday to Christmas because children get new white clothes and parents serve them a special meal, usually involving vanilla ice cream.

Light/dark was a missionary homology for white/black: it coded a veiled implication of color superiority. As in so many areas of cultural life, missionaries saw sex/gender customs in Samoa as "primitive," in the Social Darwinist sense of the term. Indeed Social Darwinism permeated the missionary enterprise, which was conceived of as bringing God's dark children into the light. Thus, George Cousins writes of Samoa in an evangelical family magazine, *Sunday at Home*, "The islanders were in gross moral and spiritual darkness. Light came streaming in upon them; the darkness fled; and for the time their eyes were completely dazzled with the brightness" (1889, 406).[8] This light/dark symbolism was to a large extent incorporated along with Christianity. Shore (1982, 279), for example, records the following Samoan song:

> The life from the ancient days of our ancestors
> In the days of darkness, was very harsh.
> But the morning came with the good news. . . .
> Samoa is enlightened, and now people all love one another. . . .

Here missionization is touted as increasing the light of loving kindness—that is, as increasing moral virtue, like the virtue of the kind, smiling, white robed UFO prince. This heathen/Christian opposition bifurcated Samoans historically—between a dark cultural past and an enlightened present. Darkness became a sign for those elements of Samoan culture out of line with Christian moralism. Precontact Samoans' sexual ways were especially dark in mission symbolism. Out-of-church marriages were named "the way of the black night"; children born from them were "children of black night." As one Samoan put it, "It's okay if [a girl and I] talk . . . and if we don't have any of those dark, Samoan thoughts, but just sit and talk straight in the light and don't do anything. But if we sit and whisper in the darkness, that's bad" (Shore 1982, 279).

Mission light/dark oppositions were meant to distance Samoans from their dark side. While my Samoan dreamers have internalized mission symbolism, they seem to experience themselves in a medial position. Another student I call Tutu (light), ruminating about the meaning of a dream, described what she called her light and dark sides. The Samoan model of the self is that people have "sides" (Shore 1982, 137). Tutu's dream also shows how Samoans saw the mission light/dark division as a matter of sides and how this light/dark symbolism is subjected to the conceptual slippage that Derrida describes. Tutu described herself in the dream as walking fast in the dark with faces flying past her when she saw "a bright light at the end and a shadow." She then commented,

> My dark side can be cold and unemotional. Yet, I prefer that side because in my dream I seem to be a lot happier in the dark walking than I was in the light. My light side seems to be opened to anybody and everybody. So my chances of getting hurt are greater. I feel so gullible, so open, that people will look at me and know every single thing about me. . . . I have a pleasant side I show a lot but [that] part of me is so unlike the real me. [The] real me . . . likes to keep hidden. You know, away from crowds. Yet, I force myself to go to public places and to be [with] everyone. If I had it my way, I would rather stay by myself . . . to know my real light side. . . . Like at that end of my dream, I was in the dark feeling happy. The point is, why am I in the dark again? Yet, I'm happy. Maybe . . . I should be more private. Maybe I'll be happier.

Tutu first tells us her dark side is cold and unemotional, but it turns out to be the only place Tutu is happy because she is insulated from others. Her light side is open and pleasant—like the kind, smiling UFO prince. Yet she experiences this social openness to others as vulnerability. In the dream, darkness represents this sociality: it is as crowded with faces as "public places." But then Tutu thinks that her private self is her "real light side," although it is hidden in the dark. Is it the light at the end of the tunnel? This distinction between her apparent light side and her real light side is significant. We will see that real/feigned was yet another key opposition imported by missionaries. Tutu's complex feelings about sociality/private life and about hiding/showing herself are shared by other dreamers in my collection, as we will see later in the essay. Here I only want to note that the symbolic tumult visible in the color revolutions of the car dream can be found in Tutu's dreaming/musing about her sides. Tutu is caught in an identity slippage in which she vacillates between identifications with light and dark, and in which the meaning of both keep changing. She can arrive at no fixed point to which to anchor her sense of self.

Dream #2: Hurricane Tusi

This next dream might be said to continue the symbolic history of whiteness in Samoan fantasy life.

I was running up these stairs. I was running faster and faster. I got to the top. A man dressed in white was waiting for me. He asked me, "Are you Malaga?" I said yes. "Well, sit down. Buckle up your safety belt." Now we were in this spaceship . . . going to heaven. When we got to heaven, there he was my great-grandfather Manga, the Paramount Chief. Then I seen him sign a piece of paper with this navy white guy. The paper was the treaty between Samoa and the United States. My grandfather told me to go to Samoa and get ready for a big hurricane that was about to come. The hurricane . . . hit Manu'a—it was Hurricane Tusi. *Tusi* in English means writer.

Racing up stairs faster and faster to get to the top might be seen as the project of Western modernity. What Malaga discovers at the top is a man dressed in white. In the first dream, the white-robed prince descends from the sky in a spaceship. Here Malaga ascends to heaven in a spaceship and finds a white-robed man. Again, whiteness is first signified by garments, tying it to the missionary experience. This mission significance is overdetermined by the heavenly destination of the spaceship. Indeed, going to heaven in a spaceship wonderfully conflates missionization and modernity. Yet in his dream report, Malaga is quick to associate white and heaven with military rule by mentioning that the naval officer who represents the United States is a "white guy."

Moral Hurricanes

Manu'a, the island hit by the dream hurricane, is the oldest traditional center of Samoan culture. In his novel *Pouliuli* (1977)—"Black Night" in English—Albert Wendt represents Samoan culture as a ring of white stones around a black stone. The novel is about the disappearing center of the modern Samoan cultural world. Colonialism was a moral hurricane that devastated what one might call Samoans' cultural center. The colonial hurricane had two prominent dimensions (both referred to in the dream). The first was linked to literacy and the second to foreign military presence.

First, the dream hurricane is named Tusi—"writer" in English—which Malaga accents by making the translation for me. Remember in the UFO prince dream, too, literacy was an important element in defining whiteness: the UFO prince "writes things down on his small writing pad." For Samoans, literacy often involved a violent awakening to a new sense of self.

The London Missionary Society (LMS) Christianized Samoa. Ten years after whites had become a significant social presence in Samoa circa 1830, Reverend Murray of the LMS held revival meetings in Tutuila that were characterized by violent emotional outpourings and states of transport (Freeman 1983, 213). Consider one of Reverend Murray's letters to the

home office in London, about a Samoan servant, that provides insight into
the source of this emotional storm: "I found her exclaiming . . . 'Woe is me!
Woe is me' and in answer to my enquires she stated that the words that had
gone to her heart were these 'where is the hope of the hypocrite when God
taketh away his soul,' adding that she had just discovered that she had all
along been a hypocrite" (March 20, 1840).

This woman is converting to more than a religion: she converts to a discourse of sincerity laden with what one might call a "white" sense of self. The
idea of hypocrisy derives from a model of the self as inner. "Formerly . . . we
uttered love . . . with our mouth while our hearts were full of hatred and
murder" says another of Murray's converts (1839). One is insincere or hypo-
critical inasmuch as one's words are congruent with one's heart—that is, with
one's private sensibility and intent. One is sincere inasmuch as one's words are
congruent with the inner self—one's "soul" in evangelical terminology.

"Soul," referring to the individual's inner life, was an aspect of self in
vogue in eighteenth- and nineteenth-century England. The Industrial
Revolution broke down many stable agricultural communities, precipitating
the migratory employment pattern that characterizes capitalism. Values that
had once resided within the community had to be internalized (Levy 1973,
347–54; 1974). Evangelical religious practices played a role in the internalization process. Evangelicals preached surrendering the soul to God, but
because people were sullied by original sin, this surrender dictated a habit of
vigilance towards one's own internal life (Davidoff and Hall 1987, 88). The
minute and unflagging attention thus directed helped to create an internal
space in which values might be ported, making subjectivity a site of identification and a basis for identity.[9]

Samoans take role-playing as the primary site of identification and
basis for identity (Mageo 1989a, 1995, 1998). Many individually oriented
terms for the self were pivotal in Christian religion's beliefs and practices.
Missionaries translated them by appropriating Samoan self terms that had
previously had a socially-oriented character and giving these terms new
nuances and meanings (Mageo 1998, 141–163). Mission services became a
daily social event at which people gave speeches that used these terms
(Holmes 1974, 60–62). Mission usages were inscribed in the texts that the
LMS translated into Samoan. Reading the Bible was the very signature of
the independent churches that made up LMS (Gunson 1987). Missionaries,
therefore, were as dedicated to teaching reading and writing as they were to
moral and religious education (Mills 1844). Postcontact Samoans came to
harbor a white sense of self because, until well into the twentieth century,
missionary sects were singular in their interest and ability to publish texts in
the Samoan language.[10]

Second, the U.S. Navy governed American Samoa during the first half of the twentieth century (Gray 1960). High Chief Manga was one of the signatories to the original treaty ceding American Samoa to the United States. In the dream, the "navy white guy" with the treaty bears a metonymic relation to the hurricane: the hurricane follows the signing as the night follows the day. The American military presence in Samoa during the twentieth century was a kind of moral hurricane, particularly during World War II.

In the early 1940s, the American military used the Samoas as bases of military transport. On some islands American GIs outnumbered the indigenous population of men, women, and children (Franco 1989, 386; Mageo 1996a, 70–72; 1996b, 47; 1998, 151–52). One result of the occupation was a tidal wave of illegitimate children. "Roam, roam with the army guys," said one limerick about girls of the period, "The guys leave and left them with a little army." The local population associated this moral hurricane with arrival from the sky: during the war "the entrance-gates to the airport . . . became known among the Samoans as 'the gates of sin'" (Stanner 1953, 327). In World War II, then, the meaning of whiteness changed.

Let us take a moment to pull together various symbolic strands. In the UFO dream, white is associated with kindness, wealth, the context-free self, and freedom as an unmitigated good. In this hurricane dream, white is associated with the American military and literacy. We also saw that in Christian symbolism blackness and darkness were associated with heathenism and more generally with aspects of the Samoan self unacceptable in Christian terms—sexual elements in particular. During World War II, however, unchristian sexuality also came to be powerfully associated with white visitors.

The image of Hurricane Tusi in the dream suggests the stirring up or intermixing of symbolic elements as well as a dangerous acceleration. Inasmuch as the hurricane follows the trip to heaven and the ceding of Samoa via a signature by a traditional high chief to the U.S. navy, the dream symbolizes religious and military colonialism by catastrophe and thereby darkens whiteness.[11] Here color difference begins doubling back on itself, as in Derrida's model of *différance*, but rather than being a normal semiotic process, it threatens devastation. Hurricane Tusi was an actual hurricane that took place in 1987 in the Manu'as. Winds reached up to 180 miles per hour. Afterwards the islands looked as if they had been atom bombed.

Dream #3: Glittering Jewelry

The two prior dreams revolve around whiteness. A window on blackness is opened by the following dream. I call the dreamer Penina (Pearl) and have changed some locations to which she refers. Penina's dream evinces a conceptual slippage of black symbolism, which is the counterpart of the white slippage I have traced throughout this chapter. Penina's work on the dream also provides insight on how transnationalism increases the psychological salience of *différance* in postcolonial places and on the consequences of this salience for identity.

In Penina's dream only her aunt appears, sometimes called "aunt" or "aunty" and sometimes called "mother." Samoa has a generational kinship system. Aunts are called by the Samoan word for "mother," uncles by the word for "father," and so forth. Children traditionally, and still to a degree, circulate between the homes of these other "mothers" and "fathers," sometimes being brought up by them for part or all of their childhoods.

> I was walking down the hallway of my old school in east Los Angeles. I was going through my schoolmates' lockers and stealing everything I could put my hands on like coins, money, jewelry, diamonds, pearls, and gold necklaces. . . . When I got home, my mom was there waiting for me. Together, we walked into my room and I emptied my pockets . . . and let all the money and jewelry fall. . . . My aunty was [as] surprised as I to see so much money and beautiful, glittering jewelry. . . . I gave her half of what I stole and she quickly ran . . . to her room to put it away. But before I could do anything else, there came a heavy knock on our front door and the man behind yelling, "Open up, it's the police!" . . . Without any other word, my mom took my hand and led me to her room. . . and shoved me into her bedroom closet. . . . The police . . . asked my mom if she saw me today; my aunt just stood there nodding her head "no." . . . [M]y aunty came back . . . [and] began to yell at me as though I had the nerve of bringing those stolen things in this house! . . . [W]hat she was saying made me feel like saying, "Hey, you took half of it, so don't complain!" But that would be too disrespectful. . . . I went into my room and cried . . . for the whole day and night.

In this dream, as others recounted here, one finds a cargo theme: glittering wealth falls from Penina's pockets. But here there is no illusion that one can legitimately get without giving. Theft has become a negative cultural identity issue for Samoans. In some places where Samoans have migrated, they tend to be regarded as lightfingered. Not surprisingly, Samoans are embarrassed by this image. It has supplanted a former negative cultural identity image of Samoan girls as promiscuous. Samoans have been erasing the latter perhaps since Mead published *Coming of Age in Samoa* (1928), and certainly since World War II.

Dream Work

First Penina free-associated to the dream. Again in this next passage, when she says "mom" she means "aunt" in nuclear family terminology.

That was my first public school. . . . [S]ince pre-school, I've gone to Catholic schools. . . . I liked the school very, very much because I felt more free, unlike Catholic schools which always gave orders. . . . In my childhood, I remember playing in the streets and finding money and jewelry and giving it to my aunty. She gave back the money, but she kept the jewelry. . . . [T]o be honest, I've stolen little things before, not from stores, but from my mom's purse.

Samoans' reputation for theft derives from treating the possessions of groups to which they belong as communal. Several times over the years of our marriage, Sanele told me of a gigantic pearl that his mother kept in her chest. One day his youngest brother took the pearl and gave it to a friend. While regretted by family members, this action was not considered stealing. A capitalist economy, as opposed to a gift economy, is a factor in the redefinition of taking as stealing and is implicated in the money that Penina drops on the bed. Penina takes "little things," meaning small amounts of money, from her mother's purse, which she too has learned to call "stealing."[12] The venue of her dream theft is a school she liked because she felt more free there. As in the UFO prince dream, "not being poor but rich" and "free will to do anything" are symbolically affiliated. But as Penina continues, we will see that freedom and wealth have lost their previous moorings in whiteness and have become associated with blackness—or more precisely blackness has splintered fractal-like, reproducing the old black/white opposition within itself:

> The stealing does bring to mind a friend of mine named Eartha. She used to go to school with me in Sacred Heart High School. This friend was very close to me; she'd go anywhere we go as a group; she's black and she's a thief. One day, as we were walking into a store to look around, she stole some things . . . and showed it to us when we got out. I hated her a lot for stealing, but she was still my friend. I hated the way she would ask for something straight out, like if she was to watch you eating and she was hungry too, she wouldn't feel so embarrassed ask straight out, "Can I have some?"

In Penina's dream it is she who steals, but in her associations stealing is represented by a black girl, Eartha. She is close to Eartha: Eartha represents what in Christian symbolism would be Penina's dark side. In part, Christian light/dark symbolism took root in Samoa because it was superimposed upon an indigenous skin color contrast between fair and dark.

Samoans have always been various shades of brown.[13] In precontact times, like other Polynesians, they attributed fair skin and hair to aristocratic genealogies (Luomala 1986, 139–40). Gossips impute fair-haired children of common families to philandering aristocrats. When I asked my Samoan students to role-play their dream characters, they would describe themselves as dark when (as one dreamer put it) they played "average looking" people. They described themselves as fair if they were playing an especially attractive figure, particularly if that figure was female.[14] In folklore, the archetypal heroine is named Sina; *sina* means "glistening white" like moonlight on water. Sina was also the conventional name of the village princess who had a major role in ceremonies (Krämer [1902] 1994, 34). Today Samoan girls are often named Sina or variations thereof. Samoans, furthermore, have none too positive feelings about dark skin. *Uliuli* means "black." Family members may tease the darkest child by calling them "Black Lizard" (*Piliuli*) or "Black Thing" (*Meauli*). In Samoan proverbs *uliuli* is a synonym for "ugly" (Schultz 1994, 102).[15]

Ironically, for Penina, Eartha also represents that individualistic form of self, which during missionization became associated with whiteness. This individualism is symbolized by Eartha's relation to eating. Eating is of primary symbolic significance in Samoa.[16] Polite Samoans never ask for food. They wait for others to offer them some. The polite Samoan would then decline; the other would press them to accept; eventually the Samoan would accept. This little drama is symbolic of placing social demands for respect above one's own personal desires. Eartha's relation to eating represents personal expressiveness: "She can . . . ask for anything she wants straight out," Penina says, "without having to be afraid or scared of being rejected or scolded at."

Eartha may be fearless but she evokes Penina's fear of authority. One time when Eartha stole, a clerk called the police.

> The police took all of us back in the storage room and asked us to empty our pockets and read us our rights. . . . [T]hey found nothing on us and we were set free. But I was so scared I cried in the store. . . . My real father is . . . very demanding and he scares me . . . just like the police. My dad always gave orders. . . . Everything he says goes no matter what. . . . My first encounter with policemen happened when . . . we used to live in an apartment in San Francisco downtown. . . . [A]s I was walking down the hallway, I witnessed a policeman shooting a black man for a crime. I have been scared of policemen ever since then. If a policeman told me to move, jump, or dance I would probably do it.

Policemen are scary to Penina because they shoot black men, suggesting that she associates them with the white side of a black/white polarity. But Penina's Samoan father is like a policeman because he represents the strict, real *fa'aSāmoa* (Samoan way). The opposites, real/feigned, come from the discourse of sincerity originally imported by white missionaries. In Penina's remarks, "real" refers to what one might call a white valuation of one's nuclear/biological father as an authentic parent. It follows that this policeman's version of the "real *fa'aSāmoa*" is the colonial/mission version, which consolidated parental power. In the nineteenth century, sisters had rights to their brothers' children (Turner [1884] 1984, 83). Well into the 1920s, Samoan children, like those elsewhere in Polynesia, moved of their own volition among extended family households in search of a congenial situation—particularly when authority figures became demanding (Mead [1928]1973, 24; 1959, 61; Levy 1969; Carrol 1970; Brady 1976). As Penina indicates, today sisters' rights to their brothers' children and children's own rights are assessed more lightly than they once were. Penina says that she was forced back to Samoa by her dad, but says "I have deep feelings for my aunty in Atlanta. I've lived with her all my life and she means more to me than anyone else."

Penina's relationship with her aunt is under the sign of thievery in the dream; this is what they share; this is what they hide. The dream thereby delegitimates and makes precious (like jewels falling on the bed) an association that would have been legitimate in old Samoa. But Penina's bond with her aunt is also one based on a discourse of personal feelings that is unlikely to have existed in premission times. Money and glittering jewels also evoke the trope of treasure: it is these two objects one finds in discovery scenes in movies about treasure hunts. Here, however, the treasure is a newly discovered resource: deep personal relations/sentiments that for Penina stand opposed to tradition. Penina explained,

> It was hard for me to get along here in Samoa with my . . . real mother and father. They're mostly into the real *faa'Sāmoan* way of raising their kids. They teach them . . . not to *kalakiki* . . . not to talk back to your elders. . . . [M]y aunty always listened to what I had to say, even if it was wrong and she always trusted me enough to have my own boyfriend. . . . But here . . . I can't talk to them to explain a problem I'm having. I can't even look at a guy because they say I'm being *kalakiki*! I hate it! I want to express myself the way I do with my aunty and that's why we're so close.

Kalakiki is a modern colloquial version of *tautalaitiiti*. *Tautalaitiiti* literally means "to talk above one's age." Samoan children are supposed to listen to elders' orders rather than being listened to (Sutter 1980; Mageo 1991b, 410–12; 1998, 41–51). *Tautalaitiiti* also refers to illicit precocious sexuality (Mead[1928]1961, 88, 137, 140). Thus the term conflates respect for elders—perhaps the most primary tenet of Samoan ethics—and sexual propriety. As a private symbol, Penina's aunt is linked to personal expressiveness and also to sexual freedom. Not only did she let Penina have a boyfriend, Penina remembered that her aunt and uncle hid X-rated films in the closet where she hid in the dream.

Projective Exercises

In class, I presented my version of Freud's theory of dreams as wish fulfillment ([1900]1953): dreams represent a forbidden wish and are often anxiety-provoking because they also dramatize the anticipated punishment for enacting that wish. As a first projective exercise, I asked Penina to guess what the forbidden wish and the punishment might be. Penina believed the dream's forbidden wish was "to be with my aunty again." Indeed at another time Penina dreamed of this wish explicitly; it was again linked with stealing and, curiously, with an outer-space image like the two major dreams explored earlier:

> I was facing our bedroom fan when I heard my brother walked in. He was complaining about me always taking his stuff without asking for it from his room. I had my own room too. It was my room from Atlanta. I had this book on my bed and I was looking back and forth for it. My brother just finished telling me that my aunty is coming down from Atlanta to see me. I turned to him as if he just came from outer space and I saw her standing there in the blue. I felt as though I was brought back from the dead and then I started to jump up and down with joy. I couldn't believe she was finally here to get me away from Samoa. I hugged her so hard she could have died from suffocation. I felt I couldn't let her go anymore, so I fell to sleep again while I was holding her.

In reference to the glittering jewelry dream, Penina said that the price for fulfilling her wish was to be like Eartha: "Straightforward with people. To not fool around, but to ask for something straight out. To be able to face policemen, my father, and tell them what I feel without being afraid of stealing from someone or hurting the other's feelings and disregarding mine." Penina described her punishment:

> I am stuck here in Samoa until I learn to have the courage enough to go up to my real father and tell him straight out . . . "I want to go back to my aunty." . . . I'll have to live . . . putting other people's feelings before mine. Sort of like being afraid of what the others might feel about me. . . . [A]sking myself, "God, what will they think I am, a thief, a real selfish person, or just a plain, ignorant, spoiled brat?" And ignoring my true feelings.

Penina misconstrues the idea of dream punishment (an unpleasant event within the dream). One might surmise that this punishment was represented in the threat of being taken away by the policeman or by confinement in the closet. The life events that Penina considers the punishment seem to have these meanings. She is taken away from her aunt because she doesn't have the courage to tell her father what she wants: she must closet her feelings.

We saw earlier that a discourse of sincerity was imported to Samoa by missionaries and founded upon a white sense of self as inner. For Penina, however, the white discourse of sincerity has splintered. It is distilled in the adjective "real," which has become Penina's way of thinking about her biological parents and about the currently canonized version of the *fa'aSāmoa*.

But it is also distilled in the phrase "true feelings" and has become Penina's way of thinking about her personal relationship with her aunt. To complicate matters further, that aspect of the discourse of sincerity Penina associates with her aunt—personal expressiveness—is represented by Eartha, a black girl. White missionaries are still importing discourses and practices meant to produce sincere personal interrelationships to Samoa. I lived in Samoa for eight years. One year I resided next door to a Mormon family. Under instructions from their church, they had a nuclear family encounter group every week in which each family member shared their feelings toward one another! Normally Samoan custom dictates that those lower in status do not share their personal feelings with those above them. Those who do are *kalakiki*—the failing that Penina is accused of by her biological parents.

Penina has a developing interior life, but the result seems mainly to be a sense of herself as a "real selfish person." Like Tutu's real self in the dream discussed earlier, Penina's "ignorant," "brat" self must be hidden. Tutu's interior self is hidden in the dark; Penina's is not hidden in the dark per se, but in the closet, which presumably is dark, and not an inapt metaphor for interiority. Penina is uncomfortable in it. She commented that when her aunt pushed her into the closet in the dream, she thought, "How could I fit in here?" Is this how interiority actually feels to people in cultures like Samoa, which traditionally have been intensely social? Yet Penina does not imagine that this interior is an unknowable territory, as Samoans once did. For her, interiority is an intensely valued space with which she identifies, however furtively. Bhabha (1984) and Taussig (1993) maintain that postcolonial identities are hybridized: they combine local elements of culture with mimetic appropriations of colonial alters. While problematic, Penina's interiority is not mimetic, but passionately her own.

A second projective exercise I gave Penina was to select polarities from the dream and role-play the two sides. One of the two polarities she chose to play was between her father and her aunt.

AUNT: I love Penina very much, and since she was a baby of only a year and a half, I've been taking care of her. . . . She's like my own child, she belongs with me. I was her mother then, so I should be her mother now. We've become so close to each other. . . . She doesn't get along with her real family because they don't know her as well as I do. I have to get her back!

FATHER: No! She belongs with her real family. When you have children of your own, where will she stand in your life? You'll feel different about Penina . . . and you'll only hurt her. She's also growing up too fast for you to handle. When she gets to be a young adult she'll never listen to you . . . because she's getting to be too *kalakiki*. . . . Only her real parents can stop her, because if she goes off-course, we'll straighten her right away. . . . With us, Penina will . . . give us a good name for our family. She's my only hope for a good name with Samoan people. I expect her to be successful in everything she does and I want all my children to give a good name to the family.

In this dialogue the two versions of the discourse of sincerity we have encountered—one emphasizing close feeling and intimate knowledge, the other "real" nuclear family ties—are personified by aunt and father respectively and confront one another.

Sa'o, meaning "straight," but also "right," "correct," and "direct," is a Samoan value and is of key significance in this dialogue where Penina's father uses it to mean all these things.[17] But Penina has also used this term. Remember, she thought the solution to the dream problem was to be straightforward with her father and tell him "straight out" about her desire to be with her aunt. To Penina's father "straight" means proper deference; to her it means telling her true feelings. This divergence is not just between generations; it is yet another example of the postcolonial fissioning of meanings and identities that is my concern here.

Penina keeps telling us how much she and her aunt trust one another. Role-playing is a projective exercise: we can assume that through it she expresses not only her father's doubts, but her own as well. It is also Penina who fears she cannot trust bonds that go beyond her nuclear family and, therefore, the intimacy she shared with her aunt. These doubts are clearly reflected by her aunt's inconsistent and ambiguous behavior in Penina's dream.

In class, I also presented my version of Jung's model of dreaming as compensation: dreams reverse life situations in ways that indicate how we need to change them. As a third projective exercise, Penina was supposed to guess how the dream reversed her present life situation. She found two reversals in her dream. The first revolved around the figure of her aunt, whom she again calls her "mom":

I was *hiding* from it all. When the police came to get me, I hid instead of facing my problems. This is a great reversal for me because I was always taught by my mom to never hide from your problems because that won't help anything. And worse than that, my mom helped me to hide in her room closet.

The second reversal was around the figure of her father:

[I]n my dream the police only scared me, but didn't take me away. . . . [M]y aunty was able to hold me back . . . but in real life she wasn't able to do that. . . . Maybe she should have done what she did in my dreams . . . hide me away from my dad, then maybe I would still be with her.

Penina's aunt is a Janus-faced figure who keeps doubling back on herself. In the dream and in life, she privately shares a de-legitimated form of intimacy with Penina. In life, this is a relationship of mutual listening that entails granting another freedom of expression and the freedom to pursue a personal romantic relationship. In the dream, this is an honor-among-thieves relationship (thievery being associated with cultural shame for Samoans), which Penina associates with an African-American. In regards to thievery, the aunt *publicly* disavows her complicit relationship with Penina to the dream policemen. By doing so, she protects Penina and stops the policeman from taking her away. Yet this dream aunt also privately denies her complicity in theft to Penina by yelling at her for "bringing those stolen things in this house!" In waking life, Penina's aunt *publicly* honors the "real" *fa'aSāmoa* and thereby *privately* fails to protect Penina when her father comes to take her back to Samoa. Here the significance Penina assigns to her aunt (and by extension to the once-white discourse of sincerity) is as chameleonic as the car in the first dream we considered. If this instability doesn't drive Penina crazy, it does drive her to despair: within the dream she cries for a whole day and night. In life, this instability also leaves Penina in an identity crisis: before others, she must hide and ignore feelings that are as precious to her as glittering gems. This is Penina's *experience* of being a person in a postcolonial transnational world. Her dream is a "royal road" to this experience.

The *Différance* of Black and White

In the home worlds of Western colonialism and in worlds that have been colonized, few symbols are as public as black and white. We know what these symbols mean, even as contested as these significances now are. But black and white are also the stuff that dreams are made of: they orchestrate personal desires in the UFO dream, personal anxieties in the hurricane dream, and the negotiation of personal identity and personal relationships in Penina's dream. Black and white are not merely subjects of interpersonal communication in culture but also of intrapersonal communication within the self. Obeyesekere (1981) argues that public symbols become invested with personal significance in the fantasies and practices of some religious specialists. But black and white are commonly reinvested with personal significance by Samoan young people who suffer the normal stresses that characterize their era, transnationalism being one.

The dreams in this chapter indicate that white and black remain salient symbols in Samoa despite neither being granted a reliable significance. In old Samoa, white was equated with high status and beauty and black with low status and ugliness. These meanings provided a base that was to a degree accordant with those missionaries imposed on white and black in early colonial times. White became associated with all that was newly good: missionization itself, literacy, the discourse of sincerity, and parts of the *fa'aSāmoa* in accord with Christianity. Missionary discourse ordained the nuclear family as real and its version of respect relations as "the real Samoan way." Black became associated with hypocrisy and darkness, along with all that missionaries considered bad—in a word, with heathenism, which itself was taken to represent parts of the *fa'aSāmoa* in discord with Christianity, particularly loosely regulated sexuality among young people.

This presumably somewhat gradual historical revolution in Samoan color symbolism began to spin in later colonial times. Whites became ever-more associated with a cargo cult mentality, the ceding of Samoa to colonial powers, foreign military presence during World War II, and the moral hurri-cane to which it lead. In postcolonial times, black has come to represent those parts of the *fa'aSāmoa* that taint the "national" image in transnational situations symbolized by thieving, which itself symbolizes a communalistic relation to group property. In Penina's associations, however, an African-American thief also represents all that she values in her relationship with her aunt: an emotionally intimate parent-child bond, respect based on mutual trust rather than on hierarchical propriety, a modern American orientation to sexuality, an ability to directly express and pursue personal desires, favoring personal relationships above family obligations, and a discourse of true feel-ings that has grown up among young people and some elder confederates.

In part, this doubling back of meaning results from the way historical events refracted black and white by revealing new dimensions of the people who represented these colors. In part, it results from the way the semiotic play of *différance* in people's imaginations reconfigures public symbols that have become personally significant to them—as reflected by dreams. In quotidian contexts, at least in Western places, people are predominately aware of and use the more stable significances of public symbols when communicating with others, just as they use the common meanings of words, as Leach holds (1958). Then primary-process thought may be principally a nighttime system that operates independently of rational, reality-testing, daily thinking (Stephen, chapter 6).[18] But in certain cultural-historical circumstances, post-coloniality being one, the primary system bleeds through the secondary system and alters symbols more abruptly. Meaning, Derrida tells us, is forever taking a detour away from any original object of specification, getting lost in a manner re-creative of semiotic systems. While colonialism and postcolonial-ism are all about invidious differences, "*différance* instigates the subversion of every kingdom" (Derrida 1982, 22). This subversion helps to dismantle racial and other forms of discrimination and the negative cultural and personal identities that derive from them. It also leaves people like Penina to discover who they are amidst a shifting "borderland" of black and white.[19]

Notes

1. While the westerly Samoas are clearly postcolonial, people may question this term in application to American Samoa. The term "postcolonial" seldom refers to pure cases. Postcolonial, psychologically speaking, is a frame in which one reflects back upon colonial experience. Admittedly, this kind of reflection begins in the colonial period itself.

2. In Samoan *nanu* means "to speak a foreign language"; it also means to badly mispronounce.

3. Nusi grew up in the westerly Samoas. Sanele's father was a catechist and was often reassigned, so Sanele grew up in both Samoas.

4. For another example of projecting superpowers on whiteness, see Dureau on the Simbo (2001, 132, 136).

5. Dalton argues in Papua New Guinea that cargo activities revolve around a belief that white bourgeois culture has mastered the magic of accumulating great wealth while giving it away to others (2001).

6. Earlier missionaries also targeted high chiefs for conversion in hopes these conversions would influence their followers (Gilson 1970, 75).

7. Shore (1982, 158–167) interviewed Samoans on freedom and constraint. These values changed in relation to social context, as implied by the way he framed the questions.

8. For other examples of this light/dark Christian symbolism, see Keesing 1992; Comaroff and Comaroff 1991; Carucci 2001; Dureau 2001; and Dalton 2001.

9. Foucault traces the role of sexual ethics in this process (1988, 1990).

10. On the mission domination of print see Huebner 1986.

11. Other dreams in my collection darken whiteness as well, for example:

> I dreamed last night that . . . I heard a knock on my door. . . . [O]ut in
> a window stood a white woman asking for help. . . . I ran to the door
> and opened it. She stood in front of me with a sharp knife. . . . Before,
> she looked helpless, but now she looks like a "killer." I ran, but she . . .
> caught me and stabbed me in the back. I felt the pain and then I scream.

12. Penina never took more than five dollars without permission.

13. Being brown accounts in part for Samoans seeing themselves in a medial racial position. A Samoan boy adopted by R. L. Stevenson's household remarked of a new black servant to a white friend, "You must not despise him because his skin is black. His soul is as brown as yours or mine" (Field 1937, 266). Another time this boy staged a battle with toy soldiers between what he called a "white" battalion and a "brown" battalion. Knocking down the white battalion, he exclaimed, "The Samoans win!"

14. When role-playing elderly Samoan males who represented traditional values, dreamers would describe themselves as dark but with white hair. Here again my point is that the poles of dark/light, black/white oppositions splinter fractal-like.

15. Fair/dark symbolism was further complicated by the mixed matings and marriages that began soon after contact and became politically important in the late-

nineteenth and early-twentieth century (Gilson 1970; Davidson 1967). Fair hair is common among possession victims in twentieth-century spirit possession stories and is imputed to descent from either a spirit girl (reputed to have fair hair) or from German ancestors. See Mageo 1998, 171–190. Germany was a major colonial presence in the westerly Samoas during the nineteenth century. Western Samoa was a Germany colony from 1900 until 1914.

16. On the semiology of eating in Samoa, see Shore 1982, 242 and Mageo 1989b.

17. On this term, see Mageo 1998, 224–25.

18. As mentioned in the introduction, Obeyesekere argues that in some cultures the imaginal mind, and hence primary processes, are not backgrounded (1990, 65–68).

19. The term "borderland" is from Anzaldeia (1991), who documents a similar psychological situation.

CHAPTER 6

Memory, Emotion, and the Imaginal Mind

MICHELE STEPHEN

Anthropological studies of dreams, trance, spirit possession, and other alternate states of consciousness have in recent decades contributed rich new understandings of how such apparently abnormal mental states are used in positive and creative ways in many human cultures.[1] Yet our models of mind used to account for and interpret such experience remain tied to assumptions and definitions that are linked to pathology, regression and maladaption (Stephen 1997). It was in the hope of developing a more open model, less tied to implicit Western cultural values, that I first formulated the concept of "autonomous imagination" as a way of talking about dreams and dream-like states (Stephen 1989a, 1989b, 1995, 1997). I originally started with the idea of a special stream of imagery thought operating outside consciousness, but for a long time I could not say precisely what was its relationship to the "unconscious" or to the mind in general, or what might be its purpose.

In this chapter I argue that there exists in the mind two separate registers of memory, one which organizes information in terms of verbal categories and semantic understandings and one which records and organizes all information according to its emotional significance.[2] What is usually available to waking consciousness is only the semantic/language register of memory. Outside consciousness is the emotionally-coded memory register,

which is linked to the stream of imagery thought I have previously identified
as "autonomous imagination." I will further argue that the function of REM
sleep, which we know to be a regularly occurring physiological state, is to
review the day's sensory input and relate it to, and encode it in, the emotional
memory system (an argument consistent with evidence indicating that dreams
are a continuation of the concerns of waking life, for example Cartwright
1981, 245; Foulkes 1993, 13). This process of storing in memory, I suggest,
involves linking new sensory information to existing emotional categories or
schemas (Bucci 1997, 197–199; Eagle 1988; Watt 1990, 504–508).

Numerous psychological and cognitive studies of memory have
demonstrated that memory is no simple matter of recording experience, but a
much more complex process of selection, evaluation, construction, and interpretation (Bucci 1997, 98ff). Thus proposing that there are two separate
memory registers in the mind presupposes two separate interpretative and
evaluative systems operating independently. The model I propose differs
from other similar models developed by several cognitive theorists in this
very respect. Others have suggested that different processing systems deal
with different kinds of information in varying ways. Left/right hemisphere
studies emphasize that different processing tasks (such as verbal versus spa-
tial) are carried out by the two hemispheres of the brain (for example van den
Daele 1994; Watt 1990). Dual (Paivio 1986) and multiple code theories
(Bucci 1997) propose that information relating to the self and emotion are
processed by a different system from that which deals with the external
world. In contrast, I suggest that all incoming sensory information is scruti-
nized and assessed independently by two evaluative systems and encoded differently in two separate memory registers. Such a model, I hope to show, can
throw considerable new light on many old issues related to dreaming and
similar states.

Thought without Words

Various cognitive psychologists have proposed that the mind is possessed of different systems of dealing with information, which roughly corre-
spond to the primary- and secondary-process thinking originally identified
by Freud ([1900], 1953). Paivio (1986), for example, has proposed that the
mind employs, in addition to a verbal system, a separate imagery-based mode
of thought. More recently Bucci (1997), on the basis of extensive research,
has produced a multiple-code theory of mind that she attempts to integrate
with psychoanalytic concepts of conscious and unconscious processes. Bucci's
work is especially valuable, I believe, because it shows how the latest developments in cognitive psychology are unraveling the complexities of the ways in

which information is translated across various modes of transmission until it can be represented in the symbolic and verbal forms which compose waking thought. She identifies a number of levels of processing by which sensory inputs (percepts) come to be represented in the mind as conscious thought: these include subsymbolic, imagery/symbolic and verbal/symbolic levels.

Information registered by the senses is not automatically represented as verbal thought but, as Bucci (1997, 174–175) shows, must be communicated to the brain and there represented in subsymbolic form before it can be translated into the symbolic or semantic representations of conscious thought. Bucci proposes that the first level of processing in the mind, the subsymbolic code, operates in sensory, visceral, and kinesthetic modalities; it is characterized as content rather than being structure determined, and employs parallel distributed processing systems. The second level of processing, the nonverbal symbolic code, consists of images that, Bucci argues, combine some of the features of both the subsymbolic system and verbal symbols. Images, like words, can represent other entities and be used in rule-governed ways. They may represent the thing they stand for, or bear a completely arbitrary relationship to it. Sequences of images can depict episodes and events, or stories. Images can be processed in parallel or in sequence and are modality specific, like the subsymbolic system. The imagery system, she argues, provides an intrinsic basis for organizing and representing subsymbolic experience and also provides the basis to connect nonverbal experience to words. The final level of representation is language, the verbal symbolic code, which is amodal, allows sequential, logical processing and the representation of complex, abstract thought (Bucci 1997, 175–176).

Bucci is concerned primarily with the processing of emotion and the problems of translating feelings into words. She proposes that representations of self, and self in relation to others, are constituted in self schemas, the basis of which are laid down before the acquisition of language. The difficulties of moving from one processing level or mode to another, from the subsymbolic, through the imagery/symbolic to the verbal, can thus result in emotional schemas being dissociated from, or simply not connected to, the verbal level of thought, leading to emotional disturbance and pathology (Bucci 1997, 200ff). The aim of psychoanalysis, she argues, is to reconnect the dysfunctional emotional schemas with the verbal system, and with the help of the analyst, to reframe and restructure it in consciousness (Bucci 1997, 212).

Although concerned with emotional processing, and multiple codes of processing, Bucci's model is quite different from the model I propose in that Bucci sees emotional processing as a separate task, leading to the formation of self schemas, but which passes through the same levels of processing as all thought. In contrast, I am proposing two separate systems of memory and evaluation, one based on verbal/semantic coding, and one based on emotion. In my model, emotion is recorded and interpreted in both systems, but in different ways. Bucci provides extremely valuable insights into the ways in which information is represented in the mind before it becomes verbal thought, but in my view, fails to recognize that there are two independent systems evaluating all incoming information. The emotional schemas she describes would, from the perspective of my model, belong to the semantic system, since they are able, under favorable circumstances, to be represented in consciousness in the form of language.

A model that comes closer to what I am proposing has been suggested by van den Daele (1994). Combining recent cognitive and neurophysiological perspectives, van den Daele (1994, 410–411) attempts to reformulate psychoanalytic concepts concerning the structure and topography of the mind. He proposes a two-tiered structure approximately corresponding to the phylogenetic "old brain" and "new brain," each level of which is separated into specialized subsystems. The primary system, corresponding to the "old brain," is composed of three parts: an endogenous, a relational, and an exogenous subsystem (van den Daele 1994, 411–426). Each subsystem deals with information relating to different aspects of experience that can be roughly equated with the concerns of the id, the superego and the ego, as formulated by psychoanalysis (van den Daele 1994, 438–439).

The secondary system, corresponding to the neocortex, is divided into a *logicolinguistic system*, which employs language and sequential logic, and a *configurational system*, which employs imagistic representation (van den Daele 1994, 426ff). The functions of the secondary system are to reflect upon and order the information relayed to it by the primary system. Both parts of the secondary system interact with each other and may access or communicate with the primary system. Since the imagistic representations of the configurational system are more congruent with the prelinguistic representations of episodic memory employed by the primary system, it is via the configurational system that the primary system can be influenced and controlled (van den Daele 1994, 431).

This model corresponds with mine in that it identifies two higher-level systems of evaluating and interpreting information. Van den Daele (1994, 432; 431) also points out that the configurational system can be communicated to directly without the mediation of the verbal system (as in hypnosis), and he suggests that the configurational system may play a role in the structuring of episodic memory (which he locates in the "old brain"). He does not, however, explicitly link the configurational system to a separate memory register encoded according to the emotional significance of the imagery. Nevertheless his description of the logicolinguistic and the configurational systems and their relationship to subsymbolic processes is essentially compatible with the model I propose.

Another model seeking to integrate psychoanalytic insights with new developments in neurophysiology and biological psychiatry is proposed by Watt (1990). This model also comes very close to my suggestions concerning a dual memory system, and helps to demonstrate its possible neurological basis. Evidence from studies of the relationship between brain lateralization and emotion, combined with neurophysiological studies of brain injuries and disorders, strongly indicates the "primacy of the right cortex for the activation of affect, particularly painful affect" (Watt 1990, 500). The same evidence suggests that the role of the left hemisphere is to inhibit and control affect by representing in language a "benign subset of representations" (Watt 1990, 500) of the more highly charged negative images constructed by the right hemisphere. (For example, the infant, according to Klein [1988] has vivid fantasies of devouring the mother, ripping and tearing up her body, scooping out the contents of her breasts and so on; when the child reaches the stage that this hostility to the mother can be represented in the verbal thought "I am angry with mother," horrendous imagery gives way to a much more benign set of representations.)

The dual system of processing located in the two hemispheres of the cortex as proposed by Watt almost exactly matches my suppositions about imagery, emotion and memory. He suggests that the mode of processing and representation employed by the right hemisphere is specially suited to constructing self and object representations—not conscious impressions of self and other but "the deeper, less available, and more affectively powerful impressions of self and other that inform our dreaming, are intimately tied to all wishes and fears" (Watt 1990, 501). Watt (1990, 508) envisages a set of "templates" of emotionally loaded situations involving self and other that are laid down in memory in infancy before the acquisition of language and form the basis for the construction of more complex self-representations. He concludes that our emotional life may involve a "process of analogical comparison of current self and object representations with a stored internal set of "master engrams" condensed from previous experiences of pain and pleasure" (Watt 1990, 512).

Watt's (1990, 519) identification and description of two primary systems of representation, "one lexical-semantic, the other affective-configurational," differs from my proposal only in one important respect. Watt assumes that affective experience is organized in relation to self and objects, that is the latter provide the organizing principle; I propose that all experience is processed by the imaginal mind, not just experience of self in relation to others, and that the principle of organization is emotion/feeling. Thus in my view *all* incoming information is registered according to its pleasure/pain significance and recorded in sensory imagery.

Bucci, van den Daele and Watt identify, in somewhat different ways, two processing systems, one of which employs imagery as its mode of representation and is especially concerned with emotion and feeling, the other which codes information in language. Diverging only slightly from these propositions, I suggest that all sensory information is dealt with by both systems but in different ways. Emotion and imagery exist in the verbal/semantic mind but are connected to words. Likewise, the imaginal mind registers the external, physical world, but categorizes or evaluates that information according to feeling and emotion, in other words according to its value to the self (does it cause pleasure or pain?). The imaginal mind does relate to external reality—not in an abstract, objective way, however, but rather to assess experience according to its emotional salience for the self.

A Dual Memory Model and "Autonomous Imagination"

If we work on the basis of a model of mind involving two separate registers of memory—one verbally coded, one emotionally coded—then a number of things emerge in a new and clearer light. What I have identified, on essentially phenomenological grounds, as "autonomous imagination" (Stephen 1989a, 1995, 1997) can now be given a clearer theoretical basis of understanding. I have previously described autonomous imagination as a "stream of imagery thought that operates mostly outside consciousness and beyond conscious control. Although not usually available to consciousness, it can spontaneously enter consciousness in dreams, and sometimes in waking visions, and is experienced as taking place independently of a person's conscious invention or will. With special training, a person may learn to bring the stream of imagery into consciousness and direct its unfolding, as is found in the controlled trances of shamanism and meditative practices, in hypnosis, Jungian 'active imagination' and numerous Western psychotherapeutic techniques (Stephen 1995, 99).

This proposition was based upon a host of experimental studies.[3] On these grounds I have argued that "autonomous imagination" possesses certain important characteristics which not only distinguish it from thought and imagination controlled by waking consciousness, but also suggest capacities beyond those normally available in ordinary waking consciousness (Stephen 1989a,1995,1997). I now want to show how each of these characteristics can be illuminated by a dual memory model.

1) Autonomous imagination takes the form of vividly
   externalized sensory imagery

If dreams are the products of a system that does not possess language, then the dream thought (information carried by the dream) must be expressed in some other way. Dreaming employs sensory imagery (including visual, haptic, olfactory, and auditory modes) as its means of representing information. Freud ([1900]1953) long ago pointed to the representational problems of dream thought, but my proposition goes somewhat further in that it identifies a processing system which operates without language (although not without vocalizations, as we shall see). Whereas Freud maintained that dream thoughts were deliberately disguised to protect consciousness, I propose along lines suggested by Fromm (1957) and others (e.g. Greenberg and Pearlman 1993; van den Daele 1994) that the dream thought is not disguised, but because it is represented by nonverbal means, it appears strange and unreadable to the verbal system that operates in waking consciousness. Spontaneous waking dreams or visions and deliberately induced states, such as shamanic possession or a hypnotic trance, can be understood as employing the same system of imagery thought as sleep dreams.

The difficulty of even conceptualizing the notion of thought without words—which seems almost a contradiction in terms—has been well discussed by Bucci (1997) and other cognitive theorists (Weiskrantz 1988). Indeed, we might say that our conviction is that thought is constituted of words, that by its very nature thought is verbal. Yet if we think in evolutionary terms, it is evident animals must process complex information, act upon it, and communicate to other animals, all without the benefit of language (Weiskrantz 1988). Furthermore, we know the human infant begins life without language but nevertheless demonstrates complex capacities to interact with its external environment (Bucci 1997, 138ff; Cohen 1988; Leslie 1988; Stern 1985).

As outlined earlier, recent work by Bucci (1997) and others is important in showing how information is created, registered, and communicated within the mind via nonverbal codes. Bucci (1997, 173ff) describes how information received by the senses must be relayed to the brain and there processed first of all via subsymbolic systems, including sensory, visceral, and kinesthetic modalities. These subsymbolic formulations are then represented in imagery in the nonverbal symbolic system, and finally mapped onto language. Thus language is but the final end of the process, and one which is not yet developed in animals and human infants.

However, all this is not to say that words and sounds are absent from the imaginal memory register. The important point is that words and utterances are not encoded according to their semantic meaning, but according to the feelings or emotions to which they are linked. Thus a person in a dream or trance might speak and hear voices, but these vocalizations convey emotional or symbolic significance rather than semantic content. It is for this reason, I suggest, that the mysterious utterances of prophets, healers, and spirit mediums usually require translation before they can be understood by the audience.

Autonomous imagination employs words—since words are sounds—but it uses words (and other sounds) for the feelings attached to them, and not according to their semantic meaning (Brown 1991, 38ff; Bucci 1997, 214–222; Watt 1990, 498). These feelings and emotions attached to words as sounds may be purely idiosyncratic, or may be part of shared cultural experience, for example, feelings of shame (or arousal) attached to swear words, or sexual and scatological referents.[4] Songs, chants, spells, and prayers all employ sound, intonation, rhythm, and association to evoke feelings, and thus might be easily taken up by the emotional memory system. I suspect that the phenomenon referred to as glossolalia is an example of wordlike sounds linked to feelings, or of language-like structures lacking semantic referents (a similar suggestion might be made concerning the "word salad" and language disorders present in schizophrenia, I point I will return to later).

In entering the world of dreams or waking visions we are not dealing with a system that combines imagery with language; rather we have entered a realm where words no longer have semantic meaning, but possess instead affective valence as sounds carrying emotional significance. Our problems in interpreting the products of the imaginal mind are compounded by the fact that we are locked into the linguistic/semantic system, especially, of course, when we are engaged in scholarly or scientific discourse. The reason why the configurational system has largely been ignored by cognitive science, as Watt (1990, 494) and van den Daele (1994, 428) point out, is because it is so very difficult to conceptualize a mode of thought that does not employ language. When we realize that information might be stored in the mind in two quite different ways, we can begin to understand that the mode of thought employed in dreams and dreamlike states is not regressive, disordered, or an impoverished version of waking thought brought about by the neurophysiological conditions of sleep (e.g. Bucci 1997, 248), but rather an independent system of interpretation and evaluation.

2) Autonomous imagination has a different access to memory

The nature of the different access to memory evident in dreams, hypnosis, and similar states, which has been described as "state dependent memory" by many researchers (Hilgard 1977; Sheehan and McConkey 1982; Brown 1991) now becomes obvious. It is not that a specific state of consciousness creates its own memory record, but rather that a separate memory system organized on a different basis is drawn upon in dreams, hypnosis, and other altered states.

We can understand better why dreams are so difficult to remember unless they are written down immediately after waking or else told to someone else. Because dreams are constructed without language, they are not able to be registered in the semantic system of memory unless a special effort is made to recall them in consciousness and translate them from imagery to words (Bucci's imagery/symbolic to verbal/symbolic). Only then can the dream be registered in the verbal memory and labeled as a dream. We can also see why childhood memories unavailable to conscious recall may surface in dreams or in hypnosis; these childhood experiences were laid down in the emotional memory in imagery before the acquisition of language and thus are simply not present in the semantic register. Furthermore, since experience is recorded in the imaginal memory as imagery attached to feeling, more vivid memories are contained there than in the semantic register. The same event may be registered quite differently in the two registers, due to the nature of registering and coding.

The amnesia reported by persons experiencing trance or possession (Stephen 1989a, 57) and other culturally induced altered states, such as hypnosis, is explicable in the same terms. One cannot recall experiences that took place in nonordinary states of consciousness because they do not belong to the verbal memory register. Only if there has been a special effort made to register these experiences in consciousness by subsequently representing them in language will they be recorded in the verbal/semantic memory system.

3) Autonomous imagination is responsive to external direction yet retains its spontaneity and independence in relation to waking consciousness

The hypnotic suggestion, the ritually induced possession state, and the lucid dream are all examples which indicate that the imaginal system can be communicated with and responds to external influences without the person having conscious awareness of the fact. How is this possible?

If we realize that there are two, not one, memory systems storing information, then we can understand that the verbal system will attend to information readily assimilable in verbal terms, while on the other hand the imaginal system will register images, feelings, and other information that are not easily or immediately representable in words. For example, my conscious awareness may register the sympathetic words spoken to me by a friend, but certain subtleties of the friend's tone, gestures, and other body language may impress the imaginal system in quite a different way. Since consciousness in normal waking states is attached to the verbal system, and has access only to the verbal memory, the information being registered by the imaginal system necessarily bypasses consciousness.

In the case of a hypnotic suggestion, the hypnotist's verbal instruction easily translates into imagery that then serves to access the imaginal memory. As Van den Daele (1994, 432) points out, "[T]he psychotherapeutic approach identified with Milton Erickson provides a radical example of

therapeutic discourse addressed to the configurational mind with no necessary engagement of ordinary cognitive formulations." The capacity of people
to experience hypnosis depends, I would suggest, on their ability to switch
from the verbal system to the imaginal system. This is not regression or
gullibility, or weakness of will, but a willingness to suspend verbal processing
and move to imaginal processing. In this manner, the verbal suggestion that
"you are standing in a beautiful garden smelling the roses" is taken up by the
imaginal mind and represented in sensory impressions of the sights, sounds,
and smells of gardens recorded in the imaginal memory. In order to communicate back to the hypnotist what you are experiencing, you act out for your
audience what it is you see and feel in that beautiful garden.

We can observe the same process operating in trance and possession
states induced by healers and spirit mediums in many cultures. The healer
takes the request of a client for help and then, by various means, induces a
state wherein the imaginal system is accessed and the problem is represented
and resolved, or at least some answer found, in the form of imagery or other
sensory representations. Thus the healer may see a snake lodged in the
patient's abdomen or may simply feel heat or vibrations from a particular part
of the body. The shaman may then enact the extracting of the snake from
the body, or a journey to the underworld to retrieve the patient's lost soul, or
demonstrate the vibrations from the sickness with hand movements, and so
on. The acting out of the situation, which is usually interpreted as a performance for the sake of an audience can, I think, be better understood as the
natural means of communication from the imaginal mind of the healer to
that of the patient.[5]

A dual memory model can also throw some new light on dreams and
altered states of consciousness as splits in consciousness. Consciousness is
most strongly attached to the verbal system which operates in a normal
waking state, but we know that consciousness can also attend to the imaginal
system in sleep dreams and in waking visionary states. Consciousness does
not direct but rather observes the products of the imaginal system as if they
were an external reality. The dream, the vision, the hypnotic state *happen* to
one, they are not created in or by conscious awareness. They are created by
the imaginal system. Yet while consciousness is able to focus on and attend
to the imaginal system, it remains in touch with the verbal system, ready to
revert to it at any moment if necessary. I suggest that the "hidden observer
effect" observed by Hilgard (1977) in hypnotic states represents this continued contact between consciousness and the verbal system. This has obvious,
if not essential, adaptive functions in maintaining a link with external reality.
From this perspective, the "dream censor" identified by Freud ([1900]1953)
can be seen to have a similar function; even during sleep, a fraction of con

sciousness remains in touch with the verbal system, ready to awaken the dreamer if the dream experience for any reason becomes too troubling.

Thus dreams and similar states can be regarded as involving consciousness paying attention to, or reviewing, two different memory registers—on the one hand focusing on internal imagery and the emotionally coded memory, and at the same time maintaining contact with the verbally coded system. Some states involve a minimum of attention to the verbal code, such as the REM dream. Yet even here we have the dream "censor" ready to wake the dreamer if necessary. Other states involve varying degrees of conscious attention to the verbal and the emotionally coded register—for example, the lucid dream, the hypnotic trance, or culturally prescribed possession states.

4) The special capacity to reflect and influence bodily and psychological processes outside conscious control

How does a dual memory model help to explain this potential for healing body and psyche? The phenomena is now so well attested to I think it is beyond doubt (Rossi 1993; Sarbin and Slagle 1979; Singer 1974; Singer and Pope 1978; Stephen 1989a). Yet the question remains: How and why does imagery influence bodily states? The key here is again, I think, emotion. Emotions are mental states accompanied by physical and physiological states. Indeed experientially, the feeling in the body of anger, excitement, happiness, satisfaction, or pain, is primary. We sense something in the body and then recognize it as anger—blood rushing to the head, heart beating rapidly, body tensing. These bodily sensations, associated with actual physiological changes, we verbally label in consciousness as "anger." Here the direction of communication is from the body to conscious awareness.

I am proposing that specific imagery is linked to specific feelings (along a pleasure/pain axis). When this imaginal memory system is reviewed, imagery evokes the attached feelings (just as a word will evoke its semantic meaning in the verbal memory system). Here we find communication in the opposite direction, from the mind to the body. This is not a matter of conscious concentration on a particular image, but of accessing the imaginal system that, without conscious thought or awareness even, evokes feelings in the body and thus communicates information to it. In the same way, feeling states originating in the body—that is caused by sickness or bodily malfunction and as yet unidentified by consciousness and the verbal system—may give rise to imagery in the imaginal system, and be expressed in dreams and similar states.

Bucci (1997), Van den Daele (1994), and Watt (1990) all agree that imagery thought is particularly well adapted to represent emotion and feeling, and thus provides a link between verbal thought and subsymbolic representations. Bucci (1997, 78–85, 174–175) holds that imagery thought possesses characteristics that enable it to communicate with subsymbolic systems. Van den Daele (1994, 431) observes that similarity of the mode of representation employed by the configurational mind to that of the primary system (which he locates in the old brain) enables it to influence and control this level: "To the extent that the primary system represents experience prelinguistically in terms of episodic memory, the configurational system is particularly congruent with 'primary experience,' and therefore, it is through the medium of the configurational system that the primary system is, to a significant extent, influenced or controlled. The congruence of the 'language' of the primary system and the configurational system provides an explanation for those studies which report the concentration on images, imaginal performances, or the like impact health, sports performance, and interpersonal relations."

Employing similar kinds of evidence and arguments, Rossi (1993) shows how hypnotic suggestion employs language that can easily be "transduced" to imagery and thus to subsymbolic representations which communicate to the body. Thus current work in several fields is beginning to clarify the way in which information coded in non-verbal form can influence the body and aspects of mind outside conscious control.[6]

5) Creativity and autonomous imagination

How can a dual memory model elucidate the creative potential of autonomous imagination? My previous formulations assumed simply, on the basis of the phenomenological evidence, that there exists a stream of imagery thought which deals with, presumably, internally generated information (for example, thoughts and feelings, and imagery stored in memory). Now I am proposing something more specific: a separate mode of processing all incoming sensory information that operates without language and that registers all information in a separate memory system. From this perspective, the innovative, creative potential of autonomous imagination arises from its very nature as an alternative mode of processing information that is free of the constraints of language, and employs different criteria of significance.

The cognitive theories of Bucci (1997), Van den Dale (1994) and Watt (1990), as I have already discussed, provide a new theoretical means of understanding the processes whereby creative, innovative combinations of information come about (see also Rossi 1993). They show that language-based thought is not the sole or even primary mode of processing information, but only a means of representing the final product. Bucci argues that creative persons are able to draw upon imagery and subsymbolic processes and then subsequently formulate their insights in words. In Bucci's view all kinds of creativity, including scientific discoveries and technological inventions, originate at subsymbolic levels, and then later are translated into symbolic and semantic codes (1997, 223–228). I think Bucci's arguments are very important in suggesting the kinds of nonsemantic processes that underlie verbal language-based thought, and I believe she is correct in pointing out that all significantly new formulations of knowledge draw upon such sources. But it is also important to distinguish between what Van den Daele refers to as "knowledge of" and "knowledge about" the world (1994, 433).

What language allows is the development of abstract knowledge *about* the world, whereas the imaginal system registers and stores only information that has direct relevance to the self, that is, knowledge *of* things. Animals require a great deal of knowledge of various aspects their environment in order to find food and shelter and to survive, but they do not possess abstract knowledge about how these things are constituted. Such abstract knowledge is the product of language, which can represent information in terms that have no relevance to the self. Scientific knowledge, abstract knowledge about, only becomes possible with the development of language. Thus in developing language, human beings have added to a primary capacity to gain knowledge of the world necessary for survival, a second system enabling the development of abstract knowledge. Both Watt (1990, 518–519) and Van den Daele (1994, 433–434) describe the advantages of bringing these two kinds of knowledge together to gain insight into emotional and relational problems.

Although scientific and technological discoveries have been attributed to dreams and dreamlike states, I think such is not the usual avenue to scientific advances. Rather, I believe the imaginal mind is responsible for a different kind of creativity. Once we realize that the imaginal memory operates by linking sensory impressions to emotion and feeling, then it is no mystery as to why autonomous imagination is associated with artistic creativity. Aesthetic creations—painting, sculpture, music, dance—all involve expressing feeling and emotion in a particular sensory mode—visual imagery, sound, and movement. Art involves the fusion of sensory form and feeling. The imaginal system provides the source of the artist's ideas, which the artist is able to fashion into a work of art. Poetry also, although it employs words, can be seen to flow from the same source. The poet clearly possesses a special ability to use language in all its aspects, but also a unique talent to capture language as evocative of feeling. I suggest that the poet draws upon the emotional memory register of the imaginal mind to find the language which is stored there according to its emotional valence and reference to the self (see also Bucci 1997, 214–217). Indeed often what strikes us about poetry is the way in which it defies or makes paradoxical the semantic meaning—"fire flowers exploding" has no semantic or common sense—and yet it is somehow aesthetically pleasing and striking. In such cases, the imagery created by words is quite different from the semantic sense conveyed by them.

Dreams and altered states of consciousness are widely associated cross culturally with religious experiences and innovations. Warning, guidance, communications from ancestors, spirits and deities, and instruction in ritual and religious matters are commonly attributed to dreaming (Bourguignon 1994; Stephen 1979, 1995; Tedlock 1994). Prophecies and whole new systems of belief are believed to originate from dream and dreamlike states (La Barre 1970; Lanternari 1973; Stephen 1997). Why should this be? In the first place, the imaginal mind, as we can now see, represents a different way of apprehending and evaluating the world. It does possess information not available to the semantic register, and it does communicate to levels of mind and body outside conscious awareness and control. Furthermore it is not limited to the constructs and categorizations of language. It can thus represent the incomprehensible, the unthinkable—unthinkable, that is, in language and words. It reaches to the deepest levels of desire and emotion within the self and at the same time is in touch with its highest aspirations and most refined sensibilities. Yet its processes are not available to consciousness. Its products and creations enter consciousness—in dreams and similar states—already fashioned, as if from another world or some source outside the self. These products are not the inventions of the semantic mind (that is, the verbal mind that speaks to itself as it thinks) but something quite different and external to it.

Why the association of dreams and trance/possession with radical social, cultural and religious change (La Barre 1970; Lewis 1971, 1986; Stephen 1997)? The imaginal mind, by drawing on the imagery/emotion memory register, enables the prophet to transcend the semantically created world of society and culture, and thus provides the means of formulating a new vision which can be translated into language at a later date. The frequent use of glossolalia, and other mysterious or paradoxical pronouncements, by prophets and oracles might well be understood as reflecting the process of translating from the imaginal to the semantic realm.

Precognition, telepathy, clairvoyance and other so-called ESP phenomena are also widely believed to occur in dreams and dreamlike states, and not only in non-Western cultures (Hunt 1989:114–117; Krippner and Hughes 1970; Van de Castle 1994, xxi–xxii, 427–428). Although it would be going too far to try to explain all ESP phenomena in these terms, I think a dual memory model can help to explain the widespread belief that dreams function as warnings and predictions concerning the immediate future (which we might say has already been largely determined in outcome but is not yet apparent to consciousness). I have argued that the imaginal system independently registers and evaluates all incoming information, but only as that information relates to or impinges on the self. It thus attends to information that may not be verbally labeled or registered, and it records this information in the emotional memory in the form of sensory imagery. Thus it is only logical that it contains information not available to verbal thought. Indications of danger, or imminent threat (originating from other persons or the physical environment) too subtle to be recorded by the verbal system, might be picked up by the imaginal system and represented in dreams or waking intuitions. Certainly the link between strong emotion and feeling and ESP is well known; people usually report premonitions concerning, or connections with, those emotionally close or important to them (Van de Castle 1994, 408ff). I think also of Jung's (1973) work on synchronicity and the importance of emotion and of the so-called marvels of animal intelligence: their abilities to find their way across vast distances, and such like. Animals evidently operate without verbal memory or verbal thought. Perhaps we should begin to think not of Extra Sensory Perception, but rather of Extra Semantic Knowledge.

The creativity of the imaginal system is of a special kind that arises from its capacity to represent information and express things which cannot be represented or expressed verbally, and thus are not registered in the verbal memory system. It steps in where language fails.

Psychopathology and the Imaginal Mind

Many might object that my emphasis here on the creative aspects of the imaginal mind ignores much more obvious dysfunctional and pathological aspects. Psychoanalytic theory has been concerned almost exclusively with these aspects, since it was via pathology—neurosis and psychosis—that Freud and his followers were first to discover the imaginal mind. What can a dual memory model reveal about mental disorders?

As Bucci (1997), Watt (1990), and van den Daele (1994) all point out in slightly different ways, infantile experience, which according to psychoanalytic theory is the basis of later neurotic and psychotic disorders, is necessarily recorded in memory in preverbal terms because the infant does not yet possess language.[7] Because the early events of childhood are not encoded in verbal memory they are not available to conscious recall and thus cannot be dealt with in consciousness, although they are the roots of emotional disturbance.

Only with the help of an analyst can these disturbing unconscious elements be brought into consciousness, translated into verbal terms and thus be resolved. The difficulties of translating information between different processing codes—verbal versus imagistic versus subsymbolic sensory, kinesthetic, and somatic modalities—can result in information simply not reaching the verbal system and thus consciousness. Alternatively, it can aid the process of repression, so that, as Bucci sugests (1997, 206, 269), self schemas involving painful affects can be cut off from the verbal system and not easily translated back into it.

Mental disorders might also be expected to arise if the two systems come into conflict, or if one begins to intrude too much upon the other. Since each system has different criteria of significance (feeling tone as against semantic meaning) and employs different means of processing information (for example, analogue as against digital; parallel as against sequential), it is evident that the two systems are likely to have different views of a situation and sometimes come into conflict. When the configurational system is opposed to the position taken by the verbal system (which informs consciousness and executive action) the conflict may be expressed in dreams or represented in physical symptoms. The view that symptoms are essentially a communication is basic to psychoanalysis, but what I am suggesting here is that these communications (dreams and symptoms) are not simply expressions of forbidden id desires, but rather communications from an independent evaluative system.[8]

More serious in terms of mental disturbance than conflict between the two systems is the possibility of a confusion or merging of the two. It is evident that in order to act upon external reality a person must know whether what is perceived is a physical reality or a dream or waking vision. If one's normal waking consciousness is constantly intruded upon by false perceptions that have the appearance of reality—that is, hallucinations—then one's relation to reality will be severely disrupted. The need to separate the two systems, ensuring that the executive function is confined to waking consciousness, is evident in the fact that during sleep the connection between the brain and the motoric system is switched off; thus the dreamer is not able physically to act out the events of the dream (Gillin, Zoltoski and Salin-Pascual 1995, 85). Dream happenings must be kept separate from waking reality if the person is not to be totally confused as to the status of mental events. Indeed, I suggest that one important function of REM sleep is to enable review of the configurational system under conditions where there is no possibility of the dreamer mistaking the dream images for reality and trying to act upon them. If we envisage a mind (or system of mental organization) where no verbal/semantic system exists—as in animals and human infants—then how is the organism to distinguish between what is an actual sensory perception and what is a sensory perception reviewed in memory? One means would be to develop a special neurological state wherein the body was immobilized, during which memory could be reviewed and new information integrated with it. That, I suggest, is precisely the role of REM sleep.

If the imaginal system begins to invade waking consciousness, not only will the person's orientation to reality be disrupted; the thought processes will be interrupted and will mix verbal processing with imaginal representations. What if a person becomes confused between the two systems to the extent that he or she begins to use words not for their semantic meaning, but for their emotional significance as vocalizations recorded in the imaginal/configurational system? This might well help to explain the word and language disorders observed in various forms of schizophrenia (Lipton and Cancro 1995, 974–975). It might also help to account for the fact that some therapists claim that they can understand the communications of their schizophrenic patients (Lipton and Cancro 1995, 975)—that is, the words do have emotional significance but not semantic meaning. Or perhaps the sufferer mistakes hallucinated commands for semantic statements. Thus, for example, a patient ordered by his "voices" to castrate himself, interprets this literally as a semantic statement—an order to cut off his genitals—when the statement may represent metaphorically the idea that he must control his sexual desires.[9]

If, as Watt and van den Daele maintain, the verbal/semantic system and the configurational/imaginal system are located in the left and right hemispheres respectively of the brain cortex, then we might propose that some kinds of severe mental disorders arise from either too much, or too little, communication between the two hemispheres across the corpus callosum.[10] In view of my arguments concerning the need to separate the two processing systems, the possible location of the two systems in two discrete hemispheres of the brain seems to further underline this functional necessity.[11]

The Relation of REM Sleep to Dreaming

The cognitive theory developed by Bucci (1997, 248–249) explains dreams as the result of activation during sleep of an emotion schema, with its subsymbolic processing systems. The special neurophysiological conditions of sleep—"the absence of external input, along with the high cortical arousal that is characteristic of REM periods"—facilitate the activation of subsymbolic systems. In dreams the latent content provided by an emotion schema (which may be as varied as the schemas which make up the individual's emotional world) is represented in imagery and finally in the dream narrative which is translated into verbal form. In van de Daele's (1994, 439) model, dreams originate from presymbolic subsystems—the endogenous, relational and exogenous subsystems located in the "old brain"—and are given representation in imagery by the configurational system. Finally the dream, when recalled or told to another person, is represented in the verbal system.

My dual memory model differs in some important respects with regard to dreaming. I have suggested that the psychological and cognitive function of REM sleep is to review and encode new information in the imaginal/configurational memory system. The neurophysiological conditions of REM sleep are entirely consonant with this. The fact that no new information is entering the system, the high level of cortical arousal, combined with other levels of physiological arousal (heart beat, blood pressure, genital arousal), all taking place while the connection to the motoric system is shut down (Gillin, Zoltoski and Salin-Pascual 1995, 84–85), is highly consistent with a reviewing of information, assessing its emotional significance, and linking it to the existing emotional memory code.

On this basis we can explain the difference researchers have observed between dreams reported in the laboratory, when the dreamer is awakened during or directly after REM sleep, and those dreams recalled spontaneously at home (Van de Castle 1994, 283–287). If, as I suggest, REM dreaming involves sorting, comparing, and storing recent experience in the emotionally coded register, then much of this experience is obviously by its very nature trivial or routine, like the REM reported dream. The spontaneously recalled home dream, according to this line of argument, is brought into awareness as the result of the attention of that portion of consciousness which remains attached to the verbal memory code and external reality even during sleep. What I believe happens is that where there is some difficulty in integrating new experience, this is marked by the "dream censor" (Freud [1900]1953) as needing to be dealt with in consciousness, and thus the dream thought is allowed to enter consciousness and is recalled as a dream, often awakening the dreamer in the process. This would account for the more bizarre imagery and inventive nature of spontaneously recalled dreams since the system must be extensively searched to find a match for the new information. Infantile memories may in this way surface in dreams, since the process of encoding new information involves the linking of present experience in relation to past experience carrying the same emotional significance.

Thus we all need to dream every night (or rather we all require REM sleep) but we only need to recall dreams when some kind of problem is making daily experience difficult to integrate with existing emotional schemas. One type of dream arises out of the neurological procedures of routine information processing—the REM dream. The other, the spontaneous dream, arises out of psychological or other difficulties. Thus I think that REM dreams are meant to be forgotten, as some dream researchers have insisted (Crick and Mitchison 1983), so as not to overload the memory systems unnecessarily, and that only spontaneously remembered dreams have significant relevance to our psychological conflicts or other problems.

Foulkes (1993) has recently noted that any functional explanation of dreaming must take into account the fact that a) dreams are not limited to REM sleep or even to sleep itself; b) that in early childhood REM awakenings do not generate reliable dream recall (Foulkes 1993, 11–12); and c) the information processing functions proposed for dreaming identified with REM sleep have been supported by experiments with animals only. He interprets these three facts to mean that dreaming is in no sense reducible to REM sleep but in fact depends upon "an advanced and self-reflective consciousness generally lacking in other species and in human infants" (Foulkes 1993, 17). The model I have proposed resolves these difficulties.

REM sleep is present in both human and higher animals, and in human infants, since all three possess sensory/emotional coding processing systems. Dreaming, however, can only exist (as Foulkes maintains) when the child reaches a certain level of cognitive development—that is to say, when the child has sufficiently developed the linguistic/semantic system (See Hunt 1989, 47 for a similar observation). Dreams, in my view, represent communications between the sensory/emotional system and the semantic system. Thus dreams, as such, cannot exist until the two processing systems have developed. As Foulkes (1993, 12) argues, dreams can also take place outside sleep when "voluntary control of consciousness is relinquished," and, I would add, the imagistic system is allowed to take over. Consciousness continues to observe the products of the imaginal system, but does not control them; this situation can occur spontaneously, or it can be deliberately sought or induced, as in meditative states or shamanic trance. Since human beings possess consciousness, they can attend to either processing system, the verbal/semantic or the emotional/imaginal, but for most people, as the semantic register develops and expands with the acquisition of language, the imaginal system usually fades into the background. Certain individuals, however, such as shamans and spirit mediums, seem to have a special ability to draw upon the imaginal system. Such individuals are also to be found in Western cultures (see Newman 1999 for a vivid anthropological study of an American "diviner").

REM Sleep and Memory

Many cognitive approaches suggest that dreaming serves as an alternative means of processing information (Cartwright 1981, Cohen 1979,

126–134; Fishbein 1981; Greenberg and Pearlman 1993). However, not all researchers agree that the evidence supporting problem solving in dreams is convincing (see Blagrove 1992 for a review of the debate). REM sleep has also been connected by several researchers to the processing of memory and emotion (Greenberg 1981, 126; Hartman 1981, 118; Reiser 1994;Winson 1990). A recent important objection has been raised by Foulkes (1993, 14), who points out that the evidence indicating a connection between REM sleep and learning is based only on *animal* experimentation, and that there is "no compelling evidence for the role of REM sleep in *human* information processing." This reminder serves to support my arguments concerning dual memory systems. Most tasks involved in human learning use language, or can be represented in language, since that is our preferred cognitive mode. Language-based learning is not, of course, likely to be influenced by manipulating conditions which affect only the imagistic system. Thus most experimental procedures concerned with human learning and memory would not be likely to provide positive evidence to indicate a connection with REM sleep. (A further implication of these findings is that the language-based memory system must be stored and coded in a different manner).

Following up earlier work by Palombo (1978) on dreams and memory, studies by Winson (1985), a neuroscientist, and Reiser (1994), a psychiatrist, have proposed models of emotion and memory which in important respects match my proposals, and indicate in detail how such a system might be organized in the brain (for example, Reiser 1994, 91–92). Reiser (1994, 197) contends that

> REM sleep may provide a mechanism for memory processing whereby the voluminous input of the day may be sorted at leisure during sleep, when the circuits are not otherwise busy. . . . [A]ffective connections would exert considerable influence on those neural sorting and filing operations, and the sense we make of dreams through the psychoanalytic process would reflect the influence of those affective connections as they manifest themselves in both domains. The mental memory process would consist of deciding which percepts to store and which to discard, on the basis of the relation or lack of relation to significant events already in memory, as Stanley Palombo (1973, 1978) had suggested earlier on the basis of psychoanalytic-dream laboratory studies.

Yet neither Reiser nor Winson (nor Palombo) recognizes that what they are describing cannot represent the totality of human memory.

Foulkes's point about the laboratory evidence concerning REM sleep and learning being based entirely on animal studies identifies a crucial difficulty with models of memory such as those developed by Winson and Reiser. Reiser's description of the organization of memory on an emotional basis is derived primarily from clinical evidence. Dreams and fantasies do indeed demonstrate the memory structure he outlines, but we cannot imagine that abstract knowledge of the world, such as is developed with the emergence of language, is stored in the mind in the same way. As I have already noted, the primary advantage of verbal/semantic knowledge is that it enables us to acquire information and knowledge that has no emotional significance to us, and no direct relationship to self or to instinctual needs. Winson develops his model from an evolutionary perspective, arguing that the human emotionally coded memory system has evolved out of a memory system that can be identified in lower species. My earlier comments about animal intelligence are relevant here. I agree with Winson that animals must relate to external reality and that the emotional system was originally designed to deal with it. In developing a more efficient system of relating to external reality, I believe that the language-based system in humans was not grafted onto the original memory system, as implied by Winson, but developed separately. As it proved its advantages in the game of survival, so human beings came to rely on it more and more until the imaginal system became submerged. Paradoxically, it seems, these researchers, who have both identified and described in detail an emotionally coded memory system, have not recognized that their evidence points to the existence of a dual memory system in the mind—one based on organizational principles identifiable in lower animals and one uniquely human, based on language.

Nightmare and Trauma Dreams

Nightmares and recurring trauma dreams can also be explained in terms of encoding experience in the emotional memory. Although not using a dual memory model, Koulack (1993), writing about dreams and stress, and Domhoff (1993), writing about the repetition of dreams, including nightmare and trauma dreams, both propose that such dreams represent attempts to integrate stressful or traumatic experience with existing emotional schemas. Koulack (1993, 322) observes that a "mastery hypothesis" has been suggested by several theorists: "Although the mechanism for adaptation is never precisely identified, the underlying theme of these notions is that dreaming provides an opportunity for the dreamer to integrate affectively charged material with past, similar material that has already reach successful resolution."

I think a dual memory model can help to explain this mechanism for adaptation. The nightmare or trauma dream is not an attempt to solve a problem, but rather an effort to link new emotionally charged experience to the existing emotional memory system. Some experiences arouse feelings so powerful and so overwhelming that they are impossible to integrate. The same material will thus be processed again and again until it can be accommodated; in some cases this may never be achieved and the nightmare continues. The fact that children are more prone to nightmares than adults, and that children usually grow out of them, is also consistent with the notion of integrating new emotionally troubling experience in nightmares (Domhoff 1993, 312). Whereas adults already possess an extensive emotional code, children are still in the process of developing theirs. Recurring nightmares in adults are likely to be associated with extraordinary events such as wartime experiences, rape, torture, or other severe traumas (Domhoff 1993). In such cases, even the adult emotional code is unable to accommodate the experience. The constant entry of these dreams into waking life is drawing attention to the need to deal with this material in consciousness. (This point seems supported by the finding that when sufferers of trauma dreams start to discuss them in therapeutic contexts, the severity of the dreams begins to diminish, Domhoff 1993, 297).

Some Dream Examples

The cognitive function of REM sleep, then, is the reviewing and coding of sensory information in the emotional/configuration memory system. Dreams arise when consciousness is alerted to something in the imaginal system that needs to be dealt with in consciousness by the verbal system. Dreams thus provide a bridge between the two processing systems, and that, I suggest, is their function in human cognition. A few simple examples may help to clarify these points.

The first two dreams were told to me by Balinese, the third dream is my own after returning from fieldwork in Bali, and the fourth is a dream omen reported in a newspaper, the *Bali Post*. The three Balinese dreams were reported in Indonesian and translated by me.

Dream of the White Dog

One morning Wayan, the Balinese girl who keeps house for me, arrived early and in a hurry, and as she passed me she related the following extremely brief and apparently simple dream: "Last night I dreamed that Timpal (our dog) had nothing to eat." Although I could elicit no more information from Wayan about the dream or its meaning, her actions spoke volumes. Prompted by her dream, she had come to work early to make sure that Timpal was getting enough to eat.

Timpal, which means "friend" in Balinese, is a big beautiful white dog that my housekeeper has helped me raise from a puppy. At the time of the dream Wayan was being kept very busy by preparations for important forthcoming ceremonies in her family, and as a result was finding it difficult to keep up with her duties in my house. She and her three siblings were about to be formally adopted, after years of neglect and avoidance by their extended family, and her younger siblings were to have *masangih*, or tooth filing, a ceremony that constitutes the major rite marking the passage from adolescence to adulthood. Wayan herself had already been through this ritual. A few weeks before Wayan came to work for me, now more than two years before, her mother had died in very sad circumstances. When still grieving for her mother, Wayan had told me that she sometimes dreamed of her mother and then she knew her mother needed food or offerings and the next day she would actually take food to the cemetery for her. The dream of Timpal the dog follows the same pattern, the dream alerting Wayan to some neglect, which she then immediately attempted to correct in waking life.

The pattern of associative links here begins to emerge now, which shows how the image of the dog is indeed overdetermined in psychoanalytic terms. The dream image of the neglected and loved dog in Wayan's present circumstances links to dreams of her dead mother's spirit coming to ask for food, and to the white "friend" (Timpal), myself, who since her mother's death had, by virtue of age and status, acted as mother for the past two years. Then there is the upcoming tooth filing ceremony, which always arouses anxiety and fears of physical pain and supernatural attack at the time of the operation. As the eldest sibling, Wayan had already experienced this ordeal, but no doubt she felt anxious about her younger siblings, whom she treats like a mother. Indeed, mother and nurturer is *her* present role. She is responsible for feeding her siblings, her mother in the cemetery, and as well Timpal, the white dog, and his mistress, the white friend who now acts as substitute mother. Aggressive elements are also apparent. Indeed the tooth filing ritual is intended to symbolically remove aggressive and animal characteristics in the young person by filing off the points of the upper canine teeth. The hungry dog in the dream also links to her own aggressive feelings towards those who have in the past neglected her. In her childhood, because of her family situation, she often did go hungry. She was in fact treated little better than a dog by her family, and she has sometimes commented to me that Timpal, the dog, is fed better than many people. Her painful childhood experiences thus lead her back to a time when she was like a hungry dog but lacked the sharp fangs, which Timpal possesses to bite her aggressors. We can see then that her current, adult experiences are linked in the imagery of the dream to childhood aggressions, arousing guilt concerning destructive desires towards her family and protectors. The dreamer is both nurturer, who has neglected the loved dog, and the hungry dog itself who wants to attack those who have neglected it.

In my view, the process of connecting present emotional experiences with past emotions, linking them back to templates or emotional schemas laid down in early childhood (we could of course take the above back to early infantile experience of oral aggression towards the mother's breast, and depressive fears of destroying the good object) is clearly shown in this example. In terms of REM sorting and coding of information, the current emotional experiences are given a place in the emotional/imaginal memory system. With respect to the remembered dream reported in consciousness, I would suggest that the part of consciousness that reviews the REM process, what Freud referred to as the "dream censor," took notice of the REM image of the hungry dog, and the feelings of guilt attached to it, because these related significantly to conscious feelings about neglecting duties in waking reality. Thus the image of the dog was registered by consciousness and brought into waking awareness, whereupon the guilt attached to this image prompted the dreamer to attend to the issue in waking life. The dream is what consciousness is drawn to in reviewing the REM imagery, and what consciousness brings into waking awareness. It is not a message from the imaginal mind but rather something that the dream censor identifies as relevant to waking concerns.

Although this example of the hungry dog might easily lend itself to a classic Freudian wish fulfillment interpretation, I think the dream was produced in the process of linking present emotional experience with similar past experience, according to patterns or schemas laid down in early childhood. Thus of course, any dream might be traced back to infantile roots, if one knows enough about the circumstances of the dreamer's life. But the process involved is not one of satisfying id desires through hallucinatory wish fulfillment, but rather of encoding information in the emotional memory system. The hungry dog is a condensation of the dreamer's present adult feelings of responsibility and identification with the role of nurturer, with early infantile feelings of being neglected and frustrated herself. Infantile feelings of aggression linked to guilt are linked again to adult feelings of guilt for neglecting others. This intensification of guilt, brought about by superimposing her present adult experience onto emotions she experienced in childhood, draws the attention of the dream censor, and brings the image of the hungry dog into consciousness. There is something here that needs to be dealt with in consciousness. Our dreamer deals with the image provided by the imaginal mind in an adult way, renewing her efforts to play the adult role of nurturer and not neglect those in her care. I am not suggesting that the imaginal mind itself is communicating this message or moral, but that the dreamer's conscious mind, by reflecting on the dream image, draws this meaning from it.

Dream of Carrying an Heirloom Kris (Ceremonial Dagger)

This dream was reported by Wayan's younger brother Komang shortly after the tooth filing and adoption ceremonies had taken place. This dream report is more complex and presents a brief narrative. The young man who reported this dream had, like his elder sister, suffered childhood neglect. His feelings were compounded by a deep sense of humiliation and inferiority because of his position in his extended family, feelings made more intense by the fact that he is a male, and theoretically the one responsible for his three siblings now that he had reached adulthood. This is the dream:

> I dreamed I carried a kris from Mengwi [the ancestral home of the family] to our house temple. While I was carrying the kris I felt extremely strong, extremely big and that I was extremely knowledgeable about the state of the family. When I reached the family temple I pointed the kris at each member of the family gathered there, this was the whole family. I sat on the *pelinggih* [the shrine for the gods to sit on when they descend from heaven] and watched all who were assembled in the house temple. Then all the family bowed on their knees before me. Then the dream ended. I think this dream is connected with our place of origin [*kawitan*] and the ancestors. I feel the ancestors have given me the task of protecting the family as a parent protects his children.

Like the hungry dog, the heirloom dagger image is overdetermined. The kris has important symbolic significance in Balinese culture, and magical or supernatural powers of all kinds are attributed to it. Krises are often kept by aristocratic families as heirlooms and as symbols of power and authority, both secular and spiritual. They are also explicit symbols of male power, potency, and virility, which figure prominently in Balinese marriage rituals. Mengwi, the ancestral home of the dreamer's family, is the seat of royalty and of a powerful kingdom in the past. The dreamer's family has in fact a proud aristocratic heritage and possesses several heirloom krises. In the dream, the young man, who for all his life has been humiliated and treated with contempt by his family and community, now possesses this ultimate symbol of spiritual and family pride, he occupies the seat of the gods, the *pelinggih*, and all who formerly humiliated him now lower themselves and bow before him. In waking life, Komang had just been recognized as a family member through a formal adoption ceremony; and having also completed the tooth filing rituals, he has been publicly recognized as passing beyond adolescence into manhood. The kris also can be seen to symbolize his manhood and sexuality. He is no longer a hungry, powerless little boy whom nobody wants, but a tall, strong man to whom the whole family pays homage, as to a god or deified ancestor.

Infantile sexuality and aggressive desires are not difficult to find here—the pointing of the kris at each family member suggests these dual aspects of oedipal desires. Yet in my view the dream reflects not simply infantile wishes, but rather its imagery is depicting the new emotional situation in which the dreamer finds himself in waking like. The adoption ceremony has in fact completely changed his status in the family and in the community. This is not a question of wish fulfilment of the ego—the young man's status has in fact been completely changed by the two rituals he has just been through. What the dream seems to be doing is constructing a metaphorical statement about this important change, trying to link a new emotional experience to existing emotional schemas. Having over a period of more than two years listened to the stories of this young man's family problems, and witnessing countless times the distress he constantly felt as a result of his family's previous treatment of him, I am well aware of how dramatic was the statement made by the dream. Furthermore, since the adoption ceremony, I have seen the young dreamer's confidence and poise grow enormously. The dream did in fact mark a turning point in his emotional life. This is not to say that the dream brought about this change, but that it represents part of the process of emotional accommodation whereby new emotional experiences are incorporated into existing emotional schemas, while expanding and changing them at the same time. The role of metaphor in achieving such modifications of emotional schemas has been well described by Brown (1991, 129–135)

For the dreamer, this dream of carrying the kris has the character of an omen, a message from the ancestors about his new role in life. From the point of view being argued here, the dream arises out of the imaginal mind's efforts to register, evaluate, and store new experiences according to their emotional significance to the dreamer. Thus the imaginal mind invests the dreamer with royal symbols of potency, and places him in the position of a deified ancestor or god, because he has no commonplace experience in his life to which his new status can be linked. The imaginal mind is searching for a match for the new feelings of pride, strength, and superiority he now feels in relation to others. The dream imagery attracted the attention of consciousness because it related directly to the dreamer's conscious efforts to take his rightful place in his family and community. I think we see here the role of the dream in forming new self schemas, as radically new emotional experiences are successfully accommodated.

Dream of Taking a Shower

The following is an example of the rather prosaic dreams usually reported after wakenings from REM sleep; however, it evoked strong feelings of frustration and tiredness in me when I awoke from it. At the time of this dream I had recently returned from fieldwork in Bali and was finding returning to my usual mundane routine very frustrating: everything seemed to be more difficult and take more effort than it should. This was my dream:

> I wanted to take a shower and I didn't have a lot of time. I had to hurry. But when I entered the bathroom (in my own house but that now seemed quite different) I found it piled high with stacks of clean dry towels and clothing. In order to shower I would first have to remove all these stacks of dry items or else they would get wet. Then after showering I would have to clean up all the water and replace everything.

When I awoke from this dream it seemed to me that the feelings of frustration and weariness in the dream were identical with my feelings in real life, where even the simplest things seemed to be taking far too much time and energy. The dream was a simple but accurate metaphor of my waking experience. It solved nothing—there was no answer or resolution offered by the dream. But reflection on it did perhaps help to deflate the angst I was feeling at the time, putting my simple daily frustrations into perspective. In this sense the dream served as a kind of compensation to my conscious attitude at the time. I do not see this as the purpose of the dream, but rather as the consequence of a part of my consciousness attending to the imaginal mind's processing of recent experience, and focussing in on imagery which had direct relevance to my waking concerns.

Freud ([1900] 1953) long ago showed us the way in which our daily concerns and thoughts are taken up and imagistically represented in dreamwork in all kinds of artful and ingenious ways. The dream of taking a shower is a very simple example of how actual real-life concerns and feelings are translated into the imagery of dreams. From the viewpoint being argued here, REM sleep involves registering, evaluating, and storing recent experience in the emotional memory system. One important part of this work is the representing of conscious thoughts and feelings in imagery form so that this information can then be linked to existing emotional schemas wherein information is stored not in verbal form, but in imagery or other subsymbolic codes (Bucci 1997). All recent experience is subjected to this processing by the imaginal mind but only a very small part of it is likely to give rise to a dream remembered on waking. This is in accordance with the fact that we know that a large proportion of a night's sleep is spent in REM sleep, but usually we recall only a brief fragment of imagery, such as the dream of the white dog, or a short narrative, such as carrying the kris. The imagery that we recall on waking and describe as a dream is the result of a part of consciousness, along the lines of Freud's dream censor, scanning the REM imagery and attending to imagery that is for some reason particularly striking or relevant to waking ego concerns. Thus the vast bulk of REM imagery goes unregistered by consciousness, and is not entered into the verbal semantic memory.

A Dream of Disaster

That the majority of recalled dreams are those relating to our daily concerns is supported by extensive research findings (Cartwright 1981, 245; Foulkes 1993, 183) indicating dreams represent a continuation of waking life. But there are some dreams which seem to have a very different character and, either by the bizarreness of their imagery or their unexpectedness and lack of relation to daily concerns, draw our attention. Hunt (1989, 128–140) has called these "Titanic" or archetypal dreams, pointing out that traditional cultures usually make a clear distinction between ordinary dreams that arise just from personal concerns and worries and the "big" dreams that seem to have a kind of transpersonal significance. The final dream example I wish to discuss is illustrative of this kind of dream.

In early 1999, when I was on fieldwork in Bali, several severe landslides occurred in which many people died or were injured. Balinese journalists interviewing survivors often referred to dream omens which various people claimed to have received shortly before the disasters took place. In Balinese belief, as in many nonwestern cultures, some dreams are thought to provide omens and warnings concerning the future, particularly relating to the deaths of family members.

On February 16, 1999, a landslide occurred at Tegallalang, Gianyar, killing five people and injuring six. The event was reported in the local newspaper, the *Bali Post*, on February 17, 1999, and the following dream prediction of the event was noted. I should add that I am not assuming or vouching for the accuracy of this dream omen. Clearly it was reported after the event occurred. My point is that it represents an example of a type dream which could be explained in terms of a dual memory model.

> Before the landslide which took five lives at Banjar Belong Desa Taro, Tegallalang, took place, it appears that some of the citizens had already received a sign that a disaster would occur. Some admitted that this was through a very strange dream. "People were approached by several naked children at the place where the landslide took place," stated several people in a frightened tone of voice.
>
> According to Ni Kora and Ni Masni who everyday excavate for pumice stone on that cliff face, some friends told them that they had been visited by naked children. These children chased them away so that they would not look for pumice stone in that location again. But the people whose livelihood depended heavily on obtaining the pumice stone apparently later paid little

attention to the message of this dream. For them, the most important thing was to feed their families, and so they continued to dig in that place. "Before continuing work we put some offerings at that place," stated Ni Kora who that morning had only briefly dug for pumice at the location of the landslide.

It needs to be understood here that the "naked children" in the dream represent in Balinese belief spirits (*tonya, gamang*) who live in rivers, rocks, ravines, and other places free of human habitation. If left undisturbed these creatures do not harm human beings, but if their territory is invaded they are likely to cause trouble. In this dream we find the *gamang* warning the human beings to leave them alone, with punishment implied if their warnings were ignored.

The message of this dream is clear but unwelcome. People depend for their livelihood on excavating in the place indicated in the dream. The dream is unexpected in the sense that people had long been excavating at that place and only now was there a warning to leave it. The imagery of naked children chasing adults away is a striking and unusual one. The dreamer and others believe the dream represents a message from the spirit world. This is not something that has come out of their daily thoughts and desires. Indeed it so radically goes against them that people chose to ignore the dream's message. Here the dream imagery attracts consciousness because it is bizarrely at odds with the dreamer's conscious concerns. The dream points to something the imaginal mind knows but the verbal memory system has not registered.

My arguments about dreams and ESP, or rather Extra Semantic Knowledge, are clearly illustrated here. All incoming sensory information is processed by both systems, the verbal/semantic system and the imaginal system, but in different ways and according to different criteria. The verbal system registers what makes sense in terms of its preexisting language-based structures of knowledge and understanding. The imaginal system operates according to feelings and perceptions not necessarily registered by the verbal system. Thus it seems entirely possible to me that people working at the locations where landslides later took place might have registered subtle signs and indications that something was wrong, that some danger was present, without those indications being sufficiently clear to make sense in terms of conscious waking knowledge and experience. The imaginal mind, however, represents these subtle signs that something is wrong at the workplace in the form of supernatural beings chasing people away. In this case the imaginal mind is attempting to communicate with consciousness and the dream originates with it. This is not to claim that all precognitive dreams are true, or that all can be explained in this manner, but I believe many can be accounted for in this way, particularly dreams of impending death and illness in the family, where the outcome is not yet apparent to our verbal/semantic based understanding, but is already sensed by the imaginal system. Nightmares, trauma dreams and repetitive dreams are also examples of dreams where the imaginal mind is trying to bring to conscious awareness something which needs to be dealt with in consciousness.

From the perspective argued here, spontaneously recalled dreams are communications between the configurational/imaginal processing system and the verbal/semantic system. Since they arise from an independent interpretative system using different modes of processing, they may contain information or an evaluation of a situation not available to the verbal/semantic system. In this sense, my model supports views widely held cross-culturally that some dreams are warnings and prognostications. Jung's (1978) theory that dreams bear a compensatory relationship to consciousness is likewise indicated here. Yet, as we have seen, dreaming also involves a linking backwards in memory, as Freudian theory suggests. And finally the fact that the majority of dreams relate primarily to the daily waking concerns of everyday life is also explained.

Conclusion

The evidence and arguments presented in this chapter point to the existence in the mind of two separate evaluative and interpretative systems attached to two separate memory registers. Such a model, as we have seen, can throw new light on the following puzzles:

- What is the relationship between REM sleep and dreams?
- What is the function of dreaming?
- Why does the evidence from animal experimentation only support a link between REM sleep, learning, and memory?
- Why the difference between laboratory-reported dreams and home dreams?
- Why do the majority of dreams represent a continuum with real-life concerns?
- What purpose do nightmares, trauma dreams, and repetitive dreams serve?
- What is the source of "big" or "Titanic" dreams?
- Why are dreams interpreted so widely across human cultures as omens and prognostications?
- Why are dreams and altered states linked to sickness and healing?
- Why are dreams and altered states connected with individual creativity, especially artistic creativity, and with large-scale social and cultural change?
- Why are dreams and altered states also linked to pathology and madness?

- What is the nature of the dream censor and of the "hidden observer effect" in hypnosis?
- How do hypnotic suggestions bypass consciousness, and what is the nature of "state-dependent memory"?
- What is the reason for the period of infantile amnesia?
- Why do the pronouncements of shamans, mediums, or prophets take the form of acting out or of incomprehensible utterances?
- What is the nature of glossolalia or "speaking in tongues"?
- Why are some forms of psychosis marked by severe disturbances of speech and language usage?

These and many other issues have been discussed in this chapter. What I originally identified as "autonomous imagination" I now see as the mode of thought employed by an imaginal mind possessing an independent memory system and operating on different principles from the memory processing that underlies language-based thought. It is a system that, in evolutionary terms, is prior to language-based thought and continues to function in the mind alongside it, serving to balance and enrich it, and to step in and take over when the language-based system fails—sometimes with disastrous consequences.

Van den Daele (1994, 440) raises the intriguing question as to whether cultures vary in their reliance on what he refers to as the "configurational system" and the verbal/semantic system. Doing fieldwork in a culture like that of Bali, I can have little doubt as to my answer. So much of Balinese life seems directed towards developing a sensitivity to and control of forces, powers, and capacities that lie beyond the boundaries of waking, sequential, logical, language-bound thought. Every aspect of daily life seems permeated by the products of the imaginal mind. Balinese commonly describe this as the spiritual or immaterial (*niskala*) aspect of existence. It is through anthropological understanding of diverse cultures that our awareness is drawn to the creative potential of the imaginal mind—a potential that the language-based system, so assiduously developed in Western scientific and scholarly discourse, finds extremely difficult to recognize. However, now that cognitive science is addressing itself to the problem of how information is represented without words, and as attention is directed to the role played by feeling and emotion in the construction of memory, I believe we will soon have an even firmer evidential basis on which to support the arguments tentatively outlined here.

Notes

I thank Katherine O'Connell and Shanee Stepakoff for alerting me to Bucci's important work, and to Leland van den Daele for drawing my attention to his own work and to that of Douglas Watt. My thanks also to Jeannette Mageo, for her guidance in revising this chapter for inclusion in this volume.

1. The literature on the topic is now extensive. For some reviews see Bourguignon 1994; Peters and Price-Williams 1980, 1983; Noll 1985; Stephen 1979; and Tedlock 1987, 1994.

2. It should be noted that in using the terms "emotion" and "feeling" throughout this chapter, I do not employ the distinction sometimes made by anthropologists between feeling as the "bodily component of affect" (Csordas 1994, 341) and emotion as referring to the symbolic, cultural construction of affect (Jenkins 1994, 102). Rather I am using "emotion" to mean strong affect across a pleasure/pain axis, and "feeling" to refer to less specific and less marked forms. Those who object that all emotions are culturally constructed should read "emotion" where it occurs in this text as "affect" or "feeling."

3. For supporting studies on sleep and dreams see Cartwright (1969, 1978, 1981) and Cohen (1979); on studies of waking fantasy see Singer (1974, 1979), Singer and Pope (1978), and Watkins (1984); on senory deprivation see Siegal and West (1975) and Bowers and Meishenbaum (1984); on studies of brain laterality see Dimond (1972) and Springer and Deutch (1981); on hypnosis see Bowers (1976), Fromm and Shor (1979), Sheehan and McConkey (1982) and Brown (1991); on alternative states of consciousness see Tart (1972), Davidson and Davidson (1980) and Wollman and Ullman (1986); on cross-cultural studies of trance and possession see Bourguignon (1973, 1976, 1994), Herdt and Stephen (1989), Noll (1985), Peters and Price-Williams (1980, 1983) and Price-Williams (1987).

4. The involuntary repetition of obscenities or scatological referents that occurs in mental disorders like Tourette's Disorder (Wirshing 1995, 230) may be linked to some involuntary shifting between the two processing systems that I describe.

5. Evidence from brain laterality studies referred to by Watt (1990) indicates that the right hemisphere can communicate through action, as for example the left hand pointing to something that the subject verbally claims not to see. My observations of Balinese mediums indicated that mediums were impersonating the spirits, but when questioned about their experience, the mediums replied that what they saw was the spirits in front of them acting in a certain way. The mediums thus did not seem to be aware that in their trance/possession "performance" they were acting out what they saw—or rather what they saw in trance was their own body controlled by the possessing spirit entities.

6. Previously I have pointed out that in the Western therapeutic context the patient is in trance, as in hypnosis, whereas in other cultures it is the healer who is in trance (1989b, 218). On the basis of my observations in Bali, I am now convinced that both Balinese healer and patient are often or usually in trance. The evidence just discussed concerning the influence of the imaginal mode on the body explains why, since it indicates that both patient and healer can employ imagery thought in the healing process.

7. The large proportion of time spent by the newborn in REM sleep is consistent with the fact that there is no language system in existence at this stage and that the foundations of the emotional memory are being laid down at this time. By

the age of three or four "a child's REM will have fallen to the adult levels of 20 to 25 percent and will remain in this range for the rest of life" (Gillin, Zoltoski and Salin-Pascual 1995). Thus as the language register begins to take over and become dominant, the amount of REM sleep falls to the normal adult rate.

8. This is perhaps similar to but not identical with Jung's (1978) concept of the compensatory function of the unconscious.

9. Erikson in *Childhood and Society* (1993) describes the attempts of schizophrenic children to communicate, and the terrible frustration and distress they demonstrate when these attempts fail. His account suggests to me just such a confusion between a verbal/semantic code and a nonverbal code as I have tried to describe here. The specific kinds of speech disorders connected with schizophrenia seem to reflect the same confusion or mixing of the two different processing systems:

> Formal disorders of speech and the inferred underlying disorders of thought processes are manifested by a variety of pathological features. Most important, the integrity of the thought process becomes distorted and continuity is disrupted. The associations are logically unrelated to antecedents (loosening of associations). Separate ideas can be incomprehensibly combined, apparently based on sound rather than on meaning (clang association). New words may be formed (neologisms). Words or statements may be stereotypically repeated (verbigeration), or the examiner's words may be repeated (echolalia). The patient may experience sudden and inexplicable blocking of thoughts and may be unable to pursue the original train of thought. (Lipton and Cancro 1995, 974–975)

10. Dysfunction of connections across the corpus callosum has been proposed as a possible cause of schizophrenia, but the evidence remains inconclusive (Levin et al. 1995, 576).

11. Watt's (1990, 498–501) arguments suggest that the left hemisphere and the logico/semantic system need to be protected from too much emotion, especially negative emotion. This would help to explain those types of psychopathology where consciousness is overwhelmed by emotion. It also suggests why ego consciousness seems to feel itself threatened by excessive emotion, and the generally negative view of emotion as interfering with, rather than contributing to, cognition.

PART 3

Self-Revelation and Dream Interpretation

CHAPTER 7

Dreams That Speak: Experience and Interpretation

ERIKA BOURGUIGNON

[W]ithout the psychic processes of dreaming, human group life
could not have evolved or been maintained.
—Murray L. Wax, *Western Rationality and the Angel of Dreams*

*T*his bold statement is directly relevant to my central thesis, as I hope
to demonstrate in what follows. With it, Wax builds on Hallowell's
important earlier work with regard to human evolution and language development, which made it possible for "the inner life of individuals . . . [to] be
communicated to others. . . . Dream experiences could become the object of
reflective thought and become socially significant" (Hallowell 1976, 451).
Wax argues that the importance of dreaming to group life is indeed central—
even without telling and sharing—because, among other things, the process
of dreaming allows the self to assume the roles of others, thereby enabling
the dreamer "to adjust his or her conduct" (1999, 89). This argument suggests that dreaming has a crucial role in the individual's ability to cope not
only with life's difficulties in general, but, more specifically, with problematic
aspects of interpersonal situations.

It is precisely the question of how the self assumes the roles of others in dreams that interests me here, and with it, how dreaming enables group life. Related to this is the question of how dreams are experienced, rather than the more traditional ones in anthropological research, such as "How are dreams told?" or "How are dreams interpreted?" or even "What does a particular dream mean for this dreamer, in this cultural and social setting?" Crapanzano (chapter 10) points to the gap between the dream as dreamt and the dream as narrated, an observation that Mageo (chapter 1) underlines. Yet, as we shall see in the following, in some societies—perhaps in all—cultural understanding plays a significant role also in how the dream is experienced. Consequently such understanding, together with the dream's content, affects the impact of the dream on the dreamer's subsequent behavior and attitude and, at least for some, on the social consequences of the dream. Furthermore, we need to consider how dream experience and dream interpretation are related to the larger sociocultural context, to the understanding people have of the world in which they live, what Hallowell called their culturally constituted behavioral environment (1955).

The focus of my discussion is a class of dreams I refer to as "preinterpreted." The phenomenon of preinterpretation has not come to the attention of the anthropological literature, perhaps because it does not seem to play a role in "respectable" types of dream interpretation current in Western societies. And yet it probably exists in this country, for example, among people for whom dream symbols are easily translated into numbers to be played in the lottery, or for whom dream elements translate into specific religious symbols. Many examples of the instant recognition of cultural symbols are found in the various contributions to this volume (see, for example, Hollan chapter 4). My own discovery, if I may call it that, is an example of serendipity in the field.

Before turning to some specific examples of preinterpreted dreams some background and context need to be sketched in.

Dreaming, A Characteristic Mammalian Phenomenon

While it appears that almost all mammals dream, for humans dreaming is a culturally structured experience and activity. That is, dreams are not only variously interpreted (or neglected) in different cultural traditions, but cultural content enters into the content of dreams, as does life experience more generally. Freud ([1900]1956, 163) distinguished between two sorts of dream contents, writing that analysis "disclose[s] a *latent* content in [dreams] which is of far greater significance than the *manifest* one" (italics in original). Although Freud does not offer a definition of his terms, the manifest content of the dream is best understood as the remembered dream. He does note that dreams are remembered only partially ([1900]1956, 280). (The "dream as remembered" should not be made synonymous with the "dream as told" for this, as will be seen below, may turn out to be something else all together.) More generally, the manifest content of dreams is conceived of in psychoanalytic thought as the result of complex processes, which disguise the underlying latent content that analysis seeks to discover.

Some anthropologists have given particular attention to the manifest content of dreams (for example, Bilu 1989; Eggan 1952; Schneider and Sharp 1969). Regardless of local conventions of dream interpretations, these anthropologists have found significance in the patterns revealed by an analysis of the manifest content of dreams. A different approach is offered by Meggitt (1962), who, speaking of the Mae Enga of New Guinea, considers the meaning discovered by native dream interpretation an intermediary level between the manifest content and the latent content as revealed by a psychoanalytic approach. This is a point to be considered more closely below.

There is every evidence that dreaming and the experience of dreaming are shaped by waking experience, and by individual and cultural learning. And, of course, the traditions of dream interpretation are part of culture: as part of a belief system, rituals, skills and larger institutions, be they religious, medical or other. As far as the manifest content of dreams is concerned, here are two rather different examples: Eggan (1952) shows how the dreams of a Hopi man contain extensive references to the myths and rituals of his culture. But such use of cultural materials is found not only in so-called traditional societies. Reading Freud's reports of his own dreams makes this clear. In the manifest content of his "specimen dream" (Freud [1900]1956, 101–122), which he used to illustrate his analytic method, we learn a good deal about medical practice in Vienna at the end of the nineteenth century. The central character is a woman, Irma, who is both a family friend and a patient. There is, for instance, reference to tuberculosis, a disease which was rampant and without effective therapy. There is mention of the fact that physicians had to examine women patients through their clothes. There is also reference to conversion hysteria (now called "conversion disorder"), then a widespread affliction. This presented the problem of differential diagnosis in the absence of the diagnostic technology available a century later. In the dream, Freud expresses concern about misdiagnosing organic disease as hysterical conversion. For Freud his own culture and society were his natural environment. What we can now see as characteristics of a particular time and place are reflected in his dream. They form no part of his lengthy and complex analysis of his dream.

Thus experience, and hence learning of various kinds, are involved in dreaming as well as in the reaction to dreams. The experience of the dream, or its interpretation, may validate and reinforce beliefs. The theory and practice of dream interpretation may be part of a system of divination, whether to foretell the future or to diagnose disease and recommend, even direct, therapy. Some examples are cited below. On the other hand, the content of dreams may, in the case of some individuals, become the shared heritage of a community, part of its mythology and the basis for common action. In this connection, reports often do not distinguish between waking visions and dreams in sleep. Schwartz (1976 183) had the rare good fortune to be able to observe a Melanesian cargo cult, involving dream revelations, early in its development. He comments that "the dreams were not necessarily reported as they were dreamt, nor were they necessarily dreams at all. . . . Incoherent dreams were rejected as uninteresting. . . . On hearing . . . [dream narrations], one realizes that the dream or vision was long in preparation and finds its moment in the telling, not the dreaming."

Interpretation and Culture in the Dream

Remembered dreams are often unclear in meaning and therefore appear as puzzles to be solved. Such a search for unraveling the meaning of a dream is particularly important if the dream is experienced with some emotional intensity, among people who believe that dreams have a message of significance. The message, once understood, may concern an action to be taken or avoided, a warning, or a promise. In a religious context, the message may be thought to come from divinities or deceased ancestors. In a secular context, as in psychoanalysis and psychoanalytically informed practices, the message is understood as one from the self to the self or, perhaps, to the therapist, that is, the audience of the dream narration. Because the dream has often been seen as the paradigmatic vehicle for communication between humans and powerful spiritual entities, dreams are cited as authorities, sources of actions and innovations in mythical accounts and other foundational narratives. In this regard, dreams and waking visions serve interchangeably (Bourguignon 1972). Yet there is a significant difference: In the dream, a dialogue between the dreamer and the entities who appear is possible. In the vision, by contrast, communication flows primarily in a single direction: from the entity seen, or, more often, heard, to the visionary. In the Western tradition, the biblical authors made extensive strategic use of dream and vision narratives.

The telling and sharing of dreams enlarges the field of communication among group members, and indeed, with others, namely the entities who appear in dreams, as well as the visiting anthropologist. As Barbara Tedlock (1994, 290) has pointed out in her review of the anthropological literature on dreams, "[A]nthropologists have realized that the researcher and the subject of research create a joint social reality that links them in important ways." This too is to be illustrated below.

Basso (1987, 86) has discussed the widespread idea that "dreaming is an experience that cannot be understood literally, that dreams contain disguised meanings requiring interpretation." Anthropologists have accumulated large numbers of accounts of such interpretations. As Barbara Tedlock (1987, 105–6) has shown, however, the same dream content may be given quite different, indeed diametrically opposed, interpretations in different societies. After working among the Zuni, Barbara and Dennis Tedlock carried out research among the Quiché Maya. Here, she tells us, Dennis Tedlock dreamed of receiving an ear of roasted corn from an unknown person, a very bad dream among the Zuni, requiring an extensive cure. Among the Quiché, it turned out, this was a good dream. Thus, while the manifest content may be roughly constant, the symbolic meaning of a dream may vary among communities. Any assumption of a universal set of symbols is therefore questionable, though some symbols may have greater constancy. As Barbara Tedlock (1987, 126) notes in her conclusion, such "differences . . . are traceable to a combination of ontological and psychological differences." It is also possible that the same content, with different emotional valence, may be given different interpretations in the same society, being related, perhaps, to different degrees of physiological arousal. Regrettably, little information on this point is available in the ethnographic record. The quality of the subjective experience of a dream is not necessarily evident from its text. For example, we know anecdotally that the dream of a dead parent may range from being pleasurable to being terrifying, yet the manifest contents of such differently experienced dreams may be remarkably alike. That is, manifest content has no necessary relationship to the experiential, affective quality of the dream. Moreover, the affective quality of the manifest content may vary from that of the latent content; for example, the bland nature of the manifest content may serve as protection against the potentially anxiety producing quality of the latent content.

Against Interpretation

While many dreams are judged by the dreamer to require interpretations, not all are. The meaning of some dreams, in some contexts, appears to be self-evident. Other dreams appear to be experienced as already interpreted in the original narrative, although that narrative is discovered to be at variance with the actual dream vision, that is, the manifest content of the dream. Following are some examples of "self-evident" dreams.

A Haitian peasant may dream of his dead grandmother who tells him where treasure is buried. Such a dream requires no interpretation, although some explanation will be needed if, upon digging, no treasure is found. Nevertheless, there is a widespread belief that such treasures exist and that their location is likely to be announced in a dream by an ancestral spirit.

Genesis 37:5–10[1] tells us that Jacob's spoiled son Joseph told his brothers (or rather, half-brothers) that he had dreamt that when they were building sheaves in the field, his stood upright and those of the others bowed to it. The brothers understood this as a foretelling, or announcement, of his future reign or dominion over them, as with regard to his report of a second dream in which the sun and the moon and eleven stars (the number of his brothers) bowed down to him. And this time his father rebuked him for suggesting that father, mother and brothers would acknowledge his dominion over them. (The reference to the mother is especially interesting, since she had died a long time ago.) Although Joseph's two dreams are couched in symbolic terms, their meanings are treated as needing no interpretation. The symbols are transparent to Joseph's audience. In addition, Jacob's rebuke suggests that he sees the dreams as reflecting the young man's arrogance and that they are, in some way, intentional. They are not evaluated as messages received from a divine source. If, however, they are given to Joseph by such a source, this is now a three-way communication, involving three distinct persons or groups. It appears that Joseph's audience is the prime target of the dream.

Later, in the account of Joseph's sojourn in Egypt, he is no longer the dreamer but the interpreter of others' dreams. In both parts of the story, however, the dreams are used by the biblical writers for their own purposes.[2]

An elderly widow, who lives in a middle-sized mid-Western city, tells of dreaming of her husband who was waiting for her to get ready to leave with him. She immediately understood this to mean that she was telling herself to get her affairs in order. Asked about the affective quality of the dream, she said it was quite matter of fact, without any awareness in the dream that her husband was dead. The dream experience involved neither anxiety, nor surprise or urgency. But when she woke up, she had not finished her preparations for departure. This seemed to be an undisguised dream, apparently without symbolic quality: a direct communication from the dreamer's self to herself, one that confirms her waking concerns. It took some time for her to discover, to her surprise, that the manifest content of the dream was indeed different from the latent one: the manifest content included no reference to her husband's death nor to her own. Initially, no third party, no audience, was involved.

In contrast to the widow's dream, with its low affective quality and apparently little physiological arousal, note the rather similar content but different affective quality in the following account of the death of Margaret Mead. Jean Houston, who was with Mead two weeks before her death, writes, "She had been dozing. . . . [S]uddenly she opened her eyes and looked across the room. She pushed herself up to a sitting position and said to the wall: 'Get out of here. I'm not ready for you. Go away!' When told there was no one there, she replied: 'You can't see them but they are there alright! . . . Dead people. My mother, my father, and Ruth. They say they are here to take me with them. Please leave. Go away." (Houston 1996:228).

We cannot be certain that this was a dream, but it does seem the experience started in a dreamlike state. While the manifest content resembles that of the widow's dream, the affective tone appears radically different.

The Dream of a Haitian Woman

To explore an example of the second type, the dream experienced as interpreted, I wish to revisit the dream narrative of a young Haitian woman that I considered elsewhere in a different context (Bourguignon 1954).[3] I do so because the phenomenon presented in this account is perhaps not as unusual as I originally thought and yet, as far as I know, it has not been given attention in the literature.

Here it is necessary to provide some background regarding the cultural context. The folk religion of vodou and its worldview is shared by the great majority of Haitians, including many now living in the United States and elsewhere (Brown 2001). This religion was initially built up during the period of slavery when people from many traditional groups of West and Central Africa where brought to what was, in the eighteenth century, a French colony. The Catholic Church, the official and only religion of the French state, converted them, without, however, much instruction. Thus there arose an amalgam of the beliefs and practices of several African peoples, and these were further identified with those of the Catholic Church. This phenomenon of syncretism also took place in other parts of Catholic Afro-America, most prominently in Cuba, where the resulting religion is known as *santería*, and in Brazil, where we find several Afro-Catholic religions, such as *candomblé, xangô, umbanda*, and others.

In Haitian *vodou*, there is no central religious authority; each cult center, whether consisting primarily of a kin group or, in urban centers, of individuals attracted to a *oungan* (priest) or *manbo* (priestess), is autonomous and will have its own somewhat different practices. There are innumerable spirits, some of whom are universally known. The spirits mentioned in the following discussion are among these. Others are unique to a given cult house, family, or individual. Some are neglected and forgotten over time; new ones reveal themselves. The major spirits have identities that involve a fusion of African and Catholic features. As such they represent elements of history and memory but also the current social structure and its ideology, class distinctions, and skin color preferences. The traditional spirits are grouped into *nachon* (nations), reflecting the origins of the people and, to a greater or lesser extent, that of the spirits. Most are West African: Rada (from the Fon of Dahomey [now Benin]), Nago (Ketu Yoruba), Ibo, and some others, but also Congo and Pétro. This last group has been thought to be mostly of local origin but may include spirits with Bantu (Congo) names. Awareness of these diverse origins is at best uneven among *vodouists*. On the other hand, both known historic figures and family ancestors have appeared as spirits. *Vodou* pantheons may thus be seen, in part, as reflections of Haitian history.

Spirits (*lwa*) choose their faithful. Although various life difficulties attract people to the service of the *lwa*, *vodou* is not primarily a healing system. *Lwa* are invited to participate and they do so by "possessing" ("mounting") their servants. The person "mounted" is referred to as the spirit's "horse" (*chwal*). Such mounting involves a psychophysiological state, for which the individual will later be amnesic. This altered state of consciousness has been referred to as "trance." The trancer, who acts out the complex behavior of a particular *lwa*, is believed to be possessed by that entity; that is, the person's identity is replaced by that of the spirit. The great majority of possession trancers, but by no means all, are women.

Annette was a woman in her middle twenties, born in a rural area, but living at the time in the city of Port-au-Prince. Among her kin, who still lived in the country, was her paternal uncle, a *vodou* priest of some renown, who was the effective head of the family. He had identified the spirit (*lwa*) who had possessed her some years before and had carried out a first-stage initiation, the "washing of the head" (*lave tèt*). She had since then installed a *repozwar* (small shrine) in her room in a Port-au-Prince slum. This was a box containing three chromolithographs,[4] one representing the Mater Dolorosa, referred to in this account as Ezili or Metrès Ezili, another showing St. Jacques, referred to as Ogou. Ogou in *vodou* mythology is one of Ezili's two husbands. The third representation is of St. Patrick (the snake spirit Danbala), the other husband, who is not named in this narrative.

With the encouragement of Annette and Ogou (when she was possessed by this spirit) I decided to spend some time with her family in the sugar area near the town of Léogane. We attended various rituals and discussed Annette's religious experiences. Periodically we also went to Port-au-Prince. When she described her initiation experience, which had involved an overnight stay at her uncle's center, I asked Annette whether she had dreamed. She replied, "I did not dream a single dream." This presumably referred to the events we were discussing. Then, however, she continued, "We went to Port-au-Prince Sunday. Monday night they reproached me because I am not in Port-au-Prince, because I am not taking care of the *repozwar.*" Mid-sentence, as it were, she had shifted reference to more recent events and more urgent concerns: "Mystè Ezili spoke to me, like this: that I don't need her, neither her nor [her husband] Papa Ogou. She said Jacques, well St. Jacques, that's Papa Ogou. 'Well, I am very happy you came—I need you very much.' That's how she said [it] to me."

As noted, in the initial response to my question there is a move from past to recent present. Current events intrude. This suggests that the dream was important. It involved Annette's relationship with the spirits in her shrine, two of whom are mentioned although only one speaks. Ezili complains somewhat petulantly yet expresses pleasure at Annette's coming. This seemed to say that Annette felt guilty at neglecting her duty. That was the complete spontaneous report of this dream. The rest of the account resulted from my questions. Note however that Annette does not say, "I dreamt that I saw the spirits and they said to me. . . ." She tells it rather as a real life encounter. Later, however, she does specify that the interaction with the spirit occurred in her sleep.

Since the spirits, although invisible, are thought to have human physical characteristics, I asked what Ezili, a female spirit, looked like. This was of particular interest to me since Annette at a previous time had commented on the *lwa*'s characteristics in term of the Haitian hierarchy of class and race. The reply was a surprise: "She came as a man. She can do that, any way she wants to." And to the further question about the man's identity she replied, "Yes, the face of someone I know. She said that I didn't take care of her, that I despise her. She needs the shrine to be arranged." That the Ezili in the dream vision was a known person is not given importance by the narrator; instead, she returns to a fuller account of what Ezili said: she made demands. Yet my questions appeared to give Annette pause, to send her back to the actual dream vision. In spite of her earlier assertion that female spirits can take the form of men in dreams, as indeed they can do when they possess individuals, Annette now chooses a different understanding: "It was not she herself who came. She sent [her husband] Papa Ogou, since it was a man. He did not come as a gendarme. Sometimes he comes in yellow clothes.[5] But he came all dressed in white." Her words suggest a groping to recapture the original dream experience. My further question concerned how she had known whom she had seen in her dream. Ogou, known as a warrior, would appear in a military (khaki) uniform, but this man wore white. She replied, "Since he made me that reproach, I know it was he himself [that is, Ogou]. When you see a single *lwa* making you reproaches, that is all of them. They sent one to make reproaches for all of them."

My curiosity not yet appeased, I probed further. It turned out that the man in white was someone she knew and his name was Maurice. To illustrate the relationship between spirit identities and their appearances in dreams—and perhaps also in the shape of the people they choose to possess—Annette explained, "Maurice is a dark Negro, a big fellow, so you know it is Papa Gede." That is, Gede is visualized as just such a person in the Haitian system of race and class: Gede is not only black but also one of the poor. This linkage of Maurice with Gede flagrantly contradicts her earlier identification of him as Ogou! As to Ezili Annette said, "If you dream of a beautiful reddish woman, with beautiful hair, you know it is Ezili. Any good-looking man, with beautiful hair, any mulatto, that is Danbala." (Danbala is the snake spirit, identified with St. Patrick, who is Ezili's other husband.) Annette's explanation here clarifies the relationship between spirit identities and their appearances in dreams. To understand dreams, then, one needs to know not only religious beliefs, but also the Haitian social structure! And yet, the *lwa* can choose to possess whom they wish, to take on any shape they desire.

Considering the dream narrative so far, we see that Annette tells of a female *lwa*, who complained about being neglected and wanted the dreamer to return to serve her. Probing more closely we learn that the dreamer saw and heard a man she knew who asked her to return. We discover this not immediately but only gradually, by questioning. Indeed, it is not only the questioner who finds out what was seen in the dream but, it seems, the dreamer herself. In spite of whom she actually saw in her dream, she appears to have understood the meaning of the communication and hence the identity of the person who addressed her. Finally, curious about the consequences of the dream, the actions that might now be incumbent upon her, I asked what she needed to do as a result of this dream. Nothing, it turned out, at least not immediately: "Yes, I explained in my sleep—they have to wait until I return to Port-au-Prince. They asked so much when I would return—I said I didn't know. *Lwa* come to reproach you just like human beings. When you don't light their lamp, they think you despise them." The dream is a complete event, a completed action. Not only the question, or demand, appears, but also the dreamer's response. By offering the *lwa* an answer, Annette shifts the responsibility for her lack of performance to me. Characteristically, performance (fulfillment of duties) can be delayed and relationships can be negotiated.

In spite of having seen a man known to her in her dream, Annette speaks of encountering a spirit, and a female one at that. It is her relation to this *lwa* that seems to be most salient to Annette. Yet though I saw her possessed by the male spirits Ogun and Gede, I never saw her possessed by Ezili. In the dream and the elaboration of its report, three (or is it four?) figures are involved in a communication event: Ezili (and/or Ogou or Maurice) and Annette. But of course, as the reader will have noticed, while the spirit(s) speak to Annette, the communication is (also? or primarily?) addressed by the dreamer to one who does not appear in the dream, the person who causes the trouble, the anthropologist who keeps Annette from serving her *lwa*. Though unspoken, the message was addressed to me, and rather characteristically, through indirection, given the hierarchical structure of Haitian relations. This interpretation is my own; it made sense to me. However, it is so contrary to Haitian dogma of whom or what one sees in dreams that I am quite sure it would not have made sense to Annette. Here Tedlock's (1994) remark, cited earlier, about the joint reality created by researcher and research subject is clearly relevant.

Communications by indirection are characteristic of Haitian verbal interactions, as they are of Afro-Caribbean and other Afro-American communities. These patterns have been widely documented (see Richman and Balan-Gaubert, 2001).

I noted above that Ezili was particularly salient to Annette. This refers to an episode sometime earlier in her life. She had lived in a common-law marriage with a man who then left her for another woman. When he fell ill ("went mad"), he returned to Annette's uncle for treatment. In the course of the ritual, Annette was possessed ("mounted") by Ezili, who required as a condition of the cure that the patient marry her, the *lwa*, and also her "horse," Annette. The man followed through on the ritual marriage with the *lwa*, but reneged on the human marriage.

In the dream narrative, we see Annette caught between two authorities: on the one hand, the spirits who want her in the city, and on the other, myself who keeps her in the country. She deals with this conflict by having the *lwa* tell me of their demands through her dream. And, from the perspective of the outsider, the *lwa* stand for herself. She explains, "Since I was a child, it is the city to which I am accustomed, which makes it more difficult for me here." In the context of the conversation this seems to mean, "It is more difficult for me to dream in this unaccustomed place." And then, quite clearly, "I'm rather there, in the city." Now she is no longer as eager to be in the country as she was earlier, when she sought to persuade me, with the help of her *lwa*, to go there. Then there is also the manifest content of the dream, in which it is the man Maurice who asks her to return to the city, followed by her response to me that she'd rather be there.

This dream then is a rather urgent communication event, and I suggest the urgency is so great that no symbolic disguise is required, or better, the symbolic disguise, the manifest content, can be disregarded. The dream is experienced as already interpreted. The culturally less acceptable demands of the manifest content of the dream are ignored, not acknowledged. Dreams are supposed to be about spirits, not about people you know. And when people you know appear they really aren't what they seem to be; they must be translated into spirits. And, not incidentally, spirits are more powerful and therefore more persuasive than people.

I suggest, consequently, that the communicative interaction and the way in which the dream is experienced are directly related to each other. In terms of the Haitian worldview, this is a dream message from spirits to their human servant. The *lwa* initiate the message and Annette is the receiver. From her point of view, it is her relationship to her spirits that is at issue; that is how she understands it and how she tells it. For me, as the outsider, there are two other messages: the dream image itself, which involves a man and, apparently, Annette's relationship with him. However, that is not acknowledged—it does not fit into Haitian dream theory. The other message, involving a third perspective, also is foreign to this theory: the dream is as a message from Annette's quite human self to me. But that is possible only in terms of my own theory of dreams, according to which they are messages from the dreamer's self—but in this case to the audience of the dream narrative. That is to say, this interpretation is possible only by ignoring Haitian dream theory and the dreamer's own overt understanding of the dream. It works only by taking a view quite foreign to her. My understanding, my "getting the message," which was initially quite spontaneous, is revealed by reflection to be rooted in my own worldview, my own notion of where dreams come from. If the dream involves Annette and the spirit(s) (or Maurice) and myself, we have a three-part communication, not unlike that which occurs in possession trances: the spirit takes over the human body and addresses other persons present. The "horse" has no memory for this event, because one of his or her two souls, the *gwo bonanj* (literally, "big guardian angel"), has been displaced temporarily. This spiritual element cannot remember any event at which it was not present.[6] The possessing spirit must therefore leave a message for his (or her) horse, to be conveyed after the event. In the case of this dream, the audience receives the message after the dream event, when the message is relayed.

This dream, which so clearly expresses what Annette wants—to return to the city—suggests a very compliant unconscious. However, considering her history, it is not only in dreaming that this characteristic of her psychic life is expressed. The appearance of Ogou and also Gede to convince me to go to visit her relatives in the country in the first place is another example, and so is the appearance of Ezili, mentioned earlier, that made marriage to her ex-partner a condition of his cure. Unfortunately, just putting her wishes into the mouths of her spirits doesn't always work for her.

Annette's dream narrative seemed at the time quite unusual to me with regard to the fact that the dream seemed to be experienced as interpreted, that the interpretation was part of the experience, and not a secondary elaboration. I have since found other examples.

Karen McCarthy Brown (2001, 269–70) reports the dream of the Haitian *vodou* priestess she calls Mama Lola. Here is an abbreviated version: Asked about her daughter who is in the hospital and about whom she is concerned, she says:

> Oh, Maggie going to be okay. . . . I got a dream about her. . . . [My old boyfriend] come to see me. He say, "My girlfriend in the hospital. I have to go see her. . . ." Every time I dream Gabriel, I know that Papa Gede. Papa Gede going to the hospital to see Maggie. When I dream that, I know everything going to be okay.

The dream contains a teasing conversation between Gabriel and the dreamer, but she ignores all that and focuses only on going to the hospital. Gabriel is Gede and his girlfriend is taken to be Maggie. The message is obvious, the dream is preinterpreted, materials irrelevant to that instant interpretation are ignored. Yet for the outsider, wondering about Mama Lola as a person, her imaginary contacts with her old boyfriend would be of interest. And why is it he in particular who is the regular stand-in for Papa Gede in her dreams?

Yet the men in these dreams—Maurice and Gabriel—are not arbitrary symbols of the *lwa*, although they are specific to these dreamers. They stand in for the spirits because of the theory that holds, on the one hand, that the *lwa* can choose the face and body of anyone they please, and, on the other, that they choose certain preferred physical and social types. From the outsider's perspective, it is the dreamers who select particular individuals as stand-ins for the spirits, and they do so for both personal and cultural reasons.

Obeyesekere (1981, 57), speaking of an ecstatic priestess in Sri Lanka, reports a similar instance of preinterpretation. In a dream of the divinity Isvara, she says "[H]e was wearing a cloth over his shoulder and a checked sarong held in place by a belt. . . ." Asked whom the god resembled, the woman replied, "My [dead] uncle, he wore a familiar checked sarong and broad belt." In contrast to Mama Lola's Gabriel, however, Isvara is said to have identified himself in the dream. Obeyesekere reports that after his death the uncle had spoken through her to her husband, explaining that "he has been born in the divine world as a servant of Isvara and he protects her . . ." (1981, 60). Obeyesekere comments, "Pemavati's case illustrates the tendency of ecstatics to invest ordinary events with extraordinary significance. As a result she consorts with divine beings in her dreams and participates with them in fantastic, joyful experiences" (1981, 57).

In these cases only selected elements of verbal messages are given importance; the dream image itself is treated as quite secondary.

Manifest/Latent

So far then, we have discussed dreams that are undisguised; that is, to the dreamer, there appears to be no latent, disguised meaning. The meaning or the message of the dream is immediately understood by the dreamer and the elements irrelevant to this message are discarded or ignored. These portions of the manifest content seem to disguise what the dreamer hears as the significant message. In Meggitt's (1962) terms, the "native" interpretation, which here is an integral part of the experience, is intermediate between the manifest content and, in psychoanalytic terms, the latent content. However, to Haitians such as Annette and Mama Lola, and to people in other cultures (including the biblical authors), such a latent content is not part of their worldview. They seek to understand their relations to the spirit world and what that world demands of them. To them, as to the Kagwahiv dreams "are on a par with waking experience" (Kracke 1991, 47). In them, they speak with the spirits, just as the Haitians speak with them when they are interacting with persons in possession trance. They seek guidance for their actions from these encounters, not insight into their own intrapersonal conflicts. If there is wish fulfillment, it is mediated through the spirits.

Visitational dreams are reported from a variety of cultural contexts and may, among other things, serve to initiate religious revivals (Bilu 1986, 2000.) There is, however, a difference between the Haitian dreams reported here and those that Bilu reports for the Moroccan Jews in Israel, who have developed pilgrimage traditions on the basis of their dreams. The saints who visit the faithful appear as they might have in life, not in the bodies of persons familiar to the dreamer. For this last to occur, there has to be a tradition and practice of possession trance, in which humans enact the presence of visiting spirit entities on ritual occasions.

Haitian dreams of treasure can be understood in these terms. From a Haitian point of view, they are not at all disguised, and do not require interpretation. Hence, Meggitt's middle level is missing. That people who are poor have dreams of treasure seems to involve a wish fulfillment of the most obvious kind. The only question might be why a particular person has such a dream at a particular time. In contrast to Stewart's Greeks (1999), Haitian treasure dreams are not related to historic events but only to family traditions.

The widow's dream does not involve a traditional practice of dream interpretation. At first it seemed to her that the meaning was self-evident, that no disguise of a latent content was involved. However, two elements—her husband experienced as living rather than dead, and the dream's reference to leaving with him, rather than more explicitly to joining him in death—allow for a neutral affect, a matter-of-fact approach to the need to make preparations for departure. The affectively bland manifest content of the dream masks the anxiety-charged character of the latent content. In this example the difference between manifest and latent content is not found in the message, but in the dream's affective quality.

Joseph's dreams are also immediately understood, in this case by his audience; no reference is made to his own understanding, nor does Genesis report why he told the dreams to his brothers and his father. The manifest content is expressed in symbolic terms, but the symbols are transparent. This is in contrast to the dreams Joseph interprets in Egypt. Indeed, he is so skilled at interpretation, that the prediction of his earlier dreams comes true. Dream narration is required to find explanations and, in the case of Pharaoh's dreams, interpretation leads to actions, to avoiding the predicted disaster. Beyond the purpose sought by the biblical authors, another moral seems to be implied: dreams are disguised messages; they must be told and interpreted properly to avoid disaster, in order to take appropriate actions, where possible.

The examples of preinterpreted dreams are quite different: in the narration—and apparently in the experience as well—the dream interpreted according to cultural rules is articulated first. That is, as far as we can determine, cognitively the latent content, implicit according to local theory, precedes the manifest content and outweighs it in importance. The manifest content is given no attention by the dreamer. When it is articulated, it is treated as negligible; it serves merely as a vehicle for the significant message the dream contains. A third level of analysis, the dream interpreted from the outsider's perspective, plays no explicit role in the dialogue between narrator and audience.

Mama Lola does not abbreviate the narration in quite the same way. She tells us what, of the manifest content, is important, interprets and restates it, and ignores the rest. Pemavati similarly rejects the manifest content of the dream: the identity of her uncle is treated by her as irrelevant for her understanding of what she experienced. It is not even worth reporting.

Yet in spite of what these narratives have in common the dream experiences seem to work differently for these three women. For Annette, the dream, as well as her possession trances, clearly relate to her motivations and her attempts at manipulating her social world. For Mama Lola this particular dream involves a wish and her search for a supernatural helper. For Pemavati there is a life beyond her meager earthly one.

Dreaming and the Self

In the preceding, we have looked at some examples of dreams and dream narrations in which no recourse to interpretations is taken by the dreamer; for the dreamer's purposes the meaning, or message, of the dream is clear. A variety of cultures and a number of intrapersonal and interpersonal constellations are included in these examples. Among the latter we find involvements with spirits as well as humans. In all cases cited the dreamer feels a need to understand the dream. The Haitians and the Sinhalese woman are intimately involved with their spirits and with the interpretive system, so that they immediately understand what issues the dream addresses. This enables them to shortcut the process.

The local interpretive systems involved in these examples are unlike those cited in the literature and differ in important ways. For instance, the Haitian system is not meant to reveal the "wishes of the soul," as Wallace (1958) tells us of the traditional Iroquois system. Rather, it reveals the wishes, demands, and actions of the spirits—the *lwa* and the ancestors. Yet we may consider the ways in which the spirits constitute part-selves of the dreamer. In Annette's case, quite clearly, they are part-selves that have greater authority and power than her waking, conscious self. Bilu (1986) speaks of the "wishes of the saint" that the dreamer seeks to fulfill. The psychoanalytic system, by contrast, seeks to identify the wishes of the self and evidence of intrapsychic conflict. The two coincide only, as in Annette's case, when the spirits want what the dreamer wants. Yet this is never explicitly stated. The biblical system on the other hand, foretells the future, which, if negative, can at times be avoided by appropriate actions. Still, here too, Joseph's dreams, however disguised, suggest not only a prediction but also a desire on the part of the dreamer.

Systems of dream interpretation involve various elements that, in a given tradition, make the world understandable; they are part of what Hallowell (1955) called the "culturally constituted behavioral environment." For the Haitian *vodouist*, this includes the spirits, whom one sees, hears, and speaks with in one's sleep, and who possess ("mounts") people, thereby replacing one of their souls, *gwo bonanj*. Whether in sleep or waking life, these interactions are as real as any dealings with people. Both spirits and humans have the capacity for transformation. Spirits can take on any form they wish: male or female, old or young, human or animal. Are small snakes dangerous spirits? The twin spirits (*marassa*)? Or just ordinary snakes? Humans, without changing physical form, may embody spirit entities, so that a man may be possessed by a female spirit and enact that identity, while a woman may enact a male identity. A shy person may embody and enact an aggressive spirit, and so forth. As shown in Annette's dream and that of

Mama Lola as well, in dreams as in waking life, it is important to know with whom one is dealing: Is Maurice actually Ogou? Or Ezili? Is Gabriel really Gede? These dreamers, in spite of their different levels of esoteric knowledge, are adept at knowing the true, relevant identity of the persons they see in their dreams.

Some people, moreover, are demons or *lougawou* ("werewolves"), women who eat children. That is, they cause illness and death. They are apparently ordinary people, who turn into something else at night. Stories about them are told as apparently well-known, ordinary events. Some people are zombies, victims of sorcerers; some are sorcerers. As Annette put it on another occasion, "You never know who a person is." Or in the words of another acquaintance, "You know what people are in the daytime, but not what they turn into at night." These are just a few examples of a general ethos of suspicion and ambiguity widespread throughout the region (Cf. Beck 1979 for other parts of the Caribbean). Haitians live in a dangerous world; the dangers come from human and spirit entities, spirit allies of evil humans, and so forth. These dangers are mitigated by forming alliances with spirits, being obedient to their demands. Dreams are one way in which spirits allow you to know their wishes and tell you of their conditions for giving help. Acquiring at least some knowledge of the spirit world and of magic is an important tool for survival. A trustworthy specialist must be found to help in a time of crisis.

Given this shifting field of identities, where or what is the dreamer's self, that experiences the dream, and that self who, from the outsider's perspective, creates it? We may begin by considering the Haitian notion of personhood. As we have seen, the Haitian concept is multiple, mutable, flexible. My Western concept is that personhood is singular and constant, though capable of growth and maturation as well as traumatic impairment. The English verb is one of action: "I dream." The Haitian's, "I see in my sleep," is rather more passive. Being "mounted" is also a passive experience—in both instances it is the spirits who are active. The imagery is a female one, even though men as well as women are mounted. In her study of the Gorovodu of the Ewe, Rosenthal (1998:11) says that this system of religious belief and practice is "marked by femaleness." It is strikingly similar (and historically related) to that of Haitian vodou. She speaks of the "gendered nature of possession" (1998, 113). And she emphasizes the multiplicity of the person in "the texts of Ewe personhood" but also of an "extremely individuated (not individualistic) self" (1998, 2). I cite Rosenthal's important study because she shows so clearly how multiplicity of person and singularity of self work together.

The Haitian *vodou* system, like that of the Ewe's Gorovodu, is one where personhood involves multiple, dispersed aspects of personality. I have mentioned two souls (or part-souls). People are possessed by a number of different spirits who constitute their own personal pantheons. One spirit is the *met tèt* ("master of the head"), the dominant spirit, established ritually in the head of his (or her) servant, who must be removed, ritually, after death. Arguably, each of these spirits represents part of the total self: a person's biological sex and the qualities of the other sex that complement it—perhaps an aggressive male spirit for a woman, powerful protective spirits, class consciousness, and much else. No two people have the same complement of spirits. Even the same spirit, in the head of two different people, may act somewhat differently. This multiple system, I argue, is reflected in the subjective experience of dreams. It is not only the dreamer's identity that is mutable, but also that of others: humans, spirits, animals.

The system works for the self because its underlying unity is unconscious. This unity is revealed, in part, by the constancy of motivation—the self's wishes are projected onto powerful others who are called on to work on behalf of the individual's wishes, whether in dreams or in possession trance. By the participants, spirits are seen as helpers, as long as they are obeyed. The outsider may see them as an aspect of the dreamer's or the possession trancer's self.

To return to my specific example: Actions and initiatives, in dreams or in possession trance, taken by spirits, are not the dreamer's responsibility. After all, in the dream it is not Annette who wants to return to the city (or who wants me to return); it is the spirits who want her to come. This view of the world of dreams is consistent with the world of human interactions and with the multiplicity and mutability of the Haitian concept of the person. However dangerous, it is a world of interdependence and passivity, of action by indirection and the work of others. What is constant and holds this multiple, mutable system together is a continuity of motivation. The various parts seem to work together to achieve the goals of the self.

Dream interpretation, where it exists as a formal practice, is only one example of culturally structured attempts at finding means of coping. In most life situations we all make experientially and culturally informed interpretations, enabling us to act appropriately. Sometimes, to our peril, we misinterpret. It is an American commonplace that the symptoms of a heart attack may be treated as indigestion or the initial stages of a major illness as the flu. In situations of culture contact, making sense of unfamiliar situations may be a source of both danger and of creativity.

Religious syncretism is a familiar example of this process. Annette's dream illustrates the equivalence of Haitian *lwa* and Catholic saints. Here some attributes of the saints, as shown in chromolithographs, provide the links between the saints and the spirits. The Mater Dolorosa (Our Lady of Sorrows), shown with votive offerings of bejewelled hearts, is identified with

Ezili Freda (Metrès Ezili, Mystè Ezili), the spirit of erotic love. St. Patrick, shown with snakes at his feet, is the Dahomean snake spirit, Danbala. St. Jacques (St. James the Elder, Santiago de Compostella), represented as a knight on horseback, fighting the Moors, is Ogou, the Yoruba warrior (Brown 1989). And so on through a very long list.[7] Analogous identifications are found throughout various other Afro-American religions. Syncretism has been, at one time or another, part of the missionary policy of the Catholic Church (Stewart and Shaw 1994). Whether intentional and part of a systematic policy or not, syncretism involves cognitive processes, focussing on similarities, ignoring differences.

Such iconographic identifications are only starting points for knowledge about the spirits. Their behavior in dreams and embodiments in possession trances contribute to further knowledge about them. Interestingly, the enactments of spirit identities varies with individuals: the Ogou "in the head" of one person will differ from that in another's. Representations by Haitian artists build on and develop traditional knowledge. The artists' renderings, like the enactments of possession trancers as well as the stories dreamers tell themselves and others, give rise to further creative elaborations. These narratives, performances, and visual representations may be seen as expressions of what Stephens (chapter 6) has referred to as the "autonomous imagination" at work.

Haitian art, which has flourished for almost sixty years, illustrates this. It has drawn heavily on *vodou* practices, imagery, and imagination. For example, in a 1948 painting entitled *manje lwa* (The Feasting of the Gods), Wilson Bigaud represents various elements of a complex ritual. He shows actions that occur in sequence as being performed seemingly simultaneously. Sizes of some objects are exaggerated, apparently arbitrarily. Most strikingly, the left side of the picture is dominated by a dead tree. Half way up, we see a basket and an enormous snake which is being fed by a woman who holds up a pot of liquid (see Bourguignon 1979, 251). Commenting on Haitian art, Brown (1995, 18) notes, "[T]he blighted tree, its branches lopped off, is perhaps the most often repeated image in Haitian painting. . . ." She links this to the historic crisis of slavery as well as the contemporary disastrous ecological situation. The large snake, however realistically depicted, has no match in the Haitian natural environment. It is Danbala, a key element in the Haitian mythical world. Persons possessed by Danbala, acting out the snake's habits, may climb trees. More generally, without reference to paintings, the *vodou* priest, whom I have called Jerôme, rather idiosyncratically identified the snake as Jesus on the cross (Bourguignon1982, 295).

Both the withered tree and the snake may be seen as phallic objects. Thus Jerôme speaks of the snake as entering the two Marys at the foot of the cross. The tree as a symbol of powerlessness may also be linked to the *lwa*

Legba. In Africa, this trickster spirit dances with a large wooden phallus and mimes intercourse with women bystanders. In Haiti, Legba is an old man on crutches. In Haiti, it is Gede—associated, among other things, with death and magic, but also with fertility—who is now the phallic trickster.

Haitians' interpretations of dreams appear to be consistent with their interpretations of waking reality, with their understanding of their world as lived. Dreams, however strange, are interpreted, and sometimes experienced, as conforming to their understanding of this personalized world.

Conclusions

As illustrated here, depending on our cultural neologism, the interpretation of dreams tells us what to expect, how to understand our relations with the beings in our world, how to act, perhaps how to understand ourselves. In a system where personhood involves multiple, dispersed aspects and identities, this is reflected in the subjective experience of dreams. It is not only the dreamer's identity that is mutable, but that of others: humans, spirits, animals. As argued above, the system works for the self because its underlying unity is unconscious, revealed, in part, by a constancy of motivation: the self's wishes are projected on to powerful others who are called on to work on its behalf.

Where, as in Haiti, the manifest content of dreams is believed to be a coded version of an interaction with spirit entities, the dreamer may ignore the manifest content and experience the dream as a direct interaction with spirits whose identities are only superficially disguised by the human bodies that mediate their presence. I have referred to such dreams as "preinterpreted." I suggest that the experience of interacting with spirits as embodied by humans in the case of possession trance facilitates such dream experiences. In possession trance, too, the human "horse" of the spirit is treated as largely irrelevant to the interaction between the spirit and its interlocutors.

While preinterpreted dreams may not be unusual, they have not been part of the theoretical discussion of dreams. More generally, in the anthropological literature, dreams have been seen as in need of interpretation. Yet dreams are only one category of experiences that require interpretation. Our reactions and responses to novel events or encounters depend on our interpretation, yet the only means of understanding available are derived from our past. To make sense of the new we must draw on the old. The unfamiliar and strange is understood by using the known and familiar. Africans saw Catholic saints as representations or equivalents of their spirits, much as the Romans equated the Greek Zeus with their Jupiter. Catholics and other Christians saw African spirits as devils and spirit possession as demonic. Western physicians saw possession trance as hysteria. Melanesians believed cargo came from the ancestors. Maria von Trapp, the matriarch of the Trapp family, told America on the *Tonight Show* that cargo cults were a communist plot. In each case, these interpretations reflected the observers' own understandings of the world as they sought to deal with what they had seen or learned. They would draw on the same understandings in the interpretation of their dreams or those of others, for such understandings constitute the totality of a worldview, of a culturally constituted behavioral environment.

Notes

1. Wax (1999) discusses this and other biblical dreams at length.

2. Numerous writers have used dreams for purposes of teaching or plot development. In Sholem's *Tevye the Dairyman* (1987), for example, Aleichem's Tevye invents a dream to convince his wife to agree to their daughter's marriage plans. This dream, too, is not disguised. This incident also appears in *Fiddler on the Roof*, the stage and screen adaptations of the story (Bock 1964).

3. For the purposes of the present chapter I have gone back to the original text and also updated the Creole orthography. The fieldwork was conducted in 1947–48, with the support of the Carnegie Corporation and the graduate school of Northwestern University.

4. Chromolithographs are inexpensive, mass-produced, brightly colored prints. According to White (1999–2000, 76) chromolithographs came into widespread use in Europe in the 1870s. In the 1940s they were imported to Haiti from Cuba; older ones had come from Germany. The saints represented were identified by written legends, which most of the faithful could not read.

5. Yellow, meaning khaki. Haitian gendarmes (police) had been made part of the army by the American Occupation (1915–34).

6. Lambek (1998, 106) notes that "possession is constituted by the occupation of one body . . . by more than one person . . . or mind."

7. Annette's identification of saints and *lwa* is part of a standard *vodou* repertory. Others, more assured of their esoteric knowledge, are more creative in their identifications and interpretations (Bourguignon 1982).

CHAPTER 8

Dream: Ghost of a Tiger, A System of Human Words

WAUD H. KRACKE

From this house in a far-off port
In South America, I pursue and dream you
O tiger on the Ganges' Banks.
. . . . I reflect
That the tiger involved in my verse
Is the ghost of a tiger, a symbol
and not the deadly tiger, the fateful jewel
The real thing.
We shall seek a third tiger. This
Will be like the others a shape
Of my dreaming, a system of words
A man makes, and not the
vertebrate tiger
That, beyond the mythologies
Is treading the earth.
—Jorge Luis Borges, *"The Other Tiger"* (1964:70–71)

*L*ife provides a vocabulary for our dreams. Much of it is solitary, confined to the unique experiences we store each day, that we co-opt in our dreams (Freud noted) to represent the dream thoughts to be expressed ([1900]1953). But some of the images we use in our dreams are shared with others of the same cultural community: either drawn from common linguistic usage, or from common daily experiences. Many of the images Freud cited as "symbols" (by which he meant something like "natural iconic signs," in Peirce's scheme, 1955) are based on metaphors implicit in linguistic usage ("to go down

155

in the world," "fallen woman"), or on metaphors drawn from the fabric of everyday cultural experience (raincoats or umbrellas for condoms, in dreams of Freud's Viennese patients). Such items of the vocabulary of dreaming are provided by culture.

Culture provides more: not just vocabularies of dreaming, but syntax and grammar, even perhaps pragmatics of dreaming: Do we dream alone or do we share dreams with another, communicating directly soul-to-soul in a dream? The way a dream is constituted may be shaped by the way the dreamer conceives and interprets dreams in general, in a culturally given paradigm—whether the paradigm of a particular school of psychoanalysis, scientistic negation of any significance in dreams, or a system for recommendations for the day's hunting. Poets like Borges may provide a grammar or a philology of dreams for us. Any culture that elaborates such a system provides through it a thesaurus for the construction of its members' dreams.

Many cultures provide such thesauri, in the form of systems of coded dream explications: if you dream of A, it means B will happen. These dictionaries for decoding dreams can become sources for images in dreams as well, rivaling (or at least supplementing) the "trivial events of the day" which Freud sees as a primary source of dream images; the manifest content of a dream may become quite literally a culturally coded message. If in a culture's code a certain image predicts death, for example, someone in that culture may dream about death in an encoded form, representing his or her concern in that conventional image.

That a past death is represented in dreams as future—conventional dream systems usually interpret dreams as predicting the events they refer to—may not so much be an instance of defensive displacement in time, as it represents the nature of transference: the past wish or fantasy which is repressed is experienced, in repetition (Freud 1914), as present, or as imminent.

Among the dreams I have collected from the Parintintin Indians in Brazil, I have a number of examples in which the dreamer expresses his concern directly in such symbols: concern about a parent's death, for instance, being expressed in the traditional image of a broken down house (the most popular), or dreaming of honey to refer to pregnancy.

Just as often, however, perhaps more commonly, such traditional glosses for dreams, standard prophesies read in conventional dream symbols, may have quite a different use—the reverse, in fact. Oftentimes a dream may be interpreted as predicting hunting success, or some other benign outcome, distracting from a deeper meaning representing a much more intimate wish or anxiety—a conflict. Sometimes the dreams which are subject to such distancing interpretations are dreams which deal relatively openly with highly emotional and conflict-laden content: sexual dreams, for example, or dreams of fighting, may be given benign interpretations as predicting success in the hunt. Thus Manezinho dreamed of João Boabá's "big penis," twice that I know of—once while hunting, and he immediately interpreted it as a prediction of getting tapir (he failed, because he told the dream by the fire in the morning); and again, in a highly charged dream: João was making love with his young wife Ida when her brother grabbed his (presumably erect) penis and broke it off. Again, Manezinho at first interpreted this scene as predicting that he (or someone) would kill a tapir; but I undermined this bit of secondary elaboration by pointing out the coincidence and asking if João's big penis stirred any childhood memories. (It did: an early memory of seeing a grown man's penis—João's, in fact—when he was five.) But then he reinstated the distancing effect of the traditional interpretations. He now spoke of seeing the woman's genitals in the dream, and surmised that this meant he would wound himself. He found confirmation for this interpretation in the fact that earlier in the morning he had knocked a healing machete cut on his leg and started it bleeding again. I had neutralized the effectiveness of the defense with my interpretation, but he found another that had enough impact to defuse the anxiety aroused by the childhood memory, and his rationalization was buttressed by reality (Kracke 1981).

Manezinho later made a very astute self-observation about the anxiety-reducing function of traditional interpretations. Commenting on a dream about a marital fight (I think it also involved João Boabá), he recalled, "At first when I was little I was afraid when I had dreams like that, I didn't know what it was. I told Papa. I thought it was an *añang* [ghost or malevolent spirit] that I had dreamed of. Sometimes you dream of a woman, and it is game. When you dream of a man, his prick, it's a tapir you're going to kill. All this Papa told me."

Culture provides more: not just a language for dreams, but sometimes (as Manezinho shows) considerable accumulated knowledge about them. Indeed, Freud acknowledged a debt to popular belief in his formulation of the theory of wish fulfillment ([1900]1953). Much of the world has been talking about dreams for centuries; it stands to reason that such cultures may have as much to tell us about dreams as pharmacognicists are now recognizing that indigenous cultures can teach us about pharmacology. If Amazonian cultures may open up botanical secrets to the prepared tropical botanist and open vistas of ethnopharmacology with the proverbial cure for cancer (or now for AIDS), then the multitude of cultures that have taken dreams seriously while we dismissed them as "froth" or "random neuronal firing" may well be able to amplify our vision of dreams. Looking at the lore of dreams in cultures around the world is not only of interest for understanding their diverse ways of thinking about an aspect of life that is devalued in our culture, but may be of direct value for the student of dreams in suggesting untapped approaches to dreaming.[1]

Another dream of Manezinho's gives us an example of how language structures enter the construction of a dream: Early in the day of July 11,

1968, Manezinho told me a short dream (in Parintintin): *Tamanduahu oñomeno wevikwaripe* ("Two anteaters were screwing each other in the ass.") When I asked, "And then?" he elaborated that "We pulled them out of each other" (*Ore oho wekyi oñakwai jugui*). In his interview, he went on to tell me his haircut dream:

> There is another dream, we killed a jaguar. I was skinning the jaguar. I cut the pelt and spoiled it. It turned into someone, and said to me, "Why did you skin me?" Pedro Neves was toasting manioc flour. [Someone was] with him. Pedro Neves, I told him, "Skin this jaguar, I'm afraid." I went to toast farinha for him. It seemed as if I was scraping farinha [that is, grating manioc tubers]. He was taking off the pelt. "Just now it was a jaguar!"[2]

Later in the interview, I asked how the jaguar was killed. "It was the Brazilians who killed it, left it here.[3] I took off the pelt. Caetano [said], "Cut me here on the forehead." I felt sorry for him . . . I was afraid. I called Pedro Neves. Pedro Neves . . . just cut his hair! Pedro Neves took it off with a razor, shaving him. *Ohy, omondoho ahe av.*

Right after telling this dream, Manezinho added two more:

> Zeca was fighting with his wife, and Maria do Rosario was fighting with her husband, Antônio. Zeca's wife said, "Why are you fighting with Antônio? I don't fight with Zeca." In the end, Zeca's wife married Antonio Arimã and Maria do Rosario married Zeca. . . . As if it was real.

The second was of a paca, a large, supernaturally powerful rodent that was having intercourse with a cutia, a squirrel-like rodent.

> *akutiuhu-pawêi omenó ra'u.* The paca ran after the cutia. It was the dog running after the paca. Then later the dog killed the paca. The cutia went away. I was running, running. When I got there the dog had already killed it.

Later in the interview, I commented that the first of these two dreams involved an exchange, as he traded with Diré in the haircut dream. Manezinho responded, *Ojokwepy* ["they exchange"]—when you go mess with another's wife. The others say "*ojokwepy 'nga.*" There is also like that when you screw a cousin, like me with Ida. Someone else said [if you] mess with your cousin [girl of same moiety]—only your cousin—then your daughter will die. It's no good when you screw your cousin. With *amotehe* [girl of opposite moiety], no. *Typyowy ji ojehe*—when one's child dies. If not, then one's father dies, one's mother too. If not, it hurts your child, your mother dies.

Now, in fact, he is at this point mourning the death of a year-old daughter and a five-year-old son, who died in a recent epidemic. His mother had died a few years ago, and his father was sick. I questioned him further:

> (Q: You made love with Ida?) I liked her, too. I didn't think anything, I didn't know anything, I was a child. Later I was given advice, it was later that I knew.

(Q: When did this take place?) I was size of Luis [twelve], I liked her a lot. She liked me. I didn't think anything, I thought it was like that. After they taught us, I never loved her again. Papa gave [me] advice. Now, [it's] Paolo who likes her a lot.

(Q: When single?) No, after marrying. Paolo is good because he doesn't have any connection [relationship] with her—*amotehe*. [He jumps up to catch a chicken going into the chicken-hutch to lay an egg.]

At the end, I asked:

"Did you feel guilty about sleeping with Ida? He replied, Yes, I did. Papa said to me, 'If you make love to a *kwandu*, I will die.' Now I don't do that any more—*nda'apo'javi*.

When I first heard this dream, I was puzzled by it. It was told to me in Portuguese, and I could see no reason for the pointed confusion between giving a haircut and cutting the forehead. But as I learned more Parintintin, I realized that it could be clearly understood if we think of it having been dreamed in Parintintin.

Table 8.1

Vocabulary Useful for Understanding the Haircut Dream:

o'api'rog: to skin (<*pir*, skin, + -'*og*, suffix, to cut off)
ipi'rog: with a new skin, rejuvenated
oapin'dog: to scalp <*apin*: shell (of a nut), cranium
oapin: to cut hair very short, give a crew cut
  [*apin*: means father, so *oapin'dog* could be heard as *apin* + -'*og*, "to cut off the father," though it is not literally so interpreted).
api'a: testicles
api'a'ynh: *api'a* + *ha'ynh*, seed, (semen)
api'a'y-ekyi: api'a'ynh, testicle + -*ekyi*, extract (castrate)
okwepy: repay, pay back, exchange, either in trade or in a feud. Used to refer to sister-exchange marriage, for example.
ojokwepy: exchange with one another
typyovy: to suffer the consequences of committing incest
typy: deep water + *(h)ovy*, blue or green

Here are a few vocabulary items that may help understand the haircut dream. To give a close haircut is *oapin*, from *apin*, which refers to a hard, spherical surface like a nutshell or a cranium. To scalp is *oapin'dog*, just adding the suffix -'*og*, "to cut off." But *apin* is also the word for "father," so *oapin'dog* could equally mean "to cut off the father." And *api'a* is testicle; *api'a'y-ekyi* is to extract the testicle, to geld; and complete castration is *onhakwāi'dog*. Thus the ambiguous image in the dream—cutting off the head—has a linguistic cor-respondence, via "scalping" (*oapin'dog*) to what was treated as its equivalent in the dream, a close haircut (*oapin*); but as part of a series of correspon-dences whose culmination is castration (*onhakwain'dog*). The word for "scalp," also, is a compound of two words which could literally be heard as "to cut off the father" (*o- apin -ndok*)—as he felt he had done through his incestuous affair.

These two readings are confirmed in the dream Manezinho told me the next day, literally of castration: a young man pulled the penis off an old man who was having sexual relations with the young man's sister—who was none other than Ida, Manezinho's childhood partner in incest. His associa-tions to the idea of "exchange" in the haircut dream refer specifically to the consequence of incest: it leads to the death of one's children or one's par-ents. Through his incestuous relationship, he felt responsible for the death of his five-year-old son a month before these interviews, and for the illness of his father.[4]

Let me come back to the language of dreams. How we talk about dreams tells a lot about how we conceive them and our relationship to them. A dream, for most Americans, is something we *have*, like an illness or break-fast. In Parintintin, as in many other languages, "to dream" is strictly a verb. One doesn't *have* a dream, as something external and objectified. When I say "I dream that I do such and such," I participate in the act I dream. Even more than that: in Parintintin you relate the event that happens in a dream with a grammatical tense marker that indicates one experienced this event in a dream, rather than witnessing it while awake, or hearing about it from some-one else. Dreaming is simply a modality of experiencing, another way of apprehending—even if a notoriously inconsistent, unreliable, and frankly deceptive way: "I thought I was standing on the beach. When I woke up I wasn't. I was dreaming." The Parintintin, then, take a fully intrapsychic posi-tion as they talk about dreams—as a form of experiencing.

The grammar of telling dreams reveals assumptions about the dream experience. Mahoney (1987, 8, 89–90, 108) points out that Freud's accounts of dreams are in the present tense, although Strachey translated them all in the past. This tense of exposition carries important theoretical freight: "The present tense is the one in which wishes are represented as fulfilled" Freud wrote in *Interpretation of Dreams*, ([1900]1953, 385).[5]

In Parintintin, dreams are told with a grammatical marker, a particle that marks the action or situation described as one occurring in a dream. The marker is the particle *ra'u*, and it occurs in the same place in the sentence as a group of particles that mark tense. Furthermore, it phonetically resembles a particular group of those tense-marking particles: a group of particles that mark the recounting of nonwitnessed past events—something the speaker knows from report rather than from his or her own experience.

There is a cluster of particles in Parintintin that mark a statement as being in the past tense. These particles contrast with each other on several dimensions, such as just how far in the past an event occurred (recent past versus long past, and so forth). Two separate series of past tense markers are differentiated according to how one knows about the event recounted: one series is used when the event is one the speaker has witnessed or taken part in, and a different series is used to recount events one knows only indirectly, as through hearsay. The directly witnessed past tense has two forms: *ko* for a recent event I've just seen, or that just happened to me, and *kako* for something that happened to me long past. The indirect past tense similarly has two forms: *ra'e*, something I heard about that happened recently, and *raka'e*, something I have heard of that happened in the distant past. Now, the form of past tense particle used for something that happened in a dream is *ra'u*, much closer to the indirectly heard of past event (*ra'e, raka'e*) than to *ko* and *kako* that mark directly experienced past events. Thus, dreams are represented grammatically as like something only known about from hearsay, rather than as something directly experienced. The dream is telling us about something, not revealing it to us directly. It is a symbolic communication, like language, not a direct presentation of reality.

This all brings us to conceptions of the space/time of the dream and how dream space/time relates to waking space/time. Space, ultimately, is a subjective realm. We all occupy multiple spaces—or, more exactly, we extend multiple spaces in our minds. When looking at a map, we create an imaginative space that has some kind of point-to-point correspondence to certain landmarks we walk by; when we watch a movie, or look at a representative painting that absorbs us very much, we imaginatively enter that space.

A dream creates its own space. My philosopher grandfather used to pose the question as follows: I dream I am in a canoe, heading downriver toward a waterfall. . . . I wake up just as the canoe is about to go over the waterfall: How far is the prow of the canoe from my bedpost? (Hocking 1957, 227; see also 28–29).

For him, the question is paradoxical, because the spaces are incommensurate. Yet dream space may, even for us, in some instances merge with real space. Kekulé's ring is a case in point. His dream of snakes biting their tails when he fell asleep contemplating the problem of the structure of the benzene molecule was the solution to his problem. His dream represented the structure he was seeking in waking life, the benzene ring. Lucid dreaming—being aware that you are dreaming—is even more of a case in point. In lucid dreaming, there is a partial convergence of dream space with waking space—which is one thing that makes lucid dreaming so fascinating.

For many cultures, dream space even more readily converges with living space. Indeed, it is often regarded as being a special form of perception, a road to the sacred: for the Parintintin, a way to sense (in nightmares) the presence of ghosts and malevolent spirits, but also a way to have direct access to healing spirits, as Pedro Neves did, now that shamans are gone: "January, 1968. Pedro Neves' five-year-old grandson was critically ill, at death's door. In times past, they would have performed a 'tocaia' ceremony, in which the *ipaji*, the 'empowered one'—the shaman—would call on the spirits of the sky, the waters, the forests and even the *añang* under the earth to come into the house, sing their characteristic song, and blow on the sick person with their healing powers. But since Igwaká died, and Capitao before him, without passing on their knowledge to the children they had dreamed as their successors, there were no empowered ones left among the Parintintin." (Kracke 1990, 151–52).

One evening during this time, Pedro Neves was sitting on his porch. As I walked by, I heard him singing, and asked him what the song was. "*Ka'na*," he said—"the Crippled Ones." I dreamed that the *ka'na* came to Pedrinho's house and blew on him. Now he won't die. Their song:

ji a'apó nomanomanói	[I cause not-die not-die
nomanói tußei.	Not-die indeed
ji a'apó-kwerá	I make people come alive]

The *ka'na*, explained Pedro Neves's older grandson Carlos, who sat by in my interviews with Pedro Neves translating when necessary, are human-like spirits—"they look like *añang*,"—who live in the forest, blow on people like an *ipaji* to make them better.[6]

Pedro Neves's dream recreates the space of the curing ceremony, the *tocaia* ceremony, that used to be performed by shamans. In a kind of trance, the *ipaji*, shaman, would send his spirit (*ra'uv*) or his spirit double (*rupig-wara*) out to the abodes of the spirits, and invoke them to come to help cure the patient.[7] In his dream, Pedro Neves played the traditional role of the shaman, bringing spirits in to blow on his grandson. He was able to recreate in dream space what was once a vital ceremonial space in Parintintin society.

Dreams are a lifespace—a lifespace our mind creates, true, but nonetheless a space we live in for the duration of the dream, just as we live in the spaces we are awake in. This is the import of the familiar parable of the butterfly in the *Chuang-Tze* (Chuang-Zhou, 1999 [286 B.C.]: 18). "Am I Chuang Chou who have just awakened from a dream of being a butterfly? Or am I a butterfly now dreaming I am Chuang Chou?" The mind is a link between two incommensurate spaces, that of the dream and that of waking consciousness,[8] and when dreaming we are rarely aware that we are not having a real experience. The space of dreaming is one that the mind has constructed—as is, indeed, also the space of reality. It is, as Freud has shown us, a space constructed by language: A careful reading of *Interpretation of Dreams* (Freud [1900]1953) reveals how central language is to the construction of dreams (Litowitz 1973, 1975). In Freud's conception dreams are, as Borges has put it, *un sistema de palabras Humanas,* "a system of human words" (1964, 71). But there is one more difference between dreaming reality and waking reality, though not one we all make use of. Like the virtual reality in the movie *Matrix,* the reality of dream space can be manipulated—as long as one can make oneself aware that one is dreaming. "As I sleep," says Borges in *Dreamtigers* (1964, 24), "some dream beguiles me, and suddenly I know I am dreaming. Then I think: this is a dream, and a pure diversion of my will; and now that I have unlimited power, I am going to cause a tiger."

This unlimited power to "cause a tiger" is what makes dreaming such a central image for shamanic power: dreams have the power not only to foresee, but to create realities (Kracke 1992). Shamanism is expressed through dreams: the power to cause something to happen is exercised in dream. It is done with the mediation of the same dream symbols that ordinary people use to predict events. A *pajé,* or shaman, if he wishes to cause something to happen, will dream (intentionally) of whatever it is that in most people's dreams predicts what he wishes to bring about. If he wishes to bring peccary for a man to hunt, he will dream of the man hosting a wild party; if he wants to cause a man to be attacked by a jaguar, he will dream of the man in a hammock, the dream symbol for a jaguar. In other words, rather than just receiving prescient dreams, he wills them: his dreams are lucid, and it is the control he gains through this lucidity that gives him shamanic power—he knows he is dreaming and, with the dream's unlimited power, decides "to cause a tiger."

Notes

1. "Lucid dreaming" was suggested by the claim in some cultures of being able to manipulate their dreams.

2. The text of the dream as he told it to me in Portuguese:

Tem outro, nos matamos onça. Estava tirando couro da onça. Cortei o couro. Estraguei o couro. Virou gente. Ele falou comigo, "Porque tirou couro?" Pedro Neves estava torrando farinha. [Alguem] com ele. Pedro Neves. Disse para ele "tira o couro dese onça, tenho mêdo." Eu fui torrar farinha para ele. De modo que estava ralando farinha. Ele tirava o couro. "Ainda agora estava onça." (Quem?) Finado Caetano. [Back to dream:] Caetano, "Corta aqui na testa." "Nao—doi para ti." Fiquei com pena—fiquei com medo dele. Chamei Pedro Neves. Pedro Neves—só cortou cabelo dele. Pedro Neves tirou com navalha, raspando [cabeça] dele. *Ohy, omondoho ahe 'av.*

3. The Parintintin, like many Brazilian Indians, think of themselves as a separate nation, so refer to non-Indian Brazilians as "Brasileiros," "civilizados" or—in their own language—as *tapy'yntin*, "white enemies."

4. The woman with whom he had had the incestuous affair, Ida, was the same as the young man's sister in the next day's dream with whom the older man was making love when the young man pulled his penis off. Thus, he himself was in one sense the one who was castrated in that dream—by the loss of his five-year-old son, in punishment for the incestuous relation.

5. The copyeditor of this volume, Margart Copeley, M.Ed., researched German dream-telling for Kracke. "Germans normally tell their dreams in the past tense to indicate that the entire dream is unreal. They then recount the events of the dream in the present tense, just as we do in English. Therefore I conclude that Freud most likely decided to write the dreams down in the present tense although they were told to him in the past tense."

6. Excerpt from field notes, Sarilho, January 23, 1968.

7. The cosmic space created within the *tocaia* ritual—the space of the travels of the shaman's *rupiguara* as he visits the various spirits—is in its turn a reproduction of the mythic space of the Parintintin cosmic myth: the myth of Pindova'úmi'ga, who founded the celestial world of the Sky People (see Kracke 1992, 130–137).

8. In fact, multiple incommensurate spaces. When, awake, one is immersed in a gripping novel, or contemplating a Ruisdael landscape, one is absorbed in the space of the novel or the painting. Hocking refers to this characteristic of the mind as the "vinculum" (1957, 227–229).

CHAPTER 9

The Anthropological Import of Blocked Access to Dream Associations

MELFORD E. SPIRO

$\mathcal{S}$ome fifty years ago, Dorothy Eggan, an unsung pioneer of the systematic anthropological study of dreams, published a paper stressing the anthropological importance of the manifest content of dreams (1952). Since her basic argument is no less cogent today, my aim here is not to refute, but to supplement it.

This chapter is based on dreams reported by a young American woman in the course of a two-year therapeutic analysis. I should explain that this analysis ended after two years because Ms. B. as I shall call the patient, had to leave San Diego. Nevertheless, the corpus of dreams reported by Ms. B. over the 203 sessions of the analysis, together with her associations, were sufficient to support my long-held view, based on fieldwork in three nonwestern societies, that more frequently than not there is an opposition between actors' cultural ideologies and culturally constituted (or ideal) self representations, on the one hand, and their personal desires and actual self representations, on the other. Consequently, we anthropologists commit a major methodological error when, as is often the case, we rely on the first set exclusively for constructing our psychological descriptions of the people we study. That at least is the thesis of this chapter.

A single, twenty-eight-year-old, graduate student when she entered analysis, Ms. B. is an exceptionally intelligent, highly creative, and very attractive woman. Paradoxically enough, however, Ms. B., like virtually all my female academic patients, sought treatment because of chronic depressive moods brought on by painfully low self-esteem.

At our first meeting, Ms. B. informed me that, as a feminist, she had strong reservations about entering analysis. Having been exposed to psycho-analytic theory in a course on feminist theory, she strongly objected to Freud's "male chauvinism" which, she feared, would be reflected in psycho-analytic therapy. Moreover, were she to decide, despite these reservations, to undergo an analysis, then ideally, she said, she wanted to be treated by a woman because, as a feminist, she doubted that a male could be sensitive to the sexual politics inherent in the therapeutic relationship. That being so, she had scheduled concurrent interviews with a female analyst, following which she would then decide between us. As it turned out, she reluctantly decided to work with me, for while she much preferred the female analyst, she could not afford her fees. (As a research analyst my fees are just sufficient to cover the malpractice insurance). I mention all of this to emphasize that Ms. B.'s feminism is not a reflexive academic cliché, but a strongly internalized belief system, a fact that should be kept in mind in order to understand the theo-retical import of her dreams and fantasies which follow.

The first dream reported by Ms. B. was not recounted spontaneously, but was elicited by me when, near the end of the evaluation interviews that preceeded the analysis, I asked for her earliest remembered dream. Ms. B. referred to this dream, dreamt when she was four or five, as her "Hansel and Gretel scenario."

> I was walking in the woods by myself, and there was a house, like a bakery, run by witches. I was taken inside the house, and put on a conveyor belt; it was dark and I was stripped bare by disembodied hands. . . . I was somehow strapped to the conveyor belt, and was touched all over in some way. [pause] A vague notion of penetration. It had overtones of being sexual and bad. [pause] In the finale I was thrust down a chute onto a table. All the witches were sit-ting around the table, and I was poked into, and eaten, and groped. I enjoyed it. It was all pleasant—because it was dark and naughty. It was a feast, it was exhilarating, sexual.

After recounting this dream, Ms. B. commented that when she had told it to her current boyfriend, he said that it sounded masochistic to him, to which she added, "To be lying passively on a table, and obtaining sexual pleasure from what the witches are doing to my body, now also seems masochistic to me."

Because no other materials in the evaluation interviews suggested that sexual masochism was a subject of current concern for Ms. B., I naively attached no special significance to this childhood dream. And indeed for a full seven months I heard nothing more about this subject until the thirty-fourth session of the analysis, when it came up again as an association to the following, Ms. B.'s first spontaneously reported dream.

> I'm in a museum. I see a clay sculpture of my father made by my mother—just the torso, cut off at the penis, no legs. I thought, "Huh, the same penis as C.'s" [C. is Ms. B.'s boyfriend].[1]

When asked for her thoughts about this dream, Ms. B. at first responded with various associations to (as she put it) "tabooed desires" regarding her father, and "thoughts" and "fears" regarding his penis:

> Kind of searching in my unconscious for anything taboo, so I can then have tabooed desires. I think of them [the tabooed desires] as curiosities. I don't particularly worry about them. I could have desires for my father, and I don't worry that they're too strong, and it's not an issue. [In fact, as subsequent sessions revealed, Ms. B. did have such desires, and she did worry about them because they indeed were an issue]. I sort of desire to rid myself of the taboo [laughs] of seeing my father's penis. [pause] The image of my father's penis comes into my mind occasionally as a means to relieve myself of my fears about it. Why I have such fears I don't know. Maybe as a girl I thought, "What is it? What is it like?" And I recognized it both as a symbol of power [She had read about this in her feminist theory course], and as important in itself. [pause] Also a thought of its intrusion . . . It's an obnoxious little creature that makes its presence known, and is arrogant in itself. When father is being didactic, I think "he's being a dick," and then I think of his penis. [pause] The image of father's penis pops up occasionally, but definitely there's also a fear that goes back to childhood. [pause] Actually, probably, this image is embedded in some of the [academic] work I've done.

There then followed a stream of associations that picked up the masochistic theme of Ms. B.'s childhood dream and presaged an intrapsychic conflict that was to become a dominant concern for the rest of her analysis. I therefore present them in extenso, albeit with deletions of materials not relevant to this conflict.

> I'm still nervous about talking about my sex life in here. . . . I have to cover up my sexual fantasies. . . . There's a fear that in opening myself up [by telling the fantasies] I'll be seeing myself as a type of woman I don't like to see myself—a masochist. And some of my fantasies are about not being in control—but they're not exactly about rape—and I don't want to think of myself as out of control [that is, as being subject to someone else's control]. I despise the stereotype that women desire to be told what to do, that they like to be pushed around, that they don't have sexual desires that are active, and are just objects of male sexuality. So I guess in a way it would help to reconcile my fantasy life and my conscious waking life in such a way that I don't allow myself to equate

my self with the desires in my fantasies in which I'm out of control, in which I'm told what to do. . . . I flip back and forth between my sense of identity as a woman—as aggressive, in control, not pushed around. [pause] I don't know if the connections between my sex life and my fantasies are correct. I guess they are. In my sex life, to be active is not being a sadist; it's fulfilling my desires and relating to my lover and to my source of self-esteem, i.e., that I'm attractive, and good at sex—and thank God that part of my life is fine. Sometimes I feel that to give oral sex to men is subservient, but it's the source of my pleasure and my lover's pleasure, but it's also the nub of my resentment of men's power, and their easy access to power, and their disregard for women in their desire for power, and so I view oral sex [fellatio] as being subservient. . . . In thinking of C. as being of great comfort to me, I think of that act [fellatio] as nursing, for some reason. [pause] Maybe it's because I resent the penis as power that this image [fellatio as nursing] is more acceptible to me. . . . I guess I feel resistant to talking about my sex life because . . . I'm afraid of being categorized as a masochist, and I don't want to allow that interpretation to make me feel that my identity is a masochist. I will not allow that. I'm very much a rebel in my ideology; I have no room for a weak woman.

According to Freud's dream theory, dream associations comprise the latent dream thoughts that both instigate and are represented in the manifest content of dreams. If that is the case, then Ms. B.'s lengthy and variegated associations to the present dream underscore the importance of "condensation" in the construction of dreams. Thus, whereas the manifest content of this dream can be reproduced in a text that occupies only three lines, her associations, including those I have omitted, occupy three pages. I stress this quantitative discrepancy between them because despite the significant information revealed by the manifest content of this dream—namely Ms. B.'s interest in her father's penis—her associations reveal additional information that is just as significant, if not more so.

First, however, I wish to emphasize that although Freud argued that dreams are "the royal road to the unconscious," and although for the clinical purpose of her therapy some few of Ms. B.'s associations to this dream—those that I have omitted—support that view, others, however, consist of conscious materials which, for the anthropological purpose of this chapter, are no less important. Nevertheless, before turning to the conscious thoughts and desires represented by her associations, it is perhaps useful to consider two of the unconscious thoughts and desires that they represent.

In the first place, since Ms. B.'s associations to her sexual fantasies follow upon her associations to (undisclosed) desires for her father, as well as thoughts and fears of his penis, it seemed a not unlikely hypothesis that the males who are the objects of these fantasies are unconscious symbolic representations of the Oedipal father. This hypothesis was supported by dreams and fantasies reported by Ms. B. in subsequent sessions, of undisguised sexual encounters with her father (sessions 34, 73, 153) and with me in the father transference (sessions 33, 56, 59, 63, 93, 139, 158, 168). I also speculated that unconsciously Ms. B. fantasizes fellatio (both in her fantasies and in actuality) as oral incorporation of her father's penis, but this speculation, unlike the first, was unsupported.

Second, in addition to her unconscious thoughts and desires regarding the Oedipal father, Ms. B.'s associations to her fantasy of fellatio as nursing suggested that unconsciously fellatio also represents a pull to the pre-Oedipal mother. This hypothesis was also supported by materials that emerged in later sessions. For example, in one session, Ms. B. said that in her relationships with men she has the wish to be "the little girl . . . to be comforted, petted, and held by them, and [she added laughingly] to be put inside the orb of their warmth." In another session, she expressed the desire that C. [her present boyfriend] be a "maternal person . . . who [will] take care of me and serve as a retreat from the world."

As I emphasized above, however, for the anthropological focus of this chapter Ms. B.'s conscious associations are quite sufficient, and consequently I shall concentrate on them. The latter include both thoughts—for example, the view of the penis as power, the resentment of male power, and the view of fellatio as both subservience and nursing—as well as desires—for example, sexual desires that are expressed in masochistic sexual fantasies. Although time and again Ms. B.'s associations referred to these fantasies, nevertheless she at first refused to disclose their content because while she herself, she said, viewed the masochistic desires expressed in these fantasies as ego-alien—"I don't allow myself to equate myself with the desires in my fantasies"—she feared that I, however, might view them as constitutive of her identity.

I shall focus on these fantasies because it was they that first alerted me to one of Ms. B.'s most painful conflicts, that between her masochistic sexual desires, on the one hand, and her feminist ideology, on the other. It is perhaps because of this conflict that I heard nothing more about these fantasies until, one month and thirteen sessions later, when Ms. B. alluded to one of them, but only in abstract terms, because, she said, she considered it "degrading" and she feared that I would categorize her as a "masochistic woman." Nonetheless, she began the very next session by saying she felt a need to describe the fantasy. "It will be good for me, like getting a tooth pulled out."

> I'm on this ship with horny sailors. I'm sitting on the deck, and I'm a prostitute or a servant, and I go around on my knees [she laughs] giving oral sex to these men and getting taken from behind [vaginally, not anally] at the same time, and though it's against my will, I'm enjoying it, and I have a ridiculous smile on my face, like the expression of a child. [pause] I see it as all the more humiliating because I'm enjoying it, like I'm too drunk to realize it's a cruel situation

[pause] to have my head thrust down in compliance, in servitude, in an inferior role. . . . To have such a fantasy is degrading enough in itself, but more so because I get pleasure from it.

Because by now Ms. B. had become convinced that I did not view her masochistic desires as degrading, and also because she was highly motivated to explore them, she subsequently reported similar fantasies and dreams in fifteen separate sessions,[2] though it was not until the fifty-sixth session that I learned that she employed the fantasies for masturbation. Since it would be tedious, however, to reproduce all of them here, I shall instead summarize these fantasies and dreams by saying that they all involve the theme of sexual subjugation, including both forced fellatio and intercourse by rapacious males. Moreover, in retrospect they all evoked guilt and shame in Ms. B. for having obtained sexual pleasure from behavior that violates her feminist ideology, namely, submitting to the will and control of dominant males. To quote from only one session:

> A lot of the guilt I have in telling you about my sexual fantasies is that I've been unable to accept that I give myself over to these men who are degrading to me, and that I take pleasure in relinquishing my control, and therefore I take pleasure in this masochism, which means I'm a bad woman because it shows that in my heart of hearts I want not to be in control, which is in conflict with my feminism.

Before proceeding, it might be asked why it is that although Ms. B. views fellatio as degrading when it occurs in dreams and fantasies, it is nonetheless one of her favorite sexual acts in real life. The reason, I would suggest, is threefold. In her dreams and fantasies, the men force Ms. B. to perform fellatio for their pleasure, and she enjoys it even though she is thereby subservient to their will and control. In real life, however, fellatio (a) is an expression of her will, and it is she who is in control; (b) she performs it for her pleasure, not theirs; and (c) since she views it (as she said) as nursing, the penis is a symbol not of male power but of the female breast, which means— as I discovered much later in the analysis—that unconsciously she is sucking not on her father's tabooed penis, but on her mother's permissible breast.

Let us now return to the thesis with which I opened this chapter, namely, that anthropological descriptions of the psychological characteristics of social groups that are constructed solely from cultural conceptions, or from interview protocols, or (to advert to the focus of this paper) from the manifest content of dreams, are often misleading, if not false. Thus, had Ms. B. been an anthropological informant rather than a psychoanalytic patient, I most probably would not have learned about some of her important conscious psychological characteristics, let alone her unconscious ones. As for the latter I would not have learned of her strong sexual desire for her Oedipal father, and her strong attachment to her pre-Oedipal mother. As for the former, I would not have learned that (a) although she had internalized a cultural ideology that valorizes women's sexual and emotional autonomy, she also possessed powerful countervailing desires that were inconsistent with this ideology; (b) this inconsistency was the cause of persistent intrapsychic conflict; and (c) as a consequence she suffered acute emotional pain (shame, guilt, and deflated self-esteem). What is more, I would not have learned about this constellation of psychological characteristics not because it was unconscious, but because she would not have disclosed it to me.

Thus, it was not until the seventh month and the thirty-fourth session of the analysis that Ms. B. even alluded to her conflictual sexual desires, and then only because of her associations to a dream whose manifest content bore no apparent relationship to them; and it was only in the eighth month and the forty-eighth session that she consented—at my prodding—to report the fantasies in which they were expressed. Moreover, Ms. B. withheld these fantasies despite the fact that (a) we met hourly four days a week; (b) she had a powerful motive—the wish to overcome her emotional suffering—to comply with the "basic rule" to report whatever thoughts might enter her mind; and (c) she had learned early in the treatment that, as an analyst, I was both nonjudgmental and noncritical.

I would now suggest the following. If the witholding of emotionally painful material is found even in such a favorable context, then how much more might this be the case in the ethnographic context in which most of these optimal conditions are absent. For example, (a) informants are interviewed for far fewer than 203 hourly sessions; (b) they have little incentive to report painful material; (c) dreams are often not asked for; and (d) even if they are, their latent content usually remains unknown because typically associations are neither offered nor requested.

My point, as I noted above, is not to denigrate the manifest content of dreams—it was from the manifest content of one of Ms. B.'s dreams that I first learned, for example, of her interest in her father's penis—nor is it to suggest that as ethnographers we should conduct therapeutic analyses: most of us cannot, and those who can should not. My point, rather, is that we might employ other procedures for eliciting emotionally painful material, including inter alia projective tests or other projective techniques of the kind reported in this volume by Jeannette Mageo, or we might conduct psychodynamic interviews as reported here by Waud Kracke. But if, for whatever reason, we cannot or will not employ such procedures, then we should be more modest about our empirical claims. We might, for example, introduce our ethnographies with the following caveat:

> The psychological data presented here consist only of materials that are conscious, that are culturally normative, and that are not emotionally painful (that

is, that do not arouse shame or guilt); consequently these data represent only one part—whether major or minor I cannot say—of a much more complex psychological picture.

In the absence of such a caveat, we continue to perpetuate the currently widespread, albeit misleading, view that all psychology is cultural psychology, in short, that cultural ideology and psychological reality are one and the same thing. Although the latter is the case if the ideology is internalized, it often, however, is not; and if the latter is the case, then the ideology is a cultural cliché, one to which social actors pay lip service, but which has little if any psychological—that is, cognitive and motivational—salience. Indeed, not infrequently the actors' motivational dispositions are the very opposite of their cultural ideology. Consider, for example, the Christian precept to "love your neighbor as yourself" which, though clearly incompatible with ethnic cleansing, had no influence on the psychology of the few Serbs who raped and massacred ethnic Albanians in Kosovo or on that of the many who acquiesced in, or approved of, their behavior.

I hasten to add, however, that an incompatibility between cultural ideology and motivational disposition does not necessarily signify that the former is genuine whereas the latter is spurious, that is, a cultural cliché, for despite their incompatibility the ideology may nonetheless be internalized, as is the case with Ms. B. Although her masochistic sexual desires are inconsistent with her feminist ideology, the latter is nevertheless strongly internalized as an ego ideal, as is evidenced by the painful intrapsychic conflict and the shame and guilt that these desires arouse. In short, having internalized this ideology, there is a split in Ms. B.'s self (or personality) such that one part is in conflict with another, and she attempts to resolve this conflict by wishing to believe that the ideology represents her real self, whereas the desires are an ego-alien intrusion, hence not part of her self. "It would help," as she put it, "to reconcile my fantasy life and my conscious waking life in such a way that I don't allow myself to equate my self with the desires in my fantasies."

In sum, to equate cultural ideology with psychological reality is misleading enough when, as in the case of Ms. B., the ideology is internalized; it is compounded when, as is in the case of the Kosovo Serbs, it is not.[3]

Notes

1. Although I am not unaware of the fact that dreams dreamt during an analysis and reported to the analyst have important transference meanings, as do the dreamer's waking associations, nevertheless, for brevity's sake I have omitted consideration of the transference in my discussion of Ms. B.'s dreams. I might add that transference meanings are by no means absent from dreams reported to the anthro-

pologist, though usually they are not as prominent because typically the transference itself is less intense than it is in an analysis.

2. If fantasies and dreams can be taken as evidential, these fantansies and dreams, taken together with Ms. B.'s earliest childhood dream (her "Hansel and Gretel scenario" reported earlier), give evidence of a remarkable persistence of a character trait extending over a twenty-five year period, from early childhood into adulthood.

3. For an extended explication of the meaning and processes of cultural internalization, see Spiro 1997.

CHAPTER 10

Concluding Reflections

VINCENT CRAPANZANO

> One wonders whether a grain of wheat, which carries in it the
> seed of the root, the stem, the leaf, and the ear, could dream of
> the root, the stem, etc., and become aware of that which, lying in
> it, can develop. It is certain that a grain of wheat is conscious of
> that, and that it really dreams of it. It is possible that this con-
> sciousness and its dreams are very obscure. But, without this con-
> sciousness and these dreams, it does not have life.
> —Gottfried Reinhold Treviranus[1]

*D*reams cannot be separated from their conceptualization and theorization, for that conceptualization and theorization affect, if not the
experience of the dream, than its report. This proposition is shared, in one
fashion or another, by all the contributors to this insightful and innovative
collection. It is an important insight and requires elaboration, but before
elaborating, I want to note that in most discussions of the dream in different
cultures and historical periods, there is a marked tendency to offer a relatively
systemic account of the culture's or period's dream theory. I want to question
the assumption of a single, systemic theory of the dream in any society,
including our own. It is for this reason that I begin with a quotation from the
late-eighteenth, early-nineteenth-century German naturalist, Gottfried
Reinhold Treviranus, whose attribution of the role of the dream in a grain of

wheat's development into a mature plant is as exotic an approach to the dream as any we have attributed to peoples living in far-off cultures and distant epochs. Treviranus, obviously influenced by the *Naturphilosophie* of his time, an intensely romantic one, was nevertheless a serious naturalist, whose theory of "descent with modification" may have played a role in the development of evolutionary theory. It reflects at least the beginnings of a developmental paradigm: "All living forms are the results of physical influences which are still in operation, and vary only in degree and direction."[2] The important point is that despite his "exotic" dream theory, Treviranus shared many of our cultural presuppositions, and his dream theory reflects an organicism that is by no means extinct in at least the popular imagination. The several coexisting approaches to the dream in any society, including ours, have diverse authority, but authority all the same, and resist systemic integration. They are certainly not without contradiction, as we see even in as highly a developed one as the psychoanalytic. This messiness is a social fact, and it should be treated as such, as should our propensity to give singular importance to one theory and offer a systemic account of it. The messiness is a response to the dream and no doubt facilitates the way the dream—always puzzling, producing, if you will, interpretive anxiety—is managed in different social settings.

Whatever the reality of its referent, the dream is a cultural category and subject at the discursive level at least, but at the experiential level as well, to all of the contortions of the cultural category, itself of course a cultural category. It has become de rigueur to distinguish the dream from the dream text. Like many others, most notably Jacques Lacan, I have argued that what we interpret is not the dream but the dream text (Crapanzano 1975, 145–146; Lacan 1956). Here I should like to modify this position to differentiate the dream from the dream account. I now prefer "account" to "text" because it is less restrictive. It better calls our attention to the nonverbal features of telling a dream. It removes it, if only symbolically, from the prevailing hegemony of textuality. This is not to say that dreams cannot take textual form. They certainly do and, as they do, they are subject to the prevailing construal of the text: textuality, its theorizing, and its consequent rhetorical possibility, which, in the case of the dream, we tend to naturalize in psychological terms, ignoring the fact that the psychological is itself an historically specific cultural construction. This naturalization of the dream has considerable rhetorical weight. It encourages, among other things, the universality of the dream, minimizing its culturally specific construction, the possible effect of that construction on the dream experience, and its contextual isolation and hypostatization. The dream becomes a metadiscursive category of universal presumption for the discussion—description, interpretation, and analysis—of the dream.

Let me make several observations about dreams and their accounts, which the chapters in this book have inspired. They reflect, inevitably, our categorization and evaluation of the dream. (I use the first person plural rhetorically throughout this chapter, calling on the reader to share, critically, ironically, a viewpoint.) The first point I want to make is that the dream encourages its own decontextualization, or, more accurately, its own special contextualization. Though all the contributors recognize the importance of contextualization, they have given us for the most part a very limited one. (Melford Spiro, for example, limits his contextualization to the psychoanalytic session, though he recognizes prevailing ideological influences like feminism.) They have not asked what the relevant context for dream description, interpretation, and analysis is, for the people they study or indeed for themselves. Can the dream be isolated from the discourse in which it occurs? From the discourse its recounting promotes? Jeannette Mageo, whose contribution is in fact sensitive to context, demonstrates that the dream cannot be divorced in terms either of content or interpretation from prevailing political—postcolonial—conditions in Samoa. Our conceptual isolation of the dream facilitates, I would argue, the discursive isolation of the dream. Would it not be of ethnographic, if not of psychological, significance to consider the way in which the dream features and is featured in its discursive environment? The dream, however conceived and expressed, is not without very considerable pragmatic effect. It does not just reflect or presuppose a context but casts it with varying degrees of creativity (Crapanzano 1994, 14–19; Silverstein 1976; Lee 1997, 165–167). We might well ask what the political—and the micropolitical—consequences of the isolation of the dream from its several contexts are. How does it affect, whether from our point of view or that of the dreamers, the rhetorical force of the dream, its account?[3] Here I would suggest, in line with Mageo's stress on the dream as giving critical edge to the dreamer's social and cultural world, that the framing of the dream—through dream theory and in accordance with the conventions of dream narration—masks this critical edge and thereby facilitates its expression. As Mageo writes, "In dreams the apparently seamless interdigitation of cultural schemas and our experience frays" (chapter 2).

The way we view the dream in everyday life as well as scientifically cuts off its connection with social and political discourse and action. I am speaking here of more than the way the dream has been consciously used, whether by the pharaoh whose dreams Moses interpreted or cargo cult leaders like Mambo (Burridge 1995). I am referring to the way the dream arises out of a certain political milieu, like that of Samoa, and can, though it need not, comment on that milieu and conduce action. Ernst Bloch, who was anxious to distinguish the daydream from the nocturnal dream, stressed the "world-building" role of the daydream. Unlike the night dream that is always

obscure and can never be fully communicated, the daydream is easily com-
prehended and communicated, Bloch insisted: "The daytime wishful dream
requires no excavation and interpretation, but rectification and, in so far as it
is capable of it, concretion. In short, it does not have a measure from the
outset any more than the night-dream but, unlike the spooks of the night, it
has a goal and makes progress toward it" (Bloch 1986, 99).

We need not accept Bloch's Marxist-utopian thrust to recognize the
distinction between at least certain types of daydreams and night dreams.
Bloch is reluctant, however, to consider how the night dream might also
figure in "world-building."[4] In stressing the creative potential of the dream,
the British psychoanalyst D. W. Winnicott (1971, 26) does set something of
a foundation for the dream's role in promoting social and political engagement, though he does not explicitly refer to either the political or the social
role of the dream. Less inclined to share Bloch's enthusiasm for the daydream, he finds that night dreams fit "into object-relating in the real world,
and living in the real world fits into the dream-world" in ways in which daydreams and other fantasies remain isolated phenomena, "absorbing energy
but not contributing either to dreaming or to living." Contra Bloch, they
remain static and unproductive. Obviously Bloch is either referring either to
a specific form of daydreaming, which encourages realistic fulfillment, or, as
he frequently does, he speaks metaphorically and rhetorically in and through
psychological terms.

Katherine Ewing, who stresses the manifest content of dreams in her
contribution to this volume, suggests that at least some dreams are for
migrants, and presumably other displaced people, manifestations of a
process of adaptation—"a key site where culture and identity are negotiated." Dreams manage the disjunctions produced by the experience of
migration, Ewing argues, and reconstitute self-organization in a diasporic
environment. We might add that dreams can also transform the subjective
rendition of the migrants' several worlds and the relationship between
them. As Ewing herself recognizes, some dreams actually produce—I
would say, inspire—social transformations. She mentions the famous
Seneca prophet Handsome Lake's dream. She could have cited the dreams
of any number of religious and, indeed, political leaders. In contrast to
Freud, Ewing stresses the forward push of dreaming, as it is understood in
many societies, without denying a "backward-looking approach." "When
we disentangle and foreground each of these two axes," she writes, "it is
even possible to understand how dreams can be in some sense predictive, in
the way that good hypotheses in the social sciences are predictive: because
they involve astute analysis of a social situation and hence provide a kind of
map of how people may act in the future." (See my discussion of the creative aspect of dreaming that follows.)

Whatever their predictive value, dreams can be understood as demanding interpretation that has to follow their occurrence (even if that interpretation is embedded in their first narration). Given a predictive stance, convincing interpretation is finally arrived at when the dream—its prediction—is fulfilled. This can take on harrowing proportion, as Ewing illustrates in her discussion of the dreams that were reported to have occurred before the accidental death of the son of Turkish migrants in Germany. Though the dreams ("real" or retrospectively confabulated) were taken to predict the son's death, it was only the death that confirmed—completed—them. More interested in the way in which the dream and post-mortem dream talk served to recast death "as a completion rather than a rupture," Ewing ignores other possible functions of the dream and the talk it generated. It may also have moved feelings of responsibility for the death—guilt, we might say, and ambivalence—from the "real" to the oneiric plane. It would be interesting to know how insulated the one is from the other in the Turkish family's understanding of the dream. It may have given them a way to give expression to intolerable feelings without having to acknowledge them. I encountered such deflections in Morocco and, of course, in the United States, in myself, for example.

Phenomenological accounts of the dream, like those of Ludwig Binswanger, who was not immune, it would seem, to romantic theories of the dream, stress the role the dream plays in giving us access to Being. In his introduction to the French translation of Binswanger's *Dream and Existence* Michel Foucault notes that Freud never succeeded in understanding the dream "as a specific form of experience." He never escaped the nineteenth-century postulate of the dream as "a rhapsody of images" (which, to his credit, I would add, he understood in terms of the logic of discourse) but, Foucault insists, the dream is more than a rhapsody of images, for were this the case, the dream would be exhausted through either psychophysiological mechanics or equally mechanistic symbolic analysis. The dream is, however, an imaginary experience and has, therefore, to be related to a theory of knowledge. It gives us particular access to Being or Existence, or, more mundanely, reality, or rather it is a mode by which reality presents itself. For the romantics, like the German philosopher-poet Novalis, the dream opens the dreamer to a higher reality in which the depth of the soul merges with the transcendent and foundational. Every dream is, for Novalis, "a significant tear in the mysterious curtain which falls in a thousand folds in our inner being."[5] Regardless of the shaman's understanding, it is frequently from this romantic perspective that shamanistic dreams of voyages to the netherland or the heavens, to a primordial place of origin, a ground of being, expressed in mythological terms, have been understood.[6]

We often find reports in the ethnographic literature of a split between a view of the dream as giving access to some privileged domain and a mechanistic symbology (Crapanzano 1975; Pandolfo 1995, 165–205). However arbitrary the symbol system may appear to be, it does affect, as Kracke notes in his contribution, both dreams—their reports, at least—and their interpretations. Often, I surmise, the postulated symbolic meanings relate the dream to broader cultural concerns as well as to myths and other cultural narratives. They serve, at any rate, to generalize the dream, attenuating, as it were, its particularity and the emotions associated with that particularity. I found in Morocco that the mechanical-symbolic interpretation of dreams was often accompanied by laughter. Though we might be tempted to see that laughter as simply an alleviation of anxiety produced by the dream, we should not ignore the possibility that the dream, at least its recounting, is—or can be—a form of entertainment. Often the reporting of one dream, released by a mechanical interpretation, led to accounts of other dreams by both the dreamer and his interlocutors. Such dream conversations may be an implicit form of cultural critique or the (masked) revelation of society's suppressed or secret life.

In Morocco, as in many cultures, the dream is most often understood as a wandering of the soul and what the soul witnessed is what is dreamed. The site of the soul's wandering is an indeterminate and dangerous elsewhere, which none of the Moroccans with whom I discussed it could really define. It was simply where the soul (*ruh*) wandered. They did associate it with death and some, the more philosophic of them, responding perhaps to my questioning, described it as a *barzakh*, a betwixt and between, as the great Andulusian Sufi, Ibn al-'Arabi understood the term (though none of them ever referred to him).[7] The most articulate of them said it was the *barzakh* between life and death. Many insisted on the prophetic value of dreams, though there were some skeptics who usually directed their critique against the mountebanks who claimed to be able to decipher a dream's meaning and prognostication rather than against the prophetic value of the dream itself. The site of the soul's peregrinations was from this perspective either what was occurring in some other place in the past, present, or future, which was unknown or dimly known to the dreamer, or it was squarely in the future. What was witnessed was not, however, what was directly dreamed, for the soul's experience had to be translated—*terjem*, a metaphor several used—by the mind (*'aqel*) into language. With translation came distortion and the need for interpretation, whether spontaneously by the dreamer himself or any of his immediate interlocutors or by an oneiromancer, who might depend upon inspiration or one or another of the countless dreambooks that were in circulation. These dreambooks were mechanical: if you dreamed of x, then y would occur. Practically the focus was on interpretation and not on the status of the dream.

Binswanger suggests that with Freud's stress on the latent content of the dream we have tended to minimize the role of the dream's manifest content and lost contact with the "primal and strict interdependence of feeling and image, of being attuned (*Gestimmtsein*) and pictorial realization" (Foucault and Binswanger 1994, 88). Certainly the contributors have stressed the importance of manifest content in their analysis of the dream. (Spiro is an exception, cautioning against dismissing the dream's latent content.) They have tended to relate this content, rather more in principle than in fact, to the dreamer's culture and to the circumstances in which the dreamer finds himself and to articulate their interpretation of the dream in terms of this contextualization. In most ethnographic accounts of dreams, contextualization remains particularistic and without system, in a way that is reminiscent of Claude Lévi-Strauss's use of ethnographic material in his interpretation of Amerindian mythology. Is this the effect of our particularistic understanding of the dream? The pragmatic effect of the dream so understood? Or does it relate to an American suspicion of systemic thought?

How is the affective quality of the dream image conveyed to the dreamer's audience? Like any gift, its reception always produces an emotional response in the recipient (the interlocutor) which, as I have argued elsewhere (Crapanzano 1994), produces a counter response in the gift giver—the dream narrator. Freud (1963, 140–158) referred to this as a "premium" or "forepleasure" in his discussion of jokes. Let me cite one memorable dream that was told to me and some friends when I was in the army. The dreamer—a Latino from one of the New York slums—described a nightmare he had had repeatedly as a child: He was sucking his mother's breast—later his girl friend's. Suddenly, terrified, he pulled away and saw a cockroach crawling out of her nipple. All of us were quite visibly horrified. We were all whites, highly educated, from middle and upper middle class families, and our Latino friend never let us forget it. He clearly delighted in the sensation he had produced in us, but he also seemed to take a sort of negative pleasure in reexperiencing the horror of his nightmare. Our reaction had released this pleasure, Freud would no doubt have argued. I should add that the dream spread through our company, and several men reported redreaming it. That I still remember it more than thirty years later attests to its emotional power (whatever its symbolic significance for me), and I suspect, and perhaps take delight in (who knows?) the response it produces in you, the reader, and the release that imagined response gives me.

Moroccans are well aware of the affective quality of the dream and its images, which they often understand in terms of the goodness and badness of dreams. They recognize the way this goodness and badness can be transferred to another in at least the first recounting of the dream. They say that to neutralize its effect one should first tell a bad dream to a rock. When a bad dream is told, can one be sure that it has been first told to a rock? Kracke (1978, 20) notes that Kagwahiv, or Parintintin, believe that by telling a dream in front of a fire in the morning it will not come true; it loses its power. He was surprised that his informants did not follow through on this belief, for they told him dreams indicative of both good and bad omens. He had expected that they would tell him only inauspicious dreams, to rid themselves of evil influence, but not auspicious ones, whose effect they would want to preserve for themselves. One of his informants told him that it was crucial that the dreams he heard had not been told before the fire. Dreams may indeed be dangerous in more than one respect and figure mightily in the articulation of interpersonal relations.

The dream can be understood as a series of interlocutory nestings and is, as such, essentially unstable. The initial dream experience is always illusive, if only because it is impossible to describe it without translating it into language. We experience it, we recall it, but our telling it often leaves us with a sense of betrayal, even if our telling gives us relief from the anxiety that surrounds it. It is not simply that our words do not do justice to what we dreamed; it is that they change experiential register. They create a distance between the experience of the dream and its articulation. The dream loses its immediacy, that sense of immanence, of imposition, of entrapment (so evident in nightmares) that we may perhaps liken, as an analogue, to our sense of destiny, nemesis. The distance may be understood (though need not be) in terms of the gap between word and thing, signifier and signified, symbol and symbolized, which has achieved such theoretical preeminence in recent years, and the metaphorizations, as wound, for example, or castration, it has provoked.

The illusive quality of the dream can be understood (though I do not want to insist on this) as the consequence of faulty—by the standards of waking life—communication that gives the dream experience its singular quality. It is neither addressed to a definable interlocutor nor subject to ordinary communicative and linguistic conventions.[8] It consists, as Freud among so many others has emphasized, of perceptual—mainly visual—and verbal debris, the residues of the day or days that immediately preceded it, which are conjoined by a grammar of desire, power, and taboo, which bears only a tangential relationship to the conventions of everyday narration. (I should note that among the residues are narrative chunks that sometimes give the dream experience, at least fragments of it, a sense of cohesion: an episodic quality.) Though we are wont to take the narrated dream as the dream itself, we have, as I noted above, to distinguish the account of the dream from the dream experience. And yet we must remember—a point missed by many dream theorists—that the dream account, however distorting, is itself evocative of the dream experience, perhaps even formative of it. It is appellative. It evokes our experience of the dream, and presumably those of our interlocutors. It is what is called forth—the dream—that gives the dream recitation value. It is this appellative function of language, as we understand language, that has sparked so much epistemological trouble about the status of experience and its representations. Clearly our attitudes toward language—the stress we give, for example, to its adequacy, to the split between the signifier and the signified (if we should so describe it)—affects the way our accounts precipitate the dream experience or its evaluation.[9]

Through translation, whether in self-telling or telling to others, including rocks, the interlocutory structure of the dream is defined. One tells the dream to another. Subject, as the psychoanalysts say, to the dreamer's desire, his or her projections and empathetic attachments, this other is always a complex, multireferenced other. The play of desire is of course limited by the social typification of the other (and consequently of the dreamer) and the appropriate narrative forms and conventions that are demanded by those typifications. It is obvious that the real-life interlocutors, those to whom the dreamer tells the dream, are more resistant to the projective plays of desire than the inner interlocutors who are addressed in silent—interior—recall and recounting. The tension between real and dream interlocutors is beautifully illustrated in Erika Bourguignon's account of Annette's dream in her contribution to this book. Bourguignon is both Annette's real-life interlocutor and a figure, masked, elaborated, and revealed in Annette's account which conflates, according to Bourguignon, dream and interpretation. We see similar transference-like identifications in the Samoan dreams that Mageo reports. We should not forget, however, the effect of personality style, say, an obsessive-compulsive style, on desire's freedom. It can be understood in terms of the degree of adherence to cultural or individual narrative forms and conventions.

Whatever its experiential reality, the dream, as recalled and recounted, occupies an intermediate and intermediating position in the interlocution in which it occurs. It is, in this respect, a *barzakh*. It sways; it hovers. It takes and loses shape, forms and unforms, with the progress of interlocution—with the subtly changing demands of dreamer and interlocutor over the course of its narration. It is subject, in other words, to the micropolitics—the indexical drama—of the interlocution, which psychoanalysis has described in its own metapsychological terms as transference and counter-transference (Crapanzano 1992, 115–135). It can be described in other terms as well, those of appropriation, disappropriation, and reappropriation, for example. The stakes are high. We might ask whose dream it is, anyway. It would seem that the micropolitics of dream accounts intensify the rhetorical force of the initial dream experience, now better understood as "the initial dream experience," for it has now been caught within language. It triggers—to the always ambiguous benefit of the dreamer anxious to preserve his or her ownership of the dream—the appropriate genres and conventions of dream accounts, which serve metapragmatically, we might say, to control the indexical drama of the dream account, including its ownership.

Cast in language, the dream is subject to the constraints of language as well as narrative genre. It has been observed that in many languages, as in Parintintin, discussed by Kracke, there is no substantive form of the word "dream." It is only possible *to dream*. The dreamer may be given grammatical agency, as in such phrases as "I dreamed" or he may be the passive recipient of the dream, as in the German, "*Mir träumte*" (roughly, "A dream came to me"). How far we can derive dream experience from such grammatical constructions is debatable. They do affect the way dreams, as a category, figure in the discussion and theorization of dreams and may even affect dream accounts. (These can be laid bare through the careful analysis of dream accounts and accounts of dreaming.) More striking are the ways in which some languages have a special tense for telling dreams. Kracke notes that in Parintintin there is a specific tense marker, or particle (*ra'u*), for recounting dreams, which he relates to particles that indicate that the event being described occurred either in the near or remote past and was not directly witnessed by the speaker (See also Mannheim 1987; Tedlock 1987). Dreams, Kracke deduces, are grammatically represented "as like something only known about from hearsay, rather than as something directly experienced." They are a "modality for experiencing, another way of apprehending"—one which the Parintintin apparently recognize as inconsistent, unreliable, and even deceptive. Though Kracke correlates the grammar of dream accounts with the dream's "pointing to something, not as disclosing it directly," I would stress the evidential status of a dream as indicated by its tense particle. One would have to do an extensive grammatical—and narrative—analysis of dream accounts before one could establish the relationship between the dreamer as narrator and the diagetic dreamer (the dreamer inside the dream) and the dream (see below.)

Before turning to dream narratives, I should note that many languages distinguish semantically between different types of dreams and dreamlike experiences that we tend to subsume under the dream. Doug Hollan tells us that the Toraja have a special term, *tindo*, for prophetic dreams; they are "vivid, emotionally charged, and easy to remember." Are *dream, rêve, sogno, mechta*, or *Traum* inclusive of multiple phenomena? Exclusive of others that may be incorporated in other linguistic and cultural systems? Can the daydream—*der Wachtraum, die Träumerei, la rêverie, la songerie, la rêvasserie*—be subsumed under the dream? We have noted Bloch's insistent distinction.

Ought the nightmare—*das Alptrum (der Alpdruck), le cauchemar, l'incubo, cauchemar/inkub* (in Russian)—be included in the dream—simply on an evaluative basis as a "bad dream"? And visions, fantasies, and hallucinations—how do they relate to the dream? We have to consider the possibility of different semantic fields and metaphorical extensions. In Morocco, for example—I simplify—the dream (*manama, hulm*) is distinguished from the nightmare (*bu-gettat*, a sort of nocturnal congestion, or *bu-tellis*, from *tellis*, a goatskin sack used to carry grain).[10] Nightmares are usually described in terms of a pressure on the chest, as in the *Alpendrücken*, and related on occasion to the effect of certain giant spirits (*ghula, 'afrit*). The dream is also distinguished from the daydream—*jula*, from a root referring to circulation, wandering, or *fhiya*, "distraction"—and the *ru'yâ*, a vision that might occur during dreams. The dream and the daydream are thought to be similar. As one man put it, "In the dream (*hubn*) the soul (*ruh*) wanders afar; it is outside (*kharj*). In the day dream (*flliya*) it hovers around the body."

Such semantic analysis, restricted as it usually is to the word (noun or verb) does not necessarily do justice to the way in which dream types are distinguished. They are often differentiated through figurative language, which may congeal into a substantive, as no doubt occurred with the Moroccan Arabic *bu-tellis*. We in fact know little about the way in which dream types are figuratively distinguished. I should add that we know even less about the way the dream in one guise or another is extended metaphorically to other experiences. Can Martin Luther King's "I have a dream" be literally translated in other languages? Would a vision of the future be understood in terms of a dream? How would a Parintintin mark the tense of the dependent clause that follows (were such a construction even possible)? The figurative potential of the dream encourages particular ways of construing and evaluating it evidentially, for example, prophetically.

One of the most striking metaphorical uses of the dream reported in the ethnographic literature is the Australian Aborigines figuring *alcheringa, mipuranibirina*, and *boaradja* as the Dreaming or dreamtime. The Aboriginal words do not refer to the mental experience of dreaming, according to W. E. H. Stanner (1965), but to something like "men of old." The Dreaming, if it can be generalized across Aboriginal society, refers to "a sacred, heroic time long ago when man and nature came to be as they are" but, as Stanner insists, though referring to the remote past, it is still part of the present. It was and is at all moments. Like myth, the Dreaming is a narrative about things that happened, a charter for things that still happen, and "a kind of logos or principle of order transcending everything significant for aboriginal man." And yet, at least implicitly, the dream appears to be an indigenous metaphor for the Dreaming. Though Stanner offers us no hard evidence for this, he gives us a clue: "Why the blackfellow thinks of dreaming as the nearest equivalent in

English is a puzzle. It may be because it is by *the act* of dreaming, as reality and symbol, that the aboriginal mind makes contact—thinks it makes contact—with whatever mystery it is that connects the Dreaming and the Here-and-Now" (1965, 159–160).

He notes further that there is a unity between waking life and dream life. It is not by sexual intercourse but by dreaming about a spirit-child that a man fathers a child. Through dream contact with a spirit an artist composes a new song. The dream is then, for the Aborigines, an instantiating force, and like the dream, the Dreaming is, I suggest, an instantiating account of the creation of the world, nature, and social institutions. The relationship then between the poles—the vehicle and the tenor—of a metaphor is not simply descriptive but performative or dynamic: the one creates the other. It is, I suggest further, this dynamic relationship that is metaphorized as a dream and so translated into English as the "Dreaming." In other words, as the dream relates to what is dreamed, so the narrative relates to what is narrated, so the *alcheringa* relates to the English "dreaming." The dream is doubly metaphorized.

Dream accounts are, as I have noted, subject to generic and narrative constraints. Here we have to carefully distinguish between the narration of the dream, a performance, and its narrative, or diagetic, content. The two are often confused in dream accounts, and this confusion should be taken as a datum. Included in narrative performance—the narration—would be the way the dream figures in and figures the discourse in which it occurs. Dreams have, as I have suggested, enormous rhetorical or pragmatic force. They may help make a point; they may, as any psychoanalyst knows, subtly, ironically, wittingly or unwittingly, undermine that point. They may change levels of discourse and concern, much the way citing a proverb, telling a joke, or reciting a myth does. They may allegorize—or in some other reflexive way comment on—the lead-up or ensuing conversation. They may give stress to ambiguities in those conversations. They certainly help define or redefine the participants and their relationship in the conversation, for the dream account characterizes the dreamer as minimally a trusting dreamer recounting a dream, and the audience as worthy recipients of such an account, such a gift. Of course the dreamer may not be trusting and the audience worthy of the dream gift.

Included in the narrative performance of a dream would be all sorts of paralinguistic phenomena, such as emotional intensity, voice tone, volume, pacing, rhythm, stress, eye contact, physical contact, and gesturing. These are usually missing from dream reports in the psychological and ethnographic literature. So strong is the self-isolating effect of the dream text (in the West at least) that these paralinguistic phenomena are often ignored even in literary accounts of the dream. They do have important, pragmatic effect. They are principal determinants of the way relations between the dreamer and his or her audience are constituted and construed. A dream told in anger, as a vehicle of aggression, certainly has a different effect than the same dream told with loving care or dutifully to an inquiring ethnographer. It promotes a different interpretation.

Erika Bourguignon describes her attempt to discover the dream of her Haitian informant. Annette is possessed by the female spirit Mystè Ezili, and is, therefore, intimately involved with Ezili's two "husbands": Ogou, or Saint Jacques, as he is sometimes known, and the snake spirit Danbala, also known as St. Patrick. Annette had taken Bourguignon to her village in the country-side, where Bourguignon asked her if she had dreamed during her *vodou* initi-ation. Annette answered, "I did not dream a single dream. We went to Port-au-Prince on Sunday, Monday night they reproached me because I am not in Port-au-Prince, because I am not taking care of the shrine [to Ezili]—Mystè Ezili spoke to me, like this: that I don't need her, neither her nor Papa Ogou. She said Jacques, well St. Jacques, that's Papa Ogou. Well, I am very happy you came—I need you very much. That's how she said [it] to me."

Annette does not describe this experience as a dream when she tells it, though she does later. She speaks as though she had had a real life encounter with Ezili. In the course of questioning, Ezili becomes—for a time—a man, someone familiar, Ogou, a man dressed in white, a man named Maurice, Danbala, another spirit, Gede. Annette elaborates, finally revealing the dream's message, as Bourguignon understands it: a reproach. By asking her to go to the countryside, Bourguignon caused her to neglect her shrine to Ezili. For Bourguignon, Annette discovers her dream as she recounts it. What is valuable to her is revealed in the elaboration of the dream. It is the unfolding communication that is important rather than the dream itself. She ignores the culturally less acceptable demands of the dream's manifest con-tent. As dreams are supposed to be about spirits and not about people, she translates people into spirits. The dream, Bourguignon insists, is experienced as already interpreted.

I am not convinced that Annette recounted anything like a dream as we normally understand it. It was only through the anthropologist's questioning that she finally admitted that she had been dreaming. It seems more like a vision—a waking vision that may extend into sleep or a sleeplike condition—which Annette took to be a message from the spirits. It is perhaps only metaphorically a dream. I have heard similar accounts in Morocco among the spirit possessed. Shifts in experiential registers—from waking reality to dream, trance, or fugue states—were often not distinguished in life historical narratives and conversations (Crapanzano 1980). This confounding of registers, which created a sense of puzzlement, mystery, and awe, was reminiscent of the tales of wonderment told by storytellers in market places and at religious festivals.

Shifts in time, the changing identity of characters, the absence of a single or multiple story line, the collapsing of narration and interpretation, and the absence of a fixed narrative point of view should not necessarily be taken as a sign of pathology. They may simply be *façons de parler*.

And yet we have to recognize that the rhetorical force of such turns of phrase reflect, indeed exploit, the understanding of the dream in the dreamer's culture and the way the dream is classified and ontologically evaluated. Does the category we translate as dream include other experiences such as visions and hallucinations, or does it exclude some of the experiences we include? Nightmares, for example? Are dream and waking reality sharply distinguished? Blurred? Though blurring has been frequently reported in the ethnographic literature, it would seem that such reports are based on a category confusion, which may or may not be shared with the members of the dreamers' culture. Dreams and waking life are, in other words, confused with the worlds to which they give access. Are the realities that waking and dream perception reveal of the same status? Is one privileged over the other? Under what circumstances? It would appear that this category confusion facilitates the rhetorical potential of the dream.

The dream text may be taken as a subset of the dream account.[11] Written, it is subject to prevailing attitudes to the written word. They may give the dream a permanence, an evidential quality, that counters its ephemerality. They may restrict the fluidity of spontaneous oral accounts, permit dramatic recontextualizations and rhetorical usage, and exploit gaps between the original narration, its textualization, and its various readings. That is to say, they give to the dream a temporality—a historicity—that is alien to, if not altogether precluded by, oral accounts. (The way this temporality and historicity are constructed and exploited rhetorically and psychologically has to be worked out in different cultural situations.) Here I want to emphasize the deferment—the temporisation—that is inherent in the written account: the loss of immediacy, a stress on the transitory, coupled perhaps with nostalgia, melancholy, and elegiac feelings. Or, indeed, the release from a strangulating immediacy, the freedom of change, and the relief that comes with distance and perspective. As text, the dream is objectified (in accordance with prevailing notions of the text as object) and this objectification may depersonalize it, exorcise it even, while preserving it and permitting its circulation; for the dream can now take on a life of its own (which is far greater than its quotational possibility in an oral culture or in a culture in which the dream is not considered worthy of being written down.) It circulates.

Think of Jacob's dream, its publication and translation, the multiple uses to which it has been put. Think of Freud's dream of Irma, the commentaries it has inspired, the several ways in which it is been integrated into an understanding of Freud's life. Think too of Freud's own reconsiderations of it in later editions of *The Interpretation of Dreams*. He first makes reference to it in his early *Project for a Scientific Psychology*, written five years before *The Interpretation of Dreams* was published in 1900. It is true, though, that dreams can spread rapidly in their oral form. I remember hearing a dream about the end of the world that would follow man's landing on the moon in several distant parts of the Navajo reservation. The dream referred, as I remember it, to the cosmic imbalance that man's landing on the moon would cause. By the time I heard it, the dream had taken on a near-mythic status (in a sense, a quasi-textualized one) which I correlated with the symbolic role of the moon in Navajo myth and legend and to the Navajos' preoccupation with harmony and disharmony in the universe. Curiously, I remember redreaming the Navajo dream several months after I had left the reservation, but in my dream I was listening to a Navajo elder telling it. However integrated into Navajo legend, the dream will never have the circulation of a written one.

This is not the place to consider all of the possibilities that textualization permits. They have been rehearsed often enough, though not with respect to the dream. As text, the dream should be subject, it would seem, to the careful reading that we give to other literary texts. (Literary critics and scholars have certainly analyzed dreams that occur in literature with very considerable literary acumen.) Anthropologists and psychologists, including psychoanalysts, have tended to restrict their analysis to the symbolic meaning of the dream or, as in the contributions to this volume, to way the dream reflects cultural preoccupations. The dream becomes a puzzle—an occasion for interpretation, as Roland Barthes might have put it—and not a mode of experience, of world presentation, as Binswanger and Foucault insist. I do not want to deny the puzzlement—the interpretive anxiety—the dream produces. They are important if only because they disembed the dreamer from his ordinary world by suggesting other possibilities—another stage, *ein anderer Schauplatz*, as Freud figured it, other (spiritual) realms, as the romantics had it. (They also pose a threat to the dreamer's autonomy, his sense of self, for either he produces, or is destined to receive, what he cannot fully grasp.) Seen this way, interpretation offers a release from anxiety—a diverting complacency. It may be seen as a response—a counterprestation—to the puzzlement the dreamer gives in telling a dream.

Dream genres structure dreams very much the way various story telling-genres structure memory. As such they reflect the dreamer's culture. Deviations from the dream genre are indicative of personal style and may reflect pathology. Among many dream theorists, Hollan relates the dream to the self. He argues that a certain set of dreams—"selfscape dreams," he calls them—update and map the self's current state of affairs, its "contours and affective resonances" with the dreamer's body and the objects and people in

his or her world. Hollan focuses on the substantive content of the manifest
dreams, their symbolism (for example, the car as a symbol of the self in
American culture) but does not consider at least in his contribution to this
volume, the possibility that the formal structure of the dream also reflects the
self's condition. (I am not questioning Hollan's theory here or his notion of
the self.) We would have to consider how the dreamer as the dream's narrator relates to the narrated dream. The dream narration may, for example,
indicate, through hedging, irony, interpretive interpolations, and various
other distancing mechanisms, a sense of a controlling, autonomous, indeed
confident self, while the dream personage may be fragmented, amorphous,
and situationally embedded, without any agency. It may be split between an
observing presence, shadowy and illusive, and an imaginal one that is vivid
and defined or itself shadowy and illusive.

If we compare the three Toraja dreams reported by Hollan from this
perspective, we see, I believe, important differences in the way in which the
dreamer Nene'na Limbong—his self—is cast in them. (My analysis can only
be suggestive since I do not know the exact context in which the dreams
were related, the language, indexical locutions, and narrative styles in which
they were told.) Consider the "I" in the first dream: "When I was still young
. . . I dreamed that there were many people, like at a feast. I sat on a mat
while the people swarmed around me, petitioning me. Then my stomach
started coming out of my mouth, pouring onto the mat in front of me. It
didn't stop until it was all out on the mat. I awoke, startled and afraid." As in
the other two dreams, the dreamer is careful to situate the dream in his life
trajectory. They are integrated in that history, marking perhaps important
turning points. The narrative "I" of the present narration—the "I" of "when I
was still young"—is, in any case, rendered quite distinct from the narrative
"I" at the time of dreaming (the "I" of "I dreamed")—though they are
anaphorically identifiable with each other. It seems (indeed they both seem)
to be relatively autonomous and controlling, well removed from the diagetic
"I" of "I sat on the mat" or the embedded "I" of "my stomach." The distinction is carried by the indirect discourse form in which the dream (at least in
its translation) starts, "I dreamed that . . . I."[12] (Tense no doubt plays an
important role in this distinction, but it is impossible to comment on it
unless one knows what the tenses of "I dreamed," and "I sat," and later "I
awoke" were in Toraja.) At the end of the nightmarish event, the dream narrator—present or past?—returns with an "I awoke," commenting that he was
"startled and afraid" and thereby further distinguishing himself from the
diagetic "I." It is perhaps the "I" of his subsequent interpretation, the "I" at
any rate that leads to the "I" of interpretation.

In the third dream reported by Hollan, the dreamer's position is far
more ambiguous—fragile and fluid. "One time I dreamed that my throat had

been cut! There was a man who cut my throat. I fell down! And I was frightened. I woke up frightened thinking, "I'm dead!" A man cut me with a machete and I fell down dead and my eyes went dark. Then my body was cut up and distributed to A and B and C [he whispers in a low, terrified tone of voice]. "Oh, this is my body being cut up!" But I could see it happen! I was cut up and distributed [Voice continues low, quiet, horrified]. I was very frightened." Even a superficial reading of this dream reveals a far less certain narrating "I"—one that gets swept up, emotionally at least, by the nightmare. Impersonal sentences (for example "There was a man who cut my throat") are interpolated between "I" sentences; their impersonality seems to obliterate or diminish the narrative "I." The narrative "I" is itself split both grammatically in the direct quotations and in such commentary as "I woke up frightened thinking, 'I'm dead.'" Is the "I" of "I woke up" part of the dream or is it the narrator making a comment? This same split is revealed as well in the content of "I fell down dead and my eyes went dark." Here the "I" of "I fell down dead" is clear and distinct from the "I" implicit in "my eyes went dark," for how could a dead person note that his eyes were dark? Unlike the first dream, this dreamer at all levels of narration is cut off from his objectified and distinguished body throughout the dream. It is never clear where the dream ends and where it is elaborated and commented on after the fact (as in "A man cut me with a machete"). It is less the content, I suggest, than the failed identifications of the various first person usages that gives the dream its terrifying quality.

In these dreams, the narrative structure I have attempted to describe reflects the dreamer's preoccupations as manifestly expressed in the dream content. As Hollan sees it, the dreams are concerned with the experience of "the boundaries among body, self, and other as fluid, permeable, and breachable—in fact, dangerously so." Hollan does find underlying resilience and defensiveness in them or in Limbong's ensuing interpretations—I would add, in the way Limbong has integrated them in his life narrative. Dreams may be rather more performative than Hollan's approach suggests. They may not only reflect the self's condition—the threat to the boundaries of Limbong's self, body, and world—but they may perform that breach, permeability, and fluidity. It is, I suspect, rather more the performance than the reflection that demands a response—life giving or life destructive. It may be private, as when one comes to terms with one's dreams, therapeutic, or ritual, as when Limbong sacrifices a pig to his dead father after dreaming that his father was trying to drag him off to the after-world.

Binswanger would find signs of pathology in Limbong's second dream, for its contents seem to be overwhelmed by emotion. He quotes a "cosmic" dream from one of his patients in which the emotional content was so dominant that the cosmic images could not bind the dream pictorially: "I

found myself in a wondrously different world, in a great ocean where I
floated formlessly. From afar I saw the earth and all the stars and I felt
tremendously free and light, together with an extraordinary sense of power"
(Foucault and Binswanger 1990, 90). Binswanger finds the dreamer's "hover-
ing without form," "the complete dissolution" of his bodily structure, and his
ambiguous stance toward the dream (as neither a bystander to, nor immersed
in, its drama) inauspicious. The patient characterized the dream as one of
dying and saw it as a turning point in his life. (He was at times suicidal.)
According to Binswanger, he preferred the emotional content of the dream,
which he relived over and over again in his daydreams, to the emotions of
everyday life. One wonders whether the dream is as indicative of pathology
as Binswanger would have it; for, from a narrative perspective, it hangs
together. The several "I's" are not as disjointed as in Limbong's third dream.
What is pathological is the dreamer's use of the dream in his waking life: the
way he responds through repetition to the dream performance.

The dream not only reflects the condition and circumstances of the Though we in the West have tended to ignore the performative nature
of dreams, the dream is seen in many societies, as among the Aborigines, as
bringing about what is dreamed. Kracke puts it this way with respect to
Parintintin shaman dreams: "The power to cause something to happen is
exercised in dream." Unlike the ordinary dreamer, though making use of the
standard repertoire of symbols of prescient dreams, the Parintintin shaman
wills his dreams intentionally—to make something happen. Other peoples
also stress the performative nature of dreams but do not give the dreamer—a
shaman even—the same power to will the dream as do the Parintintin.
Kenelm Burridge tell us that, for the Tangu people of New Guinea, dreams,
like myths and narratives, bear truth.[13] They "are not simple fantasies woven
from sleep. They are a normal technique for solving a problem or finding a
way out of a dilemma" (Burridge 1995, 219). They are the source of truth.
They "tend to pull a future into current sensible reality; they give definity to
hope, adding faith, thereby putting the dreamer in touch with a verity shortly
to be manifest" (Burridge 1995, 180). The Tangu dream is then instrumen-
tal, but, unlike the shaman's dream, it cannot be forced. Once it has
occurred, it becomes imperatives for action. The line between prescience in
and effectuation through dreams is not always clear. Its study requires consideration of the way a society understands, among other things, being,
becoming, agency, causation, manifestation, contingency, and destiny.

The dream not only reflects the condition and circumstances of the
dreamer at the time of the dream but also at the time of its recall and
recounting (if they should occur.) There are certainly some dreams, as Ewing
notes, that serve as orientation or reorientation points in a dreamer's life.
They do in fact mark a turning point and may require revision as the individual moves through life. In a paper on Moroccan dreams I wrote more than

twenty-five years ago, I discussed several of these orientation dreams and attempted to relate their role in the dreamers' life to Moroccan dream theory—the dream's authority. They were, as I saw it, primarily concerned with the resolution of conflict. What I did not consider then—I did not have the data—was the way the dreams were revised over time (if they were) and came to play different roles (if they did) in the dreamer's experience. I suspect that for several of the dreamers, their role remained relatively constant because they related primarily to their continued affiliation with a religious brotherhood, or *tariqa*, and their participation in its trance and possession ceremonies. One characteristic of dream recall is, at least in my experience, the dreamer's usual failure to consider earlier recollections and recountings of the dream unless these recollections and recountings played a particularly significant role in the dreamer's life. In this respect, dream recall is not that different from other memories. We do not usually remember remembering memories. Dream recall, though marking a moment in the past, so manifest in Limbong's three dreams, obliterates the interval between dream and recall.

As most of the contributors to this volume recognize implicitly, the dream narrator's interlocutors affect the way the dream is told, what is recalled. They serve as dream censors: embodiments of conscience and convention. This is of course true for any narrative. I would argue, however, that given the ill-defined, ephemeral nature of dreams, interlocutors—real, implied, or imagined—have a special hold over the dream. They take possession of it. They give it fixity. Burridge (1969, 416) makes this point with respect to the Tangu when he refers to the effect of the public recounting of a dream and its acceptance by the community. It becomes a narrative. It is "then seized of the community in general, expresses a cultural rather than private experience, becomes an explicit collective representation." As we know, in some societies, like the seventeenth-century Iroquois and the Senoi of Malaysia, the public recounting of a dream has considerable individual and collective confessional, therapeutic, and expiatory effect (Wallace 1958; Stewart 1969). It may serve, as Burridge implies, to lift the dream out of the private, or the minimally shared, into the public and maximally shared. Insofar as it resonates with the values of the community, however it is understood—oracularly, as a message from a spirit, a saint, a god, or the dead, as the experience of events elsewhere, or as the revelation of the unconscious— the dream gives a transcending validity, an upliftment, a sense of communal participation to the dreamer. We might say, given our excessive individualism and privacy, that the dreamer is relieved of the lonely terrors of subjective life, but I am quite certain that this observation would not apply to all peoples at all times. Of course, the publicizing of dreams, however ritualized, produces its own burdens; for, however powerful the (ritual) collectivization of the dream, the fact remains that the dream arose from an individual, or was imposed on him, and is, therefore, always symptomatic, positively or negatively, of his condition.

The dream seizes us. It does this, perhaps like any trickster, by slipping away. We have to trap it, to possess it, to obliterate the possibility, the inevitability, of its slipping away, of any slipping away, of forgetting, of the loss that comes with forgetting (and the uncertain certainty that what has been forgotten has left it trace, an effectuating trace), and most important (and most denied), here not the possibility but the inevitability, of dying itself. Dreaming is dangerous, the Moroccans tell us. It occurs during sleep, which is associated with absence (*ghaib*), night, and death. They sometimes call sleep "the little death" (*al-maut as-sughrâ*). Night of course is a time of danger, of lurking death. During sleep the soul in its wanderings slips away. It is outside, *dehors, kharj*. It has but the most tentative connection with the dreamer. It is for this reason that you should never wake someone dreaming, even if they are having a nightmare. You might break the connection: the dreamer will die.[14] Though I do not want to generalize from one cultural construction of the dream to others, I believe that the relationship between sleep, dreaming, and death has to be considered. The ephemerality of the dream has vast metaphorical possibilities.

The French writer and philosopher Maurice Blanchot (1982, 266–268; 1955, 361–362) notes that "he who dreams sleeps, but already he who dreams is he who sleeps no longer." "He is not another, some other person, but the premonition [*pressentiment*] of the other, of that which cannot say 'I' any more, which recognizes itself neither in itself nor in others" (Blanchot 1982, 267).

Think of Nene'na Limbong's "I" dreams in this respect. Think of Hollan's attempt to relate the dream to the self's condition. Blanchot would understand his effort this way. "Doubtless the force of vigilant existence and the fidelity of sleep, and still more the interpretation that gives meaning to a semblance of meaning, safeguard the outlines and forms of a personal reality: that which becomes other is reincarnated in another, the double is still somebody" (1982, 267).

Of course the constructions and interpretations resist the splitting of the I, the self, we would say in our psychological idiom: "The dreamer believes he knows that he is dreaming and that he is asleep, precisely at the moment when the schism between the two is effected. He dreams that he is dreaming. And this flight from the dream which plunges him back into the dream, in the dream which is an eternal fall into the same dream" (Blanchot 1982, 267).

The form of the dream, Blanchot suggests, is the dream's sole content, its possibility. It "dreams itself." *Il se rêve*. It cannot *really* be. It "touches the region where pure resemblance reigns. Everything there is similar; each figure is another one, is similar to another and to yet another, and this last to still another" (1982, 268).

Think of Annette's struggle to identify, to give shape to, to name her possessing *lwa* for Erika Bourguignon, who had herself taken on oneiric status, so she surmises. (I leave the referent to this "she" ambiguous.) We may seek the original, a point of departure, an initial revelation—a final referent I would say—but in the dream, at least, there is none, Blanchot insists: "The dream is the likeness that refers eternally to likeness." Le rêve est le semblable qui renvoie éternellement au semblable (1982, 268; 1955, 362).

Yes, this may be so. Or so, at any rate, can we conceive it. Though Blanchot gives a disturbing edge to our theorizing the dream—it is for this reason that I refer to him—we have to recognize his deepest failure, the failure perhaps of the last phases of modernism, to which we are not immune: the failure to recognize fully the role of the other, however constructed, in our seizure of reality, be it as illusive as the dream or as firm as the earth we stand on, and the ensuing interpretations that that seizure now entails. We have of course to remember that the other we depend on is also our construction—up to a point, the point where he or she speaks, rendering us an other and resistant. Were there no others, would we dream? Were there no dreams, would there be any others? It is, I believe, the dream's faulted interlocution that terrifies us and inspires us to give it expression and to pass it on, like a dangerous but valued gift. The dream, its account, its interpretation, and its circulation may serves as metaphors for our consolation.

Notes

Portions of these concluding reflections are included in "The Betwixt and Between of the Dream"—a much longer critical-encyclopedic discussion of dream theory (Crapanzano 2001)

1. Quoted in Beguin (1939): 81.
2. I quote from the entry "Treviranus" in the eleventh edition of the Encyclopaedia Britannica.
3. To appreciate the communicative value of the dream, its affective contagion, its pragmatic force, when no context is provided and no particular hermeneutic advocated, I recommend the German poet Wolfgang Bächler's (1972) novel *Traumprotokolle*, which records without any context or comment the dreams the author had over a twenty-year period of psychotherapy. In his afterword, Martin Walser calls attention to the way many of the dreams reflected the political reality of the period.
4. Bloch does recognize that the romantics equated nocturnal and diurnal dreams, attributing to both of them creative force. He argues that the night dream, undischarged and unfinished, may speak directly to the daydream—to forward

intention. "The labyrinth of the night-dream even aesthetically is not a stepping-stone to the castle in the air, and yet: in so far as it forms its dungeons, archaic material can communicate with waking imagination" (Bloch 1986, 102).

5. Foucault (1994, 43) ignores the German romantic poets' insistence on the accessing role of the dream in his observation that until the nineteenth century the dream was considered an absolute experience.

6. Access through the dream to other worlds, grounding or not, is found throughout the world. Ibn al-'Arabi, the Sufi philosopher, argues that the dream opens up the imaginal world (see note # 7 below). Of the three levels of consciousness postulated in the Maitri Upanishad, the second, the dreaming state, gives a glimpse, in Heinrich Zimmer's (1951, 363) words, "into the subtle, supra- and infraterrestrial spheres of the gods and demons, which are within, as well as without. . . ." As this world is as "fraught with terror, suffering, delusory forms, and incessant change" as that of perceptual reality, it is not that of perfect being. Access to that world comes with the third level of consciousness: the blissful state of deep, dreamless sleep. Zimmer notes further that heavens and hells were thought to be the macrocosmic counterpart of the dream world.

7. Al-'Arabi describes *barzakh* as something that separates (*fasil*) two other things, while never going to one side (*mutatarrif*), as, for example, the line that separates shadow from sunlight. God says, "He let forth the two seas that meet together, between them a *barzakh* they do not overpass" (Koran 55, 19); in other words the one sea does not mix with the other. Any two adjacent things are in need of a *barzakh* which is neither the one nor the other but which possesses the power (*quwwa*) of both. The *barzakh* is something that separates a known from an unknown, an existent from a nonexistent, a negated from an affirmed, an intelligible from a nonintelligible (Chittick 1989, 117–118). Strictly speaking the dream is not so much a *barzakh* (though it is that too) as it gives access to the *barzakh*, that is the imaginal world. As William Chittick (1989, 119) puts it, the dream is for al-'Arabi "a god-given key to unlock the mystery of cosmic ambiguity and the constant transmutation of existence." It requires, however, interpretation, *ta'bir*.

8. In technical terms I have used elsewhere, the function of the Third (the guarantor of communicative and linguistic convention) is faulted. See Crapanzano 1992, and especially 1998.

9. The Moroccan man who attributed dream distortion to mind's translation of the soul's experience was in fact skeptical of language's ability to describe reality—any reality, including the dream. With the exception of those words given directly to Mohammed by Allah, he said, all words—and indeed the silences between them—betray God's creation.

10. Pandolfo (1997, 169) notes that in Berber *telles* means "darkness." One who is struck by *telles* is blinded or blindfolded. It may also be used for narrow blind alleys.

11. Though we often speak of oral texts, I have preferred here to restrict "text" to the written. It seems to me that the use of "text" for oral performances is distorting since it imposes on the oral performance textual presuppositions which may not be applicable, particularly in those societies that have, or had, no literate tradition.

12. There is, as Greg Urban (1992) points out, an anaphoric relationship between the "I" of the independent clause ("I dreamed") and the "I" of the dependent

clause ("I sat"). It would seem that in dream narratives there is a dramatic tension between the identification and differentiation of the several "I's" in the dream narration.

13. We must be careful not to reduce the relationship between myth and truth among the Tangu to our notions of mimesis, *vraisemblance*, and propositional truth value. Truths borne by myths are, if I understand Burridge correctly, imperative but mediated less through interpretation than immediate application. The Tangu do not "comprehend" but "apprehend" their narratives. When they are asked to say what a tale is about, they give a long précis, repeat the last few sentences, or describe the events recounted in it. They do not interpret, perceive inner meaning, or correlate it with other experiences, these being Burridge's criteria of comprehension. The truth of dreams, insofar as they resemble myths, or indeed are narrated, have to be understood in this imperative, apprehending fashion. For a full discussion, see Burridge 1969, 415–469.

14. One of Pandolfo's (1997, 191) informants, Si Lhassan, described the connection between the wandering soul (*ruh*) and dreamer's body in terms of the *ruhani*, a sort of soul substance, which is tied to the *ruh* but remains in the body. It remains in contact, he said, "like the connection the ground-control maintains with a satellite." The *ruhani* "is like a puddle of water when it is hit by sun light," Si Lhassan said. "The light hits the water, and you see light on the wall. Or like a mirror when it reflects the sun."

REFERENCES

Alder, A. 1931. *What Life Should Mean to You.* New York: Capricorn.

Althusser. 1971. *Lenin and Philosophy and Other Essays.* Trans. B. Brewster. New York: Monthly Review Press.

Anzaldeia, Gloria. 1991. *Borderlands.* San Francisco: Aunt Lute Books.

Bächler, Wolfgang. 1972. *Traumprotokolle: Ein Nachtbuch.* München: Hanser.

Bakhtin, Mikhail M. 1981. *The Dialogic Imagination: Four Essays by M. M. Bakhtin,* ed. M. E. Holmquist. Trans. Caryl Emerson and Michael Holquist. Austin: University of Texas Press.

Barrett, Deirdre, ed. 1996. *Trauma and Dreams.* Cambridge: Harvard University Press.

Basso, Ellen B. 1987. The Implications of a Progressive Theory of Dreaming. In *Dreaming,* ed. Barbara Tedlock. School of American Research, Advanced Seminar Series. Cambridge: Cambridge University Press.

Bateson, Gregory. 1972. *Steps to an Ecology of Mind.* San Francisco: Chandler.

Battaglia, Debbora, ed. 1995. *Rhetorics of Self-Making.* Berkeley: University of California Press.

Beaglehole, Ernest, and Pearl Beaglehole. 1938. *Ethnology of Pukapuka.* B. P. Bishop Museum Bulletin 150. Honolulu: Bishop Museum Press.

————. 1946. *Some Modern Maoris.* Wellington: New Zealand Council of Educational Research.

Beck, J. C. 1979. *To Windward the Land.* Bloomington: University of Indiana Press.

Beguin, Albert. 1989. *L'Ame Romantique et le Rêve.* Paris: Jose Corti.

Benjamin, Jessica. 1988. *The Bonds of Love.* New York: Pantheon Books.

Berger, John. 1972. *Ways of Seeing.* New York: British Broadcasting Corporation and Penguin.

Bhabha, Homi K. 1984. Of Mimicry and Man. *October* 28:125–133.

Bilu, Yoram. 1986. Wishes of the Saint. In *Judaism Viewed from Within and Without,* ed. H. Goldberg. Albany: State University of New York Press.

————. 1989. The Other as Nightmare. *Political Psychology* 10:365–389.

————. 2000. Oneirobiology and Oneirocommunity in Saint Worship in Israel. *Dreaming* 10:85–101.

Blagrove, M. 1992. Dreams as a Reflection of Our Waking Concerns and Abilities. *Dreaming* 2(4):205–220.

Blanchot, Maurice. 1955. *L'espace littéraire.* Paris: Gallimard.

————. 1982. *The Space of Literature.* Trans. Ann Smock. Lincoln: University of Nebraska Press.

Bloch, Ernst. 1986. *The Principle of Hope.* Vol. 1. Cambridge: MIT Press.

Bock, Jerry. 1964. *Fiddler on the Roof.* Libretto. New York: Crown Publishers.

Boddy, Janice. 1989. *Wombs and Alien Spirits.* Madison: University of Wisconsin Press.

Borges, Jorge Luis. 1964. Dreamtigers. Trans. Mildred Boyer and Harold Morland. New York: Dutton, 1970.

Boss, Medard. 1958. *The Analysis of Dreams.* New York: Philosophical Library.

Bourdieu, Pierre. 1992. *Outline of a Theory of Practice.* Trans. Richard Nice. Cambridge: Cambridge University Press.

Bourguignon, Erika. 1954. Dreams and Dream Interpretation in Haiti. *American Anthropologist* 56:262–269.

———. 1972. Dreams and Altered States of Consciousness in Anthropological Research. In *Psychological Anthropology*, ed. F. L. K. Hsu. Cambridge, Mass.: Schenkmann.

———. 1973. *Religion, Altered States of Consciousness and Social Change.* Columbus: Ohio State University Press.

———. 1976. The Effectiveness of Religious Healing Movements. *Transcultural Psychiatric Research Review* 13:5–21.

———. 1979. *Psychological Anthropology.* New York: Holt, Rinehart and Winston.

———. 1982. Ritual and Myth in Haitian Vodou. In *African Religious Groups and Beliefs*, ed. S. Ottenberg. Marut, India: Archana Publications.

———. 1994. Trance and Meditation. In *Handbook of Psychological Anthropology*, ed. Philip K. Bock. Westport, Conn.: Greenwod Press.

Bowers, Kenneth S. 1976. *Hypnosis for the Seriously Curious.* Monterey, Calif.: Brooks/Cole Publishing.

Bowers, Kenneth S., and David Meichenbaum, eds. 1984. *The Unconscious Reconsidered.* New York: John Wiley.

Brady, Ivan. 1976. *Transactions in Kinship.* Honolulu: University of Hawaii Press.

Breger, L. 1977. Function of Dreams. *Journal of Abnormal Psychology* 72:1–28.

Breton, André. 1972. *Manifesto of Surrealism.* Trans. Richard Seaver and Helen R. Lane. Ann Arbor: University of Michigan Press.

Briggs, Charles L. 1996. The Politics of Discursive Authority in Research on the "Invention of Tradition." *Cultural Anthropology* 11:435–469.

Brown, Karen McCarthy. 1989. Systematic Remembering, Systematic Forgetting. In *Africa's Ogun*, ed. S. T. Barnes. Bloomington: Indiana University Press.

———. 1995. *Tracing the Spirit.* Seattle: University of Washington Press.

———. 2001. *Mama Lola.* Berkeley: University of California Press.

Brown, Peter. 1991. *The Hypnotic Brain.* New Haven, Conn.: Yale University Press.

Bruner, Jerome, Jacqueline Goodnow, and George Austin. 1956. *A Study of Thinking*. New York: John Wiley.

Bucci, Wilma. 1997. *Pschoanalysis and Cognitive Science*. New York: Guilford Press.

Bulkeley, Kelly, ed. 1996. *Among All These Dreamers*. Albany: State University of New York Press.

Burridge, Kenelm. 1969. *Tangu Traditions*. Oxford: Clarendon.

———. 1995 [1960]. *Mambo*. Princeton, N.J.: Princeton University Press.

Bursik, Krisanne. 1998. Moving Beyond Gender Differences. *Sex Roles* 38(3/4):203–214.

Carrol, Vern, ed. 1970. *Adoption in Eastern Oceania*. Honolulu: University of Hawai'i Press.

Cartwright, Rosalind D. 1969. Dreams as Compared to Other Forms of Fantasy. In *Dream Psychology and the New Biology of Dreaming*, ed. M. Kramer. Springfield, Ill.: Charles C. Thomas.

———. 1977. *Night Life*. Englewood Cliffs, N.J.: Prentice-Hall.

———. 1978. *A Primer on Sleep and Dreaming*. Reading, Mass.: Addison-Wesley.

———. 1981. The Contribution of Research on Memory and Dreaming to a 24-Hour Model of Cognitive Behaviour. In *Sleep, Dreams and Memory*, vol. 6, ed. William Fishbein. New York: Spectrum.

Carucci, Lawrence. 2001. Elision or Decision. In *Cultural Memory*, ed. Jeannette Mageo. Honolulu: University of Hawai'i Press.

Certeau, Michel de. 1984. *The Practice of Everyday Life*. Trans. Steven Rendall. Berkeley: University of California Press.

Chittick, William C. 1989. *The Sufi Path of Knowledge*. Albany: State University of New York Press.

Chuang Chou. 1999 [286 B.C.]. *The Essential Chuang Tzu*. Trans. Sam Hamill and J. P. Seaton. Boston: Shambhala.

Cohen, David B. 1979. *Sleep and Dreaming*. Oxford: Pergamon Press.

Cohen, L. B. 1988. An Information-Processing Approach to Infant Cognitive Development. In *Thought Without Language*, ed. L. Weiskrantz. Oxford: Clarendon Press.

Comaroff, John and Jean Comaroff. 1991. *Of Revelation and Revolution.* Vol. 1. Chicago: University of Chicago Press.

Corbin, Henri. 1966. The Visionary Dream in Islamic Spirituality. In *The Dream and Human Societies,* ed. G. E. von Grunebaum and Roger Caillois. Berkeley: University of California Press.

Cousins, George. 1889. The Past and the Present of Samoa. In *Sunday at Home,* 406–411. London: Religious Tract Society.

Crapanzano, Vincent. 1975. *Saints, Jnun, and Dreams. Psychiatry* 38:145–159.

———. 1980. *Tuhami.* Chicago: University of Chicago Press.

———. 1992. *Hermes' Dilemma and Hamlet's Desire.* Cambridge: Harvard University Press.

———. 1994. Kevin. *American Anthropologist* 96(4):866–885.

———. 1998. Lacking Now Is Only the Leading Idea, That Is—We, the Rays, Have No Thoughts. *Critical Inquiry* 24(3):737–767.

———. 2001 The Betwixt and Between of the Dream. In *Hundert Jahre "Die Traumdeutung,"* ed. Burkhard Schnepel. Köln: Rüdiger Köppe Verlag.

Crick, Francis, and Graeme Mitchison. 1983. The Function of Dream Sleep. *Nature* 312:101.

Csordas, Thomas J. 1990. Embodiment as a Paradigm for Anthropology. *Ethos* 18:5–47.

———. 1994. Self and Person. In *Handbook of Psychological Anthropology,* ed. Philip K. Bock. Westport, Conn.: Greenwood Press.

Dalton, Douglas. 2001. Memory, Power, and Loss in Rawa Discourse. In *Cultural Memory,* ed. Jeannette Mageo. Honolulu: University of Hawai'i Press.

———. 2001 Spirit, Self, and Power. In *Power and the Self,* ed. Jeannette Mageo. Cambridge, U.K.: Cambridge University Press.

Damasio, Antonio R. 1994. *Descartes' Error.* New York: Avon Books.

———. 1999. *The Feeling of What Happens.* New York: Harcourt Brace.

D'Andrade, R. 1961. Anthropological Studies of Dreams. In *Psychological Anthropology,* ed. Francis L. K. Hsu. Homewood, Ill.: Dorsey.

———. 1995. *The Development of Cognitive Anthropology.* Cambridge: Cambridge University Press.

Davidoff, Leonore, and Catherine Hall. 1987. *Family Fortunes.* Chicago: University of Chicago Press.

Davidson, J. W. 1967. *Sāmoa mō Sāmoa.* Melbourne: Oxford University Press.

Davidson, Julian M., and Richard J. Davidson, eds. 1980. *The Psychobiology of Consciousness.* New York: Plenum Press.

Davies, Horton. 1961. *Worship and Theology in England from Watts and Wesley to Maurice, 1690–1850.* Princeton, N.J.: Princeton University Press.

Degarrod, L. N. 1989. Dream Interpretation among the Mapuche Indians of Chile. Ph.D. dissertation, University of California at Los Angeles.

Derrida, Jacques. 1978. *Writing and Difference.* Trans. Alan Bass. Chicago: University of Chicago Press.

———. 1982. *Différance.* In *Margins of Philosophy.* Trans. Alan Bass. Chicago: University of Chicago Press.

Descartes, René. [1637]1952. *Discourse on Method and Meditations.* Upper Saddle River, N.J.: Prentice Hall.

Devereux, G. 1951. *Reality and Dream.* New York: International Universities Press.

Dimond, Stuart J. 1972. *The Double Brain.* Edinburgh: Churchill and Livingstone.

Domhoff, G. William. 1993. The Repetition of Dream and Dream Elements. In *The Functions of Dreaming,* ed. Alan Moffitt, Milton Kramer, and Robert Hoffmann. Albany: State University of New York Press.

———. 1996. *The Meaning of Dreams.* New York: Plenum Press.

Dureau, Christine. 2001. Recounting and Remembering "First Contact" on Simbo. In *Cultural Memory,* ed. Jeannette Mageo. Honolulu: University of Hawai'i Press.

Eagle, Morris. 1988. Psychoanalysis and the Personal. In *Mind, Psychoanalysis and Science,* ed. Peter Clarke and Crispin Wright. Oxford: Basil Blackwell.

Edelman, G. M. and G. Tononi. 2000. *A Universe of Consciousness.* New York: Basic Books.

Eggan, D. 1949. The Significance of Dreams for Anthropological Research. *American Anthropologist* 51:177–98.

——. 1952. The Manifest Content of Dreams. *American Anthropologist* 54:469–485.

——. 1955. The Personal Use of Myth in Dreams. *Journal of American Folklore* 68:445–63.

Eliot, T. S. 1971. *The Four Quartets.* New York: Harcourt, Brace & World.

Erickson, Erik, H. 1993. *Childhood and Society.* New York: Norton.

Ewing, K. P. 1990a. The Illusion of Wholeness. *Ethos* 18(3):251–278.

——.1990b. The Dream of Spiritual Initiation and the Organization of Self Representations among Pakistani Sufis. *American Ethnologist* 17(1):56–74.

——. 1994. Dreams from a Saint. *American Anthropologist.* 96:571–83.

——. 2000. Dream as Symptom, Dream as Myth. *Sleep and Hypnosis* 2(4):152–159.

Fabian, J. 1967. Dream and Charisma. *Anthropos* 61:544–460.

Fairbairn, W. Ronald D. 1952. Endopsychic Structure Considered in Terms of Object-Relationships. In *Psychoanalytic Studies of the Personality.* London: Tavistock Publications.

Fanon, Frantz. 1967. *Black Skin, White Masks.* Trans. Charles L. Markmann. New York: Grove Press.

Field, Isabel. 1937. *This Life I've Loved.* London: Michael Joseph.

Fishbein, William, ed. 1981. *Sleep, Dreams and Memory.* New York: SP Medicaland Technical Books.

Fosshage, James L. 1983. The Psychological Function of Dreams. *Psychoanalysis and Contemporary Thought* 6:641–69.

Foucault, Michel. 1977. *Language, Counter-Memory, Practice.* Trans. Donald F. Bouchard and Sherry Simon. Ithaca, N.Y.: Cornell University Press.

——. 1988. Technologies of the Self. In *Technologies of the Self,* ed. Luther H. Martin, Huck Gutman, and Patrick H. Hutton. Amherst: University of Massachusetts Press.

————. 1990. *The History of Sexuality.* Vol. 1, *An Introduction.* Trans. Robert Hurley. New York: Random House.

Foucault, Michel and Ludwig Binswanger. 1994. *Dream and Experience.* Atlantic Highlands, N.J.: Humanities Press.

Foulkes, David. 1985. *Dreaming.* Hillsdale, N.J.: Lawrence Erlbaum.

————. 1993. Data Constraints on Theorizing about Dream Function. In *The Functions of Dreaming,* ed. Alan Moffitt, Milton Kramer, and Robert Hoffmann. Albany: State University of New York Press.

Franco, Robert W. 1989. Samoan Representations of World War II and Military Work. In *The Pacific Theater,* ed. Geoffrey M. White and Lamont Lindstrom. Honolulu: University of Hawai'i Press.

Freeman, Derek. 1983. *Margaret Mead and Samoa.* Cambridge: Harvard University Press.

Freud, Sigmund. [1900]1953. *The Interpretation of Dreams.* Part I. Vols. 4 and 5 of *The Standard Edition of the Complete Psychological Works of Sigmund Freud.* Trans. J. Strachey, in collaboration with Anna Freud, assisted by Alix Strachey and Alan Tyson. London: Hogarth.

————. [1900]1956. *The Interpretation of Dreams.* New York: Basic Books.

————. 1914. *Remembering, Repeating and Working Through.* Vol. 12 of the Standard Edition. London: Hogarth.

————. 1950. *Project for a Scientific Psychology.* Vol. 1 of The Standard Edition. London: Hogarth.

————. 1961a. *The Ego and the Id.* Vol. 19 of The Standard Edition. London: Hogarth.

————. 1961b. *Civilization and Its Discontents.* Trans. James Strachey. New York: W. W. Norton.

————. 1961c. *The Limits to the Possibility of Interpretation.* Vol. 19 of The Standard Edition. London: Hogarth.

————. 1963. *Introductory Lectures on Psycho-Analysis.* Vol. 15. Part 2.

Friedman, Jonathan. 1992. The Past in the Future. *American Anthropologist* 94, 837–859.

Fromm, Erich. 1957. *The Forgotten Language.* New York: Grove Weidland.

Fromm, Erika, and Ronald E. Shor, eds. 1979. *Hypnosis*. London: Paul Elek.

Gardner, Louise C. 1965. Gautavai. Masters thesis, University of Hawai'i.

Gerber, Eleanor R. 1975. The Cultural Patterning of Emotions in Samoa. Doctoral dissertation, University of California at San Diego.

———. 1985. Rage and Obligation. In *Person, Self and Experience*, ed. Geoffrey M. White and John Kirkpatrick. Berkeley: University of California.

Gillin, J. Christian, Rebecca K. Zoltoski, and Rafael J. Salin-Pascual. 1995. Basic Science of Sleep. In *Comprehensive Textbook of Psychiatry*, 6, Vol. 1, 6th ed., ed. Harold I. Kaplan and Benjamin J. Sadock. Baltimore: Williams and Wilkins.

Gilson, R. P. 1970. *Samoa 1830 to 1900*. Melbourne: Oxford University Press.

Globus, Gordon. 1987. *Dream Life, Wake Life*. Albany: State University of New York Press.

Graham, L. 1995. *Performing Dreams*. Austin: University of Texas Press.

Gray, J. A. C. 1960. *Amerika Samoa*. New York: Arno Press.

Greenberg, R. 1981. Dreams and REM Sleep. In *Sleep, Dreams and Memory*, Vol. 6, ed. William Fishbein. New York: Spectrum.

Greenberg, Ramon, and Chester Pearlman. 1993. An Integrated Approach to Dream Theory. In *The Functions of Dreaming*, eds. Alan Moffitt, Milton Kramer, and Robert Hoffmann. Albany: State University of New York Press.

Grosz, Elizabeth. 1994. *Volatile Bodies*. Bloomington: Indiana University Press.

Gunson, Niel. 1987. *Messengers of Grace*. New York: Oxford University Press.

Hall, C. Stanley, and Robert Van de Castle. 1966. *The Content Analysis of Dreams*. New York: Appleton-Century-Crofts.

Hall, Calvin. 1966. *The Meaning of Dreams*. New York: McGraw Hill.

Hall, Stuart. 1996. Introduction. In *Questions of Cultural Identity*, eds. Stuart Hall and Paul DuGay. London: Sage Publications.

Hallowell, A. Irving. 1955. *Culture and Experience.* Philadelphia: University of Pennsylvania Press.

———. 1966. The Role of Dreams in Ojibwa Culture. In *The Dream and Human Societies*, eds. G. E. von Grunebaum and Rober Cillois. Berkeley: University of California Press.

———. 1976 [1966]. The Role of Dreams in Ojibwa Culture. In *Contributions to Anthropology*, pp. 449–471. Chicago: University of Chicago Press.

Haraway, Donna J. 1991. *Simians, Cyborgs, and Women.* New York: Routledge.

Hartman, Ernest. 1981. The Functions of Sleep and Memory Processing. In *Sleep, Dreams and Memory*, Vol. 6, ed. William Fishbein. New York: Spectrum.

Heidegger, Martin. 1996. *Being and Time.* Trans. Joan Stambaugh. Albany: State University of New York Press.

Herdt, Gilbert. 1987. Selfhood and Discourse in Sambia Dream Sharing. In *Dreaming*, ed. B. Tedlock. Santa Fe, N. Mex.: School of American Research.

Herdt, Gilbert, and Michele Stephen, eds. 1989. *The Religious Imagination in New Guinea.* New Brunswick, N.J.: Rutgers University Press.

Hilgard, Ernest R. 1977. *Divided Consciousness.* New York: John Wiley and Sons.

Hocking, William E. 1957. *The Meaning of Immortality in Human Experience.* New York: Harper.

Hofstadter, Douglas R., and Daniel C. Dennett. 1981. *The Mind's I.* New York: Basic Books.

Hollan, Douglas. 1989. The Personal Use of Dream Beliefs in the Toraja Highlands. *Ethos* 17:166–86.

———. 1992. Cross-Cultural Differences in Self. *Journal of Anthropological Research* 48:283–300.

———. 1995. To the Afterworld and Back. *Ethos* 23:424–36.

———. 1996. Cultural and Experiential Aspects of Spirit Beliefs Among the Toraja. In *Spirits in Culture, History, and Mind*, ed. Jeannette Mageo and Alan Howard. New York: Routledge.

————. 2000. Constructivist Models of Mind, Contemporary Psychoanalysis, and the Development of Culture Theory. *American Anthropologist* 102.

————. n.d. The Intersubjective Context of Dream Remembrance and Reporting. In *Dream Travelers of the Western Pacific*, ed. Roger I. Lohmann, unpublished manuscript.

Hollan, Douglas W., and Jane C. Wellenkamp. 1994. *Contentment and Suffering*. New York: Columbia University Press.

————. 1996. *The Thread of Life*. Honolulu: University of Hawai'i Press.

Holland, Dorothy, William Lachicotte Jr., Debra Skinner, Carole Cain. 1998. *Identity and Agency in Cultural Worlds*. Cambridge: Harvard University Press.

Holmes, Lowell B. 1974. *Samoan Village*. Palo Alto, Calif.: Stanford University Press.

————. 1980. Cults, Cargo, and Christianity. *Missionology* 8:471–487.

Homiak, John. 1987. The Mystic Revelation of Rasta Far-Eye. In *Dreaming*, ed. B. Tedlock. Santa Fe, N. Mex.: School of American Research.

Houston, Jean. 1996. *A Mythic Life: Learning to Live our Great Story*. New York: Harper Collins

Huebner, Thom. 1986. Vernacular Literacy. *Journal of Multi-Lingual and Multi-Cultural Development* 7(5):393–411.

Hunt, Harry T. 1989. *The Multiplicity of Dreams*. New Haven, Conn.: Yale University Press.

Jenkins, Janis H. 1994. The Psychocultural Study of Emotion and Mental Disorder. In *Handbook of Psychological Anthropology*, ed. Philip K. Bock. Westport, Conn.: Greenwood Press.

Jung, Carl G. 1963. *Aion*. Vol. 9.2 of *The Collected Works*. Trans. R. F. C. Hull. Bollingen Series. Princeton: Princeton University Press.

————. 1966. Two Essays on Analytical Psychology. Vol. 7 of *The Collected Works*. Princeton: Princeton University Press.

————. 1967. *Alchemical Studies*. Vol. 13 of *The Collected Works*. Princeton: Princeton University Press.

————. 1968. *The Archetypes and the Collective Unconscious*. Vol. 9.1 of *The Collected Works*. Princeton: Princeton University Press.

―――. 1970a. *Mysterium Coniunctionis*. Vol. 14 of *The Collected Works*. Princeton: Princeton University Press.

―――. 1970b. Civilization in Transition. Vol. 10 of *The Collected Works*. Princeton: Princeton University Press.

―――. 1971. *Psychological Types*. Vol. 6 of *The Collected Works*. Princeton: Princeton University Press.

―――. 1972a. *The Psychogenesis of Mental Disease*. Vol. 3 of *The Collected Works*. Princeton: Princeton University Press.

―――. 1972b. *The Structure and Dynamics of the Psyche*. Vol. 8 of *The Collected Works*. Princeton: Princeton University Press.

―――. 1973. *Synchronicity*. Princeton: Princeton University Press.

―――. 1978. *Man and His Symbols*. New York: Doubleday.

Keesing, Roger. 1992. *Custom and Confrontation*. Chicago: University of Chicago Press.

Klein, Melanie. 1988. *Love, Guilt and Reparation*. London: Virago Press.

Kluckhohn, Clyde, and William Morgan. 1951. Some Notes on Navaho Dreams. In *Essays in Honor of Géza Róheim*, ed. Wilbur and Muensterger. New York: International Universities Press.

Kohut, Heinz. 1971. *The Analysis of the Self*. New York: International Universities Press.

―――. 1977. *The Restoration of the Self*. Madison, Conn.: International Universities Press.

Koulack, David. 1993. Dreams and Adaption to Contemporary Stress. In *The Functions of Dreaming*, ed. Alan Moffitt, Milton Kramer, and Robert Hoffmann. Albany: State University of New York Press.

Kracke, Waud H. 1978. *Force and Persuasion*. Chicago: University of Chicago Press.

―――. 1981. Amazonian Interviews: Dreams of a Bereaved Father. *The Annual of Psychoanalysis* 8:249–267.

―――. 1987. Myths in Dreams, Thought in Images. In *Dreaming*, ed. Barbara Tedlock. Cambridge: Cambridge University Press.

―――. 1990. The Self and Kagwahiv Dream Beliefs. In *The Psychoanalytic Study of Society*, ed. L. B. Boyer and R. M. Boyer.

————. 1991. *To Dream, Perchance to Cure.* Symposium on Dreams in Transcultural Perspective. American Academy of Psychoanalysis. New Orleans, May.

————. 1992. He Who Dreams. In *The Portals of Power*, ed. Jean Langdon. Albuquerque: University of New Mexico Press

Krämer, Augustin. [1902] 1994. *The Samoan Islands.* Trans. Theodore Verhaaren. Vol. 1. Honolulu: University of Hawai'i Press.

Krippner, Stanley and W. Hughes. 1970. Dreams and Human Potential. *Journal of Humanistic Psychology* 10:1-20.

Kugle, Scott Alan. 2000. In *Search of the Center.* Ph.D. dissertation, Duke University.

La Barre, Weston. 1970. *The Ghost Dance.* London: George Allen and Unwin.

Lacan, Jacques. 1956. The Function of Language in Psychoanalysis. Trans. Anthony Wilden. In *The Language of the Self.* Baltimore, Md.: Johns Hopkins Press.

————. 1977a. *The Four Fundamental Concepts of Psycho-Analysis.* Trans. Alan Sheridan. New York: W. W. Norton.

————. 1977b. *Écrits: A Selection.* Trans. Alan Sheridan. New York: World War Norton.

Lakoff, George. 1996. Sorry, I'm Not Myself Today. In *Spaces, Worlds and Grammar*, ed. Gilles Fauconnier and Eve Sweetser. Chicago: Chicago University Press.

Lambek, Michael. 1981. *Human Spirits.* Cambridge: Cambridge University Press.

————. 1996. Afterword. In *Spirits in Culture, History, and Mind*, ed. Jeannette Mageo and Alan Howard. New York: Routledge.

————. 1998. Body and Mind in Mind, Body and Mind in Body. In *Bodies and Persons*, ed. M. Lambek and A. Strathern. Cambridge: Cambridge University Press.

Lanternari, Vittorio. 1973. Dreams as Charismatic Significants. In *Psychological Anthropology*, ed. T. R. Williams. The Hague, Paris: Mouton.

Lawrence, D. H. 1936. *Phoenix.* New York: Viking.

Leach, Edmund R. 1958. Magical Hair. *Journal of the Royal Anthropological Institute* 88:147–164.

Lee, Benjamin. 1997. *Talking Heads.* Durham, N.C.: Duke University Press.

Leslie, A. L. 1988. The Necessity of Illusion. In *Thought without Language,* ed. L. Weiskrantz. Oxford: Clarendon Press.

Leuzinger, Elsy. 1994. *Afrikanische Skulpturen (Museum Reitberg, Zürich).* Zurich: Atlantis Verlag.

Levin, Harvey S., Vicki M. Soukap, Arthur L. Benton, Jack M. Fletcher and Paul Satz. 1995. Neuropsychological and Intellectual Assessment of Adults. In *Comprehensive Textbook of Psychiatry.* Vol. 1. Baltimore: Williams and Wilkins.

Levy, Robert I. 1969. Tahitian Adoption as a Psychological Message. In *Adoption in Eastern Oceania,* ed. V. Carroll. Honolulu: University of Hawai'i Press.

———. 1973. *Tahitians.* Chicago: University of Chicago Press.

———. 1974. Tahiti, Sin, and the Question of Integration between Personality and Sociocultural Systems. In *Culture and Personality,* ed. Robert A. LeVine. New York: Aldine.

———. 1983. Introduction. Self and Emotion. *Ethos* 11(3):128–134.

———. 1984. Emotion, Knowing, and Culture. In *Culture Theory,* ed. Richard A. Shweder and Robert LeVine. Cambridge: Cambridge University Press.

Levy, Robert, Jeannette Mageo, and Alan Howard. 1996. Gods, Spirits and History. In *Spirits in Culture, History, and Mind,* J. M. Mageo and A. Howard. New York: Routledge.

Lewis, Ioan M. 1971. *Ecstatic Religion.* Harmondsworth: Penguin Books.

———. 1986. *Religion in Context.* Cambridge: Cambridge University Press.

Lincoln, J. S. 1935. *The Dream in Primitive Cultures.* Baltimore: Williams & Wilkins.

Lipton, Alan A. and Robert Cancro. 1995. Schizophrenia. In *Comprehensive Textbook of Psychiatry,* 6, Vol. 1, 6th ed, ed. Harold I. Kaplan and Benjamin J. Sadock. Baltimore: Williams and Wilkins.

Litowitz, Bonnie. 1975. Language: Waking and Sleeping. *Psychoanalysis and Contemporary Science.* 4:291–330.

———. 1977. Individual and Shared Meanings. *Papers in Linguistics* 10:341–373.

Lohmann, Roger Ivar, ed. nd. *Dream Travelers of the Western Pacific.* Unpublished manuscript.

Luomala, Katherine. 1986. *Voices on the Wind.* Honolulu: Bishop Museum Press.

Lutz, Catherine. 1988. *Unnatural Emotions.* Chicago: University of Chicago Press.

———. 1990. Engendered Emotions. In *Language and the Politics of Emotion*, ed. C. Lutz and L. Abu-Lughod. Cambridge: Cambridge University Press.

Mageo, Jeannette. 1988. *Mālosi. Pacific Studies* 11(2):25–65.

———. 1989a. *Āmio/Aga and Loto. Oceania* 59:181–199.

———. 1989b. Ferocious Is the Centipede. *Ethos* 17:387–427.

———. 1991a. *Ma'i Aitu:* The Cultural Logic of Possession in Samoa. *Ethos* 19 (3):352–383.

———. 1991b. Moral Discourse and the Loto. *American Anthropologist* 93:405–420.

———. 1994. Hairdos and Don'ts. *Man* 29:407–432.

———. 1995. The Reconfiguring Self. *American Anthropologist* 97(2): 282–296.

———. 1996a. Spirit Girls and Marines. *American Ethnologist* 23:61–82.

———. 1996b. Continuity and Shape Shifting. In *Spirits in Culture, History, and Mind*, ed. Jeannette Mageo and Alan Howard. New York: Routledge.

———. 1998. *Theorizing Self in Samoa.* Ann Arbor: Michigan University Press.

———. 2001a. Mead and Critical Cultural Relativism. Paper presented at the centennial meetings of the American Anthropological Association, Washington D.C. November 29.

———. 2001b. On Memory Genres. In *Cultural Memory*, ed. Jeannette Mageo. Honolulu: University of Hawai'i Press.

———. 2001c. Dream Play and Discovering Cultural Psychology. *Ethos* 29:187–217.

———. 2002a. Towards a Multidimensional Model of the Self. *Journal of Anthropological Research.* Vol 58:339–365.

————. 2002b. Discourse and Sexual Agency. In *Power and the Self*, ed. Jeannette Mageo. Cambridge: Cambridge University Press.

————. 2002c. Intertextual Interpretation, Fantasy, and Samoan Dreams. *Culture and Psychology* 8:417–448.

Mageo and Knauft. 2002. Introduction. In *Power and the Self*, ed. Jeannette Mageo. Cambridge: Cambridge University Press.

Mahoney, Patrick. 1987. *Psychoanalysis and Discourse*. London: Tavistock.

Manheim, Bruce. 1987. A Semiotic of Andean Dreams. In *Dreaming*, ed. Barbara Tedlock. Cambridge: Cambridge University Press.

Maquet, P., S. Laureys, P. Peigneux, S. Fuchs, C. Petiau, C. Phillipps, J. Aerts, G. Del Fliore, C. Degueldre, T. Meulemans, A. Luxen, G. Franck, M.Van Der Linden, C. Smith, and A. Cleeremans. 2000. Experience-Dependent Changes in Cerebral Activation in Human REM Sleep. *Nature Neuroscience* 3:831–836.

Markus, Hazel R., and Shinobu Kitayama. 1991. Culture and the Self. *Psychological Review* 98:224–53.

Mauss, Marcel. [1938] 1985. A Category of the Human Mind. Trans. W. D. Halls. In *The Category of the Person*, ed. S. Collins and S. Lukes. Cambridge: Cambridge University Press.

————. 1990. *The Gift*. Trans. W. D. Halls. New York: W. W. Norton.

McClintock, Anne. 1995. *Imperial Leather*. New York: Routledge.

Mead, George Herbert. 1934. *Mind, Self and Society*, Part 3, ed. C. W. Norris. Chicago: Chicago University Press.

Mead, Margaret. [1928] 1961. *Coming of Age in Samoa*. New York: Morrow Quill.

————. [1928] 1973. *Coming of Age in Samoa*. New York: William Morrow for the American Museum of Natural History.

————. 1959. Cultural Contexts of Puberty and Adolescence. *Bulletin of the Philadelphia Association for Psychoanalysis* 9(3).

————. 1963. *Sex and Temperament in Three Primitive Societies*. New York: William Morrow.

————. 1972. *Blackberry Winter*. New York: Simon and Schuster.

Meggitt, M. J. 1962. Dream Interpretation among the Mae Enga of New Guinea. *Southwestern Journal of Anthropology* 18:216–299.

Merleau-Ponty, Maurice. 1962. Phenomenology of Perception. Trans. Colin Smith. London: Routledge and Kegan Paul.

———. 1964. The Primacy of Perception. Evanston, Ill.: Northwestern University Press.

Miller, Peggy J., Heidi Fung, and Judith Mintz. 1996. Self-Construction through Narrative Practices. *Ethos* 24(2):237–280.

Mills, W. 1844. Letter to London Missionary Society Headquarters from 'Upolu. March 19. CWM Archives (17/6/B), School of Oriental and African Studies, University of London.

Moyle, Richard. 1975. Sexuality in Samoan Art Forms. *The Archives of Sexual Behavior* 4(3):227–247.

Mulvey, Laura. 1975. Visual Pleasure and Narrative Cinema. *Screen* 16(3).

Murray, A. 1839. Letter to London Missionary Society Headquarters from Tutuila. January 15. CWM Archives (12/6/A), School of Oriental and African Studies, University of London.

———. 1840. Letter to London Missionary Society Headquarters from Tutuila. March 20. CWM Archives (13/5/A), School of Oriental and African Studies, University of London.

Murray, D. W. 1993. What is the Western Concept of Self? *Ethos* 23:3–23.

Newman, Deena I. J. 1999. The Western Psychic as Diviner. *Ethnos* 64(1):82–106.

Noll, Richard. 1985. Mental Imagery Cultivation as a Cultural Phenomenon. *Current Anthropology* 26:443–461.

Noy, Pinchas. 1969. A Revision of the Psychoanalytic Theory of the Primary Process. *International Journal of Psychoanalysis* 50:155–178.

———. 1979. The Psychoanalytic Theory of Cognitive Development. *Psychoanalytic Study of the Child* 34:169–216.

Obeyesekere, Gananath. 1981. *Medusa's Hair*. Chicago: University of Chicago Press.

———. 1990. *The Work of Culture*. Chicago: University of Chicago Press.

———. 1992. *The Apotheosis of Captain Cook*. Princeton: Princeton University Press.

Ochs, Elinor. 1982. Talking to Children in Western Samoa. *Language in Society* 11:77–104.

Ortner, Sherry B. 1984. Theory in Anthropology since the Sixties. *Journal of Comparative Society and History.* 26(2):126–127.

Paivio, A. 1986. *Mental Representations.* New York: Oxford University Press.

Palombo, Stanley, R. 1978. *Dreaming and Memory.* New York: Basic Books.

Pandolfo, Stefania. 1995. *Impasse of the Angels.* Chicago: University of Chicago Press.

Peirce, Charles S. 1955. Index, Icon and Symbol. In *The Basic Philosophical Works of Charles Sanders Peirce.* New York: Dover.

Perls, Frederick S. 1971. *Gestalt Therapy Verbatim.* New York: Bantam.

Perrin, Michel, 1987. *The Way of the Dead Indians.* Austin: University of Texas Press.

Peters, Larry G., and Douglass R. Price-Williams. 1980. Towards an Experiential Analysis of Shamanism. *American Ethnologist* 7:397–418.

———. 1983. A Phenomenological Overview of Trance. *Transcultural Psychiatric Research Review* 20:5–39.

Piaget, Jean. 1985. *The Equilibration of Cognitive Structures.* Chicago: University of Chicago Press.

Price-Williams, Douglas. 1987. The Waking Dream in Ethnographic Perspective. In *Dreaming,* ed. Barbara Tedlock. Cambridge: Cambridge University Press.

———. 1999. In Search of Mythopoetic Thought. *Ethos* 27:25–32.

Quinn, Naomi and Claudia Straus. 1997. A Cognitive Theory of Cultural Meanings. Cambridge: Cambridge University Press.

Réage, Pauline. 1965. *Story of O.* New York: Grove Press.

Reiser, Morton, F. 1994. *Memory in Mind and Brain.* New Haven: Yale University Press.

Richman, Karen E. and William Leslie Balan-Gaubert. 2001. A Democracy of Words. Political Performance in Haiti's Tenth District. *Journal of Haitian Studies* 7:90–105.

Richter, Jean Paul. 1973. The Horn of Oberon. Trans. Margaret R. Hale. Detroit: Wayne State University Press.

Ricoeur, Paul. 1970. *Freud and Philosophy.* New Haven Conn.: Yale University Press.

———. 1981. *Hermeneutics and the Human Sciences*. Trans. J. B. Thompson. Cambridge: Cambridge University Press.

Ritchie, James. 1956. *Basic Personality in Rakau*. Publications in Psychology, no. 8. Wellington, NZ: Victoria University Press.

Ritchie, James, and Jane Ritchie. 1979. *Growing up in Polynesia*. Sydney: George Allen and Unwin.

Róheim, Géza. 1946. The Oedipus Complex and Infantile Sexuality. *Psychoanalytic Quarterly* 15:503–508.

———. 1949. The Technique of Dream Analysis and Field Work in Anthropology. *Psychoanalytic Quarterly* 18:471–479.

———. 1950. *Psychoanalysis and Anthropology*. New York: International Universities Press.

Rosaldo, Michelle Z. 1984. Towards an Anthropology of Self and Feeling. In *Culture Theory*, ed. R. A. Shweder and R. S. Levine. Cambridge: Cambridge University Press.

Rosenthal, Judy. 1998. *Possession, Ecstasy and Law in Ewe Voodoo*. Charlottesville: University of Virginia Press.

Rossi, Ernest Lawrence. 1993. *The Psychobiology of Mind-Body Healing*. New York: W. W. Norton.

Sacks, Oliver. 1996. Neurological Dreams. In *Trauma and Dreams*, ed. Deirdre Barrett. Cambridge: Harvard University Press.

Sarbin, Theodore R., and Robert W. Slagle. 1979. Hypnosis and Psychophysiological Outcomes. In *Hypnosis*, ed. Erika Fromm and Ronald E. Shor. London: Paul Elek.

Schieffelin, Edward L. 1976. *The Sorrow of the Lonely and the Burning of the Dancers*. New York: St. Martin's Press.

Schneider, David, and Lauristan Sharp. 1969. *The Dream Life of a Primitive People*. Ann Arbor, Michigan: University Microfilms.

Schoeffel, Penelope. 1979. Daughters of Sina. Doctoral dissertation, Australian National University.

Aleichem Scholem. 1987. *Tevye the Dairyman and The Railroad Stories*. New York: Schocken Books.

Schultz, Dr. E. 1994. *Samoan Proverbial Expressions*. Trans. Brother Herman. Auckland: Polynesian Press.

Schwartz, Theodore. 1976. The Cargo Cult. In *Responses to Change*, ed. G. A. De Vos. New York: Van Nostrand.

Selby, H. A. 1974. *Zapotec Deviance*. Austin: University of Texas Press.

Seligman, C. G. 1924. Anthropology and Psychology. *Journal of the Royal Anthropological Institute* 54:13–46.

———. 1932. Anthropological Perspective and Psychological Theory. *Journal of the Royal Anthropological Institute* 62:193–228.

Sheehan, Peter W. and Kevin M. McConkey. 1982. *Hypnosis and Experience*. Hillsdale, N.J.: Lawrence Erlbaum.

Shore, Bradd. 1977. A Samoan Theory of Action. Doctoral dissertation, University of Chicago.

———. 1982. *Sala'ilua: A Samoan Mystery*. New York: Columbia University Press.

———. 1996. *Culture in Mind*. New York: Oxford University Press.

Shulman, David, and Guy G. Stroumsa. 1999. *Dream Cultures*. New York: Oxford University Press.

Shweder, Richard A. 1991. *Thinking Through Culture*. Cambridge: Harvard University Press.

Shweder, Richard A., and Edmund J. Bourne. 1984. Does the Concept of the Person Vary Cross-culturally? In *Cultural Conceptions of Mental Health and Therapy*, ed. A. J. Marsella and G. M. White. Dordrecht, Holland: D. Reidel.

Siegal, Ronald K., and Louis J. West, eds. 1975. *Hallucinations*. New York: John Wiley.

Silverstein, Michael. 1976. Shifters, Linguistic Categories, and Cultural Description. In *Meaning in Anthropology*, ed. Keith Basso and Henry Selby. Albuquerque: University of New Mexico Press.

Singer, Jerome L. 1974. *Imagery and Daydream Methods in Psychotherapy and Behavior Modification*. New York: Academic Press.

———. 1977. *Ongoing Thought*. Ed. Norman E. Zinberg. New York: Free Press.

Singer, Jerome L., and Kenneth S. Pope, eds. 1978. *The Power of the Human Imagination: New Methods in Psychotherapy.* New York: Plenum Press.

Spiro, Melford E. 1970. *Buddhism and Society.* New York: Harper and Row.

———. 1993. Is the Western Conception of Self "Peculiar" within the Context of World Cultures? *Ethos* 21(2):107–153.

———. 1997. *Gender Ideology and Psychological Reality.* New Haven, Conn.: Yale University Press.

Springer, Sally P., and George Deutch. 1981. *Left Brain, Right Brain.* San Francisco: W. H. Freeman.

Stanner, W. E. H. 1953. *The South Seas in Transition.* Sydney: Australian Publishing Co.

———. 1965. The Dreaming. In *Reader in Comparative Religion*, ed. William A. Lessa and Evon Z. Vogt. New York: Harper and Row.

States, Bert O. 1993. *Dreaming and Storytelling.* Ithaca, N.Y.: Cornell University Press.

Stephen, Michele. 1979. Dreams of Change. *Oceania* 50:3–22.

———. 1989a. Self, the Sacred Other, and Autonomous Imagination. In *The Religious Imagination in New Guinea*, ed. Gilbert Herdt and Michele Stephen. New Brunswick, N.J.: Rutgers University Press.

———. 1989b. Constructing Sacred Worlds and Autonomous Imagining in New Guinea. In *The Religious Imagination in New Guinea,* ed. Gilbert Herdt and Michele Stephen. New Brunswick, N.J.: Rutgers University Press.

———. 1995. *A'aisa's Gifts.* Berkeley: University of California Press.

———. 1997. Cargo Cults, Cultural Creativity and Autonomous Imagination. *Ethos* 25:333–358.

Stern, D. N. 1985. *The Interpersonal World of the Infant.* New York: Basic Books.

Stevens, Anthony. 1995. *Private Myths.* Cambridge: Harvard University Press.

Stewart, Charles. 1999. Dreams of Treasure. Paper presented at the 6th biennial meetings of the Society for Psychological Anthropology in Albuquerque, New Mexico, September 24.

Stewart, Charles, and Rosalind Shaw, eds. 1994. *Syncretism/Antisyncretism*. London: Routledge.

Stewart, Kilton. 1969. Dream Theory in Malaya. In *Altered States of Consciousness*, ed. C. T. Tart. New York: John Wiley.

Stewart, Kilton. 1951. Dream Theory in Malaya. *Complex* 6:21–33.

Stich, Sidra, ed. 1990. *Anxious Visions*. New York: Abbeville Press.

Stoler, Ann Laura. 1995. *Race and the Education of Desire*. Durham, N.C.: Duke University Press.

Strathern, Marilyn. 1990. The Gender of the Gift. Berkeley: University of California Press.

Strauss, Claudia, and Naomi Quinn. 1997. *A Cognitive Theory of Cultural Meaning*. Cambridge: Cambridge University Press.

Sullivan, Harry Stack. 1953. *The Interpersonal Theory of Personality*. New York: Norton.

Sutter, Frederic K. 1980. Communal versus Individual Socialization at Home and in School in Rural and Urban Samoa. Doctoral dissertation, University of Hawai'i.

Tart, Charles T., ed. 1972. *Altered States of Consciousness*. New York: Doubleday.

Taussig, Michael. 1993. *Mimesis and Alterity*. New York: Routledge.

Tedlock, Barbara, ed. 1987. *Dreaming*. Cambridge: Cambridge University Press.

———. 1991. The New Anthropology of Dreaming. *Dreaming* 1(2):161–178.

———. 1992. The Role of Dreams and Visionary Narratives in Mayan Cultural Survival. *Ethos* 20(4): 453–476.

———. 1994. The Evidence From Dreams. In *Handbook of Psychological Anthropology*, ed. Philip K. Bock. Westport, Conn.: Greenwood Press.

Tolpin, Paul. 1983. Self Psychology and the Interpretation of Dreams. In *The Future of Psychoanalysis*, (Arnold Goldberg. New York: International Universities Press

Turner, George. [1861] 1986. *Selections from Nineteen Years in Polynesia*. Apia: Western Samoa Historical and Cultural Trust.

———. [1884] 1984. Samoa: *A Hundred Years Ago and Long Before.* London: Macmillian.

Turner, Victor. 1967. *The Forest of Symbols.* Ithaca, N.Y.: Cornell University Press.

———. 1977. *The Ritual Process.* Chicago: Adline.

Tylor, E. B. 1873. *Primitive Culture.* 2 vols. London: John Murray.

Urban, Greg. 1992. The "I" of Discourse. In *Semiotics of Self and Society,* ed. Benjamin Lee and Greg Urban. Berlin: Mouton de Gruyter.

Van de Castle, Robert. 1994. *Our Dreaming Mind.* New York: Ballantine Books.

van den Daele, Leland. 1994. The Cartography of Mental Organization. *Psychoanalysis and Contemporary Thought* 17: 407–446.

Volkman, Toby. 1985. *Feasts of Honor.* Urbana: University of Illinois Press.

Von Grunebaum, G. E. and Roger Caillois, eds. 1966. *The Dream and Human Societies.* Berkeley: University of California Press.

Vygotsky, L. S. 1978. Internalization of Higher Psychological Functions. In *Mind in Society,* ed. Michael Cole, et al. Cambridge: Harvard University Press.

Wagner, Roy. 1991. The Fractal Person. In *Big Men and Great Men,* ed. M. Godelier and M. Strathern. Cambridge: Cambridge University Press.

Wallace, Anthony F.C. Handsome Lake and the Great Revival in the West. *American Quarterly* (Summer): 149–165.

———. 1956. Revitalization Movements. *American Anthropologist* 58(2):264–281.

———. 1958. Dreams and Wishes of the Soul. *American Anthropologist* 60: 234–248.

———. 1959. The Institutionalization of Cathartic and Control Strategies in Iroquois Religious Psychotherapy. In *Culture and Mental Health,* ed. M. K. Opler. New York: Macmillan.

Watkins, Mary M. 1984. *Waking Dreams.* Dallas, Tex.: Spring.

Watson, Lawrence C. 1981. Dreaming as World View and Action in Guajiro Culture. *Journal of Latin American Lore* 7(2):239–54.

Watson, Lawrence C., and Maria-Barbara Watson-Franke. 1977. Spirit Dreams and the Resolution of Conflict Among Urban Guajiro Women. *Ethos* 5:388–407.

Watt, Douglas F. 1990. Higher Cortical Functions and the Ego. *Psychoanalytic Psychology* 7(4):487–527.

Wax, Murray L. 1999. *Western Rationality and the Angel of Dreams.* Lanham, Wash.: Rowman and Littlefield.

Weiskrantz, L., ed. 1988. *Thought without Language.* Oxford: Clarendon Press.

Wendt, Albert. 1977. *Pouliuli.* Auckland: Longman Paul.

White, Geoffrey M., and John Kirkpatrick, eds. 1985. *Person, Self and Experience.* Berkeley: University of California Press.

White, Krista. 1999–2000. Espousing Erzili: Images of a *Lwa*, Reselections of the Haitian Woman. *Journal of Haitian Studies* 5/6:62–79.

Williams, John. [1830–1832]1984. *The Samoan Journals of John Williams,* ed. Richard M. Moyle Canberra: Australian National University Press.

Williams, Raymond. 1973. Base and Superstructure in Marxist Cultural Theory. *New Left Review* 82:3–16.

Winnicott, D. W. 1971. *Playing and Reality.* London: Tavistock.

Winson, Jonathan. 1985. *Brain and Psyche.* Garden City, N.Y.: Anchor Press/Doubleday.

———. 1990. The Meaning of Dreams. *Scientific American,* November 42–48.

Wirshing, William C. 1995. Neuropsychiatric Aspects of Movement Disorders. In *Comprehensive Textbook of Psychiatry,* 6, Vol. 1, 6th ed., eds. Harold I. Kaplan and Benjamin J. Sadock. Baltimore: Williams and Wilkins.

Wollman, B. B., and Montague Ullman, eds. 1986. *Handbook of Altered States of Consciousness.* New York: Van Nostrand Reinhold.

Zimmer, Heinrich. 1954. *Philosophies of India.* Bollingen Series 26. Princeton, N.J.: Princeton University Press.

CONTRIBUTORS

Erika Bourguignon is Professor Emeritus of Anthropology at the Ohio State University, in Columbus Ohio, where she has taught since 1949. Her studies of altered states of consciousness (trance, possession, dreams) began with her fieldwork in Haiti (1947–48). This was followed by a large scale world-wide comparative study, supported by the National Institute of Mental Health. The results are reported in *Religion, Altered States of Consciousness and Social Change* (Ohio State University Press, 1973), *Possession* (Chandler & Sharp Publishers, 1976/1991) and numerous articles. Among her other publications is a textbook *Psychological Antropology: An Introduction to Human Nature and Cultural Differences* (Holt, Rhinehardt and Winston, 1979). Most recently, she co-edited with Barbara Rigney a memoir by her aunt, Bronka Schneider, entitled *Exile: A Memoir of 1939* (Ohio State University Press, 1998).

Vincent Crapanzano is Distinguished Professor of Comparative Literature and Anthropology at the Graduate Center of the City University of New York. He has done field research with the Navajo in Arizona, with the spirit-possessed in Morocco, with whites in South Africa, and most recently with Fundamentalist Christians and legal conservatives in the United States. He is the author of numerous books and articles including *The Fifth World of Forster Bennett: A Portrait of a Navaho* (Viking, 1972), *The Hamadsha: An Essay in Moroccan Ethnopsychiatry* (California, 1973), *Tuhami: A Portrait of a Moroccan* (Chicago, 1980), *Waiting: The Whites of South Africa* (Random House, 1986), and *Hermes' Dilemma and Hamlet's Desire: On the Epistemology of Interpretation* (Harvard, 1992). His latest book is *Serving the Word: From the Pulpit to the Bench* (New Press, 2000). Many of his articles and books have been translated into French, German,

223

Italian, Portuguese, Spanish, Polish, Japanese, and Hebrew. He has taught at Princeton, Harvard, the University of Chicago, the University of Paris, the Ecoles des Hautes Etudes, the University of Cape Town, and the University of Brasilia and has been a recipient of many awards in the United States and abroad.

Katherine Pratt Ewing, Ph.D. University of Chicago 1980, is Associate Professor of Cultural Anthropology and Religion at Duke University. Her areas of specialization include psychological anthropology, South Asia and the Middle East, with field research in Pakistan, Turkey and among Muslims in Europe. In her most recent book, *Arguing Sainthood* (Duke, 1997), she examined how the Sufi mystical tradition has been a focus of religious and political controversy in Pakistan and how this controversy plays out in the lives of individuals. She has also published numerous articles and the edited volume *Shariat and Ambiguity in South Asian Islam* (California, 1988).

Douglas Hollan is Professor of Anthropology and Luckman Distinguished Teacher at UCLA. He is also a senior instructor at the Southern California Psychoanalytic Institute. He has authored numerous articles on the culture and psychology of the Toraja of Indonesia, and co-authored *Contentment and Suffering: Culture and Experience in Toraja* (Columbia University Press, 1994) and *The Thread of Life: Toraja Reflections on the Life Cycle* (University of Hawai'i Press, 1996).

Waud H. Kracke is a hybrid anthropologist, with an anthropology degree from the University of Chicago and a psychoanalytic certificate from the Institute for Psychoanalysis in Chicago. He has done fieldwork with the Parintintin Indians of Amazonian Brazil, using psychoanalytic methods as well as anthropological ones. He has published a book, *Force and Persuasion* (University of Chicago Press, 1978) on Parintintin leadership using this dual approach, and has written many articles on Parintintin dream beliefs and practices and on their personal understanding of dreams.

Jeannette Marie Mageo is an Associate Professor of Anthropology at Washington State University. Professor Mageo has published numerous articles and books on cultural psychology, cultural history, and religion, as well as on sex and gender in the Pacific. She has edited several volumes: *Power and the Self* (Cambridge University Press, 2002), *Cultural Memory: Reconfiguring History and Identity in the Pacific* (University of Hawai'i Press, 2001), and *Spirits in Culture, History, and Mind* (co-editor, Alan Howard, Routledge, 1996). Her monograph, *Theorizing Self in Samoa: Emotions,*

Genders, and Sexualities (Michigan University Press), appeared in 1998. She consulted for and appeared in a documentary made for Channel 4 in Britain, *Paradise Bent: Boys will be Girls in Samoa*. The film is framed by her historical interpretation of Samoan transvestism (Mageo 1992, 1996, 1998). It won a Silver Plaque in the "Documentary-Humanities" section of the Chicago International Television Awards and toured with the Margaret Mead Film and Video Festival sponsored by American Museum of Natural History.

Melford E. Spiro taught at University of Connecticut, University of Washington, and University of Chicago before coming to University of California at San Diego to found the anthropology department. He has conducted fieldwork in Ifaluk, Israel, and Burma. In addition to anthropology, Professor Spiro maintains a part-time psychoanalytic practice. He has published numerous books and articles, ethonographic and theoretical, and is a member of the National Academy of Sciences and the American Academy of Arts and Sciences.

Michele Stephen, Ph.D. is Senior Lecturer in Anthropology at La Trobe University, Melbourne Australia. She is editor of *Sorcerer and Witch in Melanesia* (Rutgers University Press, 1987), co-editor with Gilbert Herdt of *The Religious Imagination in New Guinea* (Rutgers University Press, 1989), and author of *A'sisa's Gifts: A Study of Magic and the Self* (California University Press, 1995). She has published numerous articles concerning dreaming, "autonomous imagination," and the dialogue between culture and the imaginal mind. She has carried out extensive research over several years in Papua New Guinea and since 1996 has been doing fieldwork in Bali, Indonesia. Currently she is working on a study of dreams, mental illness, and the imagination in Bali, which focuses on her dual memory model of mind.

INDEX